Tatjana Montik

Georgia

A Tapestry of Time and Space

Tatjana Montik

GEORGIA

A Tapestry of Time and Space

ibidem
Verlag

Bibliografische Information der Deutschen Nationalbibliothek

Die Deutsche Nationalbibliothek verzeichnet diese Publikation in der Deutschen Nationalbibliografie; detaillierte bibliografische Daten sind im Internet über http://dnb.d-nb.de abrufbar.

Bibliographic information published by the Deutsche Nationalbibliothek

The Deutsche Nationalbibliothek lists this publication in the Deutsche Nationalbibliografie; detailed bibliographic data are available on the Internet at http://dnb.d-nb.de.

Cover design by Anna Arenstein

Copy-editing: Katie Ruth Davies

Unless otherwise stated, all pictures have been taken by Tatjana Montik

ISBN (Print): 978-3-8382-2021-5
ISBN (E-Book [PDF]): 978-3-8382-8021-9
© *ibidem*-Verlag, Hannover • Stuttgart 2025

Leuschnerstraße 40
30457 Hannover
Germany / Deutschland
info@ibidem.eu

Alle Rechte vorbehalten

Printed in the EU

Table of Contents

IN PLACE OF A PREFACE

Emotional notes on the documentary book
Georgia: A Tapestry of Time and Space

I never thought that a book about Georgia, about my homeland, written in Russian, could surprise and delight me so much! After all, this is the language of the empire, the language of the aggressor and occupier. But, in reality, language does not determine attitudes, does not determine the essence and character of what is said. These are determined by the person themselves, that is, by the author.

I met Tatjana Montik in 2012, in Tbilisi, in front of the House of Justice, where students were on hunger strike in protest, and I had joined them in solidarity. Tatjana, a radio journalist, came up to us and asked us to tell her what was going on. Word went round, and it so happened that she interviewed me for a program which was later broadcast in Austria and Germany. We spoke in Russian, of course, as befits a former Soviet citizen. Later, I met Tatjana many times to talk about the Soviet legacy and Georgian attitudes towards Joseph Stalin. I also translated Tatjana's essays about Georgia, read them for podcasts on the internet radio *Dario*, and interviewed Tatjana myself for the same channel.

It was our old acquaintance that shaped the fact that I was one of the first people to read this book about Georgia.

In all seriousness, I never expected it to be such a substantial, deep, truthfully sincere text; one that could present my native country as something new, as if in a new focus and from a new perspective.

For me, it is exactly that—unexpected, joyfully radiant, and irrationally surprising! That is Tatjana Montik's book—*Georgia: A Tapestry of Time and Space*.

This is an extremely versatile, multifaceted, voluminous, rich, peculiar, intriguing, lively and heartfelt book: to be convinced of the versatility and richness of this book, it is enough merely to familiarize oneself with its intriguing content.

Tatjana has been living and working in Georgia for almost 15 years—she is a radio journalist, writer, German citizen, ethnic Belarusian, and a yogi. In her book, she writes that for many years she dreamed of living in Georgia, but she knew little about our country and had never visited it even as a tourist. She explains her interest in Georgia as "some kind of magical, or maybe even karmic, attraction."

And it seems to me that she really perceives some kind of super-sensual energy in our mountains, our land. Without this feeling, she would probably not have been able to write such a book, where every word breathes love and a special, reverential respect. She sees and perceives what we, the inhabitants of this marvelous country, sometimes simply do not notice....

In the book, the author shares her memories of places she has seen, of the people she has met fleetingly or befriended, and of the events that mattered to her personally and that were important for the country. The author tries to tell as accurately as possible of the genesis of our people, of our language and cultural traditions. I should mention that she has also translated some of the poetry of Galaktion Tabidze, and continues to deepen her knowledge of the Georgian language.

Reading this book, it was as if I was traveling together with Tatjana through Georgia in space and time, giving me the chance to see anew my native country. And it was such an amazing phenomenon for me that I simply do not have enough words....

This book is a real prosaic poem, a poem about Georgia!

In the history of Georgia, there are many renowned foreigners who fell in love with the country and contributed significantly to its growth. Of the many, one can name Marjorie Wardrop, Bertha von Suttner and Arthur Leist. Tatjana Montik certainly deserves a place among them.

A huge thank you and much respect to her for that!

After reading her book, I was so overwhelmed with emotion that, for a while, I simply forgot what was happening in the world, in Ukraine, in Israel, in my country — the occupation and borderization of Georgia by the Russian army, the policy of our pro-Russian government.... The world is going to Tartarus, and how not to fall into despair? And, suddenly, there appears a book about Georgia which is so magically penetrating that it gives a new impetus to live on and to create; a book which brings back your lost self-respect, and your hope for a happy future.

I am sure that there is not a single person in the world reading this book by Tatjana Montik about Georgia who will not want to come here to see and feel it for themselves!

I would very much like as many people as possible around the world to read Tatjana Montik's *Georgia: A Tapestry of Time and Space*. The only way is to see it translated into many European languages.

To understand Georgia, one must read this book, and then come, live, and feel what the author so lovingly describes to us.

Irakli Lomouri, Georgian novelist, historian, and orientalist

From the Author

To my brother Ivan Montik

Georgia: An All-Encompassing Love

Georgia claimed my heart in 2010, the enchantment beginning with my first breath upon arrival. Stepping off the plane, I was met by a caress of sultry southern air; rich and redolent, awakening a childlike sense of wonder within me. Childhood is where we believe in a world of endless feats, glorious achievements, pure pleasures, and unexpected marvels. Each time I drew in the distinct fragrances of Georgia, a sense of joyous certainty bloomed: these were the treasures I was destined to find.

My blessings are woven from the scent of warm, crusty bread, fresh out of the clay *tone*, its fragrance a comforting embrace. They are the intoxicating perfume of ripe figs, bursting with sweetness, filling the steep slopes of Tbilisi's streets. They are the cool, still air of the *marani* (wine cellar) on a sweltering summer's day, a sanctuary of respite. And they are the spiced notes of vanilla, honey, and cinnamon that dance in the amber depths of Georgian wine — a fragrance so captivating, I'm tempted to wear it as perfume, adorning my neck and décolletage. My blessings also rise with the pine-scented incense of the mountain forests and mingle with the earthy aroma of parched soil finally quenched by a heavy spring downpour.

The images of Georgian life hold a captivating magic for me, a spellbinding charm. They are the noble, strikingly beautiful faces of farmers toiling in the fields, the sun-bronzed shepherds guarding their flocks in the hidden valleys of Tusheti and Khevsureti. They are the joyful faces of retired elderly men, their laughter echoing as they play backgammon in the sun-drenched squares and parks of the city. They are the unbroken threads of tradition that weave together generations during vibrant feasts; the passionate fire embodied in the bodies and faces of dancers whirling in traditional Georgian dances. They are the unforgettable sight of weathered Kakhetian elders, their faces etched with the stories of a lifetime, riding in donkey-drawn carts laden with brushwood, their great-grandchildren playing carefree amidst the bundles, gazing with wide-eyed wonder at the world unfolding before them. They are the serenely contented Georgian cows, even more peaceful than their Indian counterparts, commanding a respectful pause from even the most reckless drivers. They are the families of plump piglets, happily rooting through the villages. It is the golden light bathing the villages of Lechkhumi and Imereti at sunset, the soft curves of the forested Gurian mountains, and the ancient granite peaks of Svaneti and Racha, crowned with icy breath.

Georgia, called Sakartvelo by those who live here, has seduced my very hearing. The ancient resonance of Indian mantras and the passionate shimmers of flamenco now pale in comparison to the haunting beauty of Georgian polyphony—from the solemn grandeur of church choirs to the tender embrace of folk lullabies. These voices, rich and layered, unfailingly bring tears to my eyes, washing away the dust of the world. I would never exchange them for anything, these melodies that drift through Tbilisi's streets, whispering eternal stories of love, friendship, loyalty, and honor. They are a constant source of wonder, allowing me to inhabit countless lives, both real and imagined, within the span of a single song.

My Georgia is a feast for the senses, a vibrant tapestry woven from flavors and textures that dance on the tongue. The herbs alone—tarragon, pennyroyal, red basil, cilantro, forest mint, wild thyme—are a revelation, their fragrances unlike any others; a secret treasure I carry with me wherever I roam. I am captivated by the firm, milky texture of unsweetened corn, ground into flour that yields the glorious crunch of *chvishtari* and *mchadi* (cornbread with or without cheese). The cucumbers, pale and almost ethereal, possess a tenderness that speaks to the heart, paired perfectly with sun-ripened, crimson tomatoes; their juices mingling with herbs, spices, and the rich depth of crushed walnuts. I will always be moved by the gentle caress of *gebjalia*, fresh cheese steeped in milk and mint, by the bursting-with-nectar champagne apples, succulent honeyed apricots, fragrant, colossal peaches, and the tangy, strawberry-kissed feijoa. But the true elixir of Georgia is the water itself—pure, crystalline, flowing from mountain springs, rivers, and streams, offering instant refreshment and a sense of profound peace to the traveler weary from the summer sun. Georgia is indeed a land generously blessed with this life-giving gift.

It feels impossible to truly live in Georgia without heeding the whispers of the heart. I once sought the wisdom of a hermit monk, the abbot of a monastery in Lomisi, and asked him the age-old question: should we live by the dictates of the mind, or the yearnings of the heart? His enlightened response was simple yet profound: "Seek counsel a hundred times, let all thoughts sift through your mind, and then follow where your heart leads you." My years in Sakartvelo have affirmed this truth: the people of Georgia do not merely think; they feel, deeply and passionately. How else to explain their boundless love, even for the children of strangers, their unwavering desire to offer food and shelter to those in need, their selfless devotion to their homeland, traditions, and faith? How else to explain their unwavering courage in the face of even the most formidable foe, when their most cherished values are threatened?

This, I suspect, is why leaving, even on a short trip, fills me with a poignant sense of longing before I even reach the airport; my heart already yearning for this place. If I had the power, I would protect this extraordinary haven under the sun, enshrining it as a treasure in the Red Book. "Sakartvelo, mikvarkhar!"—Georgia, I love you!

Almost fifteen years now I've called Tbilisi home, and my love for this city hasn't faded—it has become a deeper, more enduring part of me. The sages say that love is the heart's remarkable ability to see all the imperfections, all the shortcomings, and yet still choose to love, perhaps even more fiercely.

Living in Georgia has illuminated a simple truth: the world is not divided into East and West, but rather North and South. The affinities between Georgia and Greece, for instance, are far more striking than those between Greece and Germany. In much of Northern Europe, rationality often takes precedence over emotional expression, creating, in a sense, an emotional scarcity. Perhaps these cultures offer fewer opportunities for individuals to fully experience and express their feelings. In contrast, Southern European cultures, like those of Spain, Portugal, Greece, France and Italy, tend to embrace a greater freedom of emotional expression. This is not to suggest that Northerners are less warm or welcoming; rather, their lives and interactions are often guided by a strong adherence to rules, laws, and regulations, even in personal relationships. Coupled with a relative lack of sunlight and warmth—natural sources of endorphins—this structured environment can inadvertently create a yearning for deeper connection, genuine relationships, and open displays of affection. I often dreamt of a sun-drenched land where heart and love reigned supreme, a place every soul instinctively craved, despite the dictates of reason. It seems I have found this blessed land: Georgia, or, as it resonates with such magic in Georgian: Sakartvelo!

Acknowledgements

My heart is overflowing with gratitude, and so I would like to take this opportunity to acknowledge all those who offered their help and support in writing this book.

First of all, my family, headed by my brother Ivan, who helped me to realize this project by setting a clear goal and fully focusing on the book. Much appreciation goes to my mother, Tamara Montik, for her companionship in discovering Georgia, emotional coloring and keen interest in the themes of this book. I am happy that all my family members have been sympathetic to my "obsession" with Georgia, helping me and encouraging me in all my endeavors. Thanks to my children, Anton and Theodor, for their cheerful company on research trips to Svaneti, Adjara, Kakheti, Imereti, and Samtskhe-Javakheti. My sons taught me to see life in all its diversity, to find joy in small things, and not to dwell on narrow aspects of existence.

I would like to express my deepest gratitude to my Georgian friends Zurab Kikodze, Eliso Rekhviashvili, Irakli Gvenetadze, Giorgi Mamardashvili, Nana Arjevanidze, Natela Tsiklauri, and Mary Ellen Chatwin, who provided me with all kinds of help in getting to know their wonderful country, giving me tips and valuable advice, and introducing me to interesting people and experts. Special thanks to Manana Gorgodze-Kvachadze, who opened the door to the mysteries of the Georgian language and poetry, as well as the mentality of her people.

Without the touching enthusiasm of Sulkhan Nizharadze, Temuri Tunadze, Emzar Kakhidze, Nino Sulava and Olga Sova, this book would not have been possible. Thank you to my friends Tamuna Pantskhava and Konstantin Shvangiradze, Khatuna Ichuaidze, Malgorzata Kalina Turkot-Janik, and the family of Eldar Bukvaidze for their hospitality, responsiveness and hearts full of love. Special thanks to the family of my late friend Larisa Margiani, her husband Murad, and sons Vakhtang, Ruslan and Murman, who also became my dear family in Svaneti.

In addition, I am deeply thankful to my wonderful editors and curators Ernest Hauer, Udo Schmidt, Karsten Gatke and Jürgen Dückers. Their keen interest in Georgia and my work contributed greatly to the production of this book.

Peasants in the vineyard of Shaloshvili Wine Cellar in the Alazani Valley. Dignity and grace define Georgians of every age and profession

Old man on his cart in a Kakhetian village

A serene Georgian cow in Dartlo, Tusheti

About this Book

This collection of tales was born over fourteen years, nurtured by my deep affection for this land. Its nature, its history shrouded in mystery, its people, flavors, and fragrances all ignited my passion. I offer you a glimpse into a particular moment in Georgia's history. While not overtly political, this work mirrors the collective psyche of our times — the aspirations, anxieties, and joys of the Georgian people. My love for this land, its pristine nature and its enigmatic past, served as my guiding star throughout the creation of this book.

Often, the inspiration for my Georgian adventures came from books, aged and worn, that chronicled this country long ago. As I prepared for each journey, I would delve into the annals of the Georgian National Library, seeking out forgotten accounts of archeologists, ethnographers, historians, and travelers from distant eras. Their words, like kindling, fueled my curiosity. Many of these historical tomes are rare, almost relics, and thus I felt compelled to share fragments of them within these pages.

And so a journey through Georgia, in both time and space, unfolded.

The book is conventionally divided into West and East, which is how Georgians most often refer to the division of their land.

The West is proximity to the Black Sea and a subtropical climate, the myths and legends of the legendary Colchis, infectious cheerfulness and a talent for irony. The East is arid climate, winemaking, hard work, the joy of the fruits of one's labor, and rest, well deserved after work. That said, hard work and the willingness to share what you have without hesitation is characteristic of all regions of this land.

In this book, I share my memories of places I have seen, of people I have met fleetingly or befriended, and that have deeply impacted me and hold significance for the country. To the best of my ability, I have also endeavored to explore the origins of the Georgian people, the beauty of the Georgian language, and the rich cultural traditions that define this remarkable nation.

A sweeping view of Tbilisi from above Turtle Lake

Prelude. Tbilisi of 2010

For many years, I had a vision of living in Georgia. While studying in Vienna, I met a Georgian friend who introduced me to Georgian cuisine and viniculture. She also taught me to cook some Georgian dishes, which I found unique and enchanting. During my time in Ukraine, during the Orange Revolution, I encountered many Georgians who were actively participating in those events. They shared stories of their peaceful Rose Revolution and the young reformer, President Mikheil Saakashvili, further fueling my interest in the South Caucasus. Curious, I immersed myself in books and news about Georgia. Yet, despite this growing fascination, I never visited Georgia, not even as a tourist. I can only explain this enduring interest as a kind of magical pull.

In August 2010, my dream came true: my family and I moved to live in Tbilisi. I was blown away by this city from my very first step into it. This is what I wrote in my diary during those first few days:

> Founded in the 5th century AD by King Vakhtang I Gorgasali, Tbilisi, the capital of Georgia, is nestled along both banks of the Mtkvari River. Its name, translating to 'warm,' is a testament to the thermal hydrogen sulfide springs that grace the city.

"We arrived at night. Stepping off the plane, our first impression was the stupefying air: southern, soft, sultry, almost 'tasty'! The evening and night are filled with the song of cicadas, instantly setting a relaxed mood. 'Life is good, and it's good to live!' – as my grandfather used to say. This, for me, is Tbilisi. It feels a pity to go to bed on such marvelous nights, but rest is necessary; I want to wake early and seize the day. We are staying near Turtle Lake, which exerts a magnetic pull on me.

"After spending time in Tbilisi, one begins to appreciate the distinction between 'fitness' – focused on physical exercise, and 'wellness' – encompassing a healthy lifestyle and overall well-being. Achieving physical fitness often involves strenuous effort, a 'no pain, no gain' mentality sometimes associated with Western cultures. In contrast, wellness in Tbilisi seems to be about dynamic movement in the fresh air, maintaining an appreciation for life's pleasures. Georgians seem to embrace this approach, perhaps more readily 'forgiving' indulgences like coffee, wine (even with the occasional hangover), and even smoking. Why? Because the famous la dolce vita, sweet life, isn't exclusive to Italians – it's very much a part of the Georgian spirit as well."

> Turtle Lake, of volcanic origin, is located 1.8 km above the Vake district of Tbilisi. The lake is surrounded by endemic turtles, hence its name. The territory of Turtle Lake is a popular recreation area for residents and guests of Tbilisi.

Between everyday life, small children, and setting up a new home, it took time to discover the true spirit of historical Tbilisi: the multi-nationality and diversity of its inhabitants, and the famous courtyards of the Old Town.

The Vake neighborhood, where we settled and which was described as one of the most prestigious places in Tbilisi, did not seem so attractive and pompous to me. When someone once called Vake "Tbilisi's Manhattan," it made me laugh.

"My general impression is that Tbilisi has its own unique face, and it is hard to confuse it with other cities in the world. It is very green and cozy, despite the large number of Soviet high-rise buildings, which, when you look at Tbilisi from above, spoil the overall picture. But somehow the panorama of Tbilisi is colorful and romantic, as the city is situated between and on the slopes of mountains."

In the prestigious Vake district, I was initially surprised by the prevalence of Soviet-era buildings: I've always preferred living in older houses. Vake's neglected front yards and broken sidewalks were also disheartening. Yet, despite these initial impressions, I quickly felt a sense of coziness and comfort within the city. This feeling was largely due to the many small food stalls that I discovered — mini-bazaars overflowing with fresh produce, herbs, spices, cheeses, and wines. These stalls became hubs for social interaction, and conversations with the vendors proved both pleasant and enriching. I later featured these charming establishments in a radio feature about Tbilisi and its people.

> The Vake district is one of the most modern districts of Tbilisi, built in the 1950-60s. The word "Vake" translates as "flat". Vake is particularly popular among expats.

"Russian is widely understood in Tbilisi. While some younger people and certain vendors, particularly in markets, may not respond to Russian, I've encountered no hostility towards the language. Tbilisians are generally courteous and friendly. My Belarusian background (coupled with my German passport!) seems to be particularly well-received, and their warmth towards Ukrainians is also evident. Thankfully, I haven't yet heard the ubiquitous Russian pop and chanson — in fact, I haven't heard it anywhere. However, I have heard Okean Elzy, and more than once! That was a real treat for me."

> 'Okean Elzy' is a famous Ukrainian rock band headed by musician and singer Svyatoslav Vakarchuk.

Another striking characteristic of Tbilisians is their immense and unwavering love for children. Here is another entry from my diary:

"Goodness, the love for children here is truly remarkable! While walking around the city with our baby in a sling, we were stopped almost constantly by people admiring him, asking his name and age, offering blessings, and wishing him health and a long life. Our eldest son, at three and a half, is also a magnet for attention. His blond hair and blue eyes draw so much admiration that it can sometimes feel overwhelming. Walking down the street with him is almost impossible; he creates quite a stir. People even come out of shops just to see him!"

Today, in 2024, the streets of Tbilisi are filled with the Russian language — a consequence of the influx of relocators from the Russian Federation, Belarus, and some refugees from Ukraine since the start of the war. However, back in 2010, Tbilisi struck me as a remarkably international city. Alongside Georgian, one could hear English, German, French, Italian, and Spanish spoken frequently. There was also a noticeable Scandinavian presence.

Somehow, miraculously, barely had my feet touched the ground when I found myself in a Spanish-speaking women's club, where I was warmly welcomed. We met weekly with women from Spain and Latin America, went to cafés and parks together, took nature walks with our children, and celebrated birthdays.

Here's what I wrote down in my first notes back then:

"There are quite a lot of foreign citizens living in Tbilisi. Most of them are representatives of international organizations, many of which deal with refugee issues. That is why I was happy when we found a place for our son in one of the international English-speaking kindergartens. Before that, we were refused in two other kindergartens due to overcrowding."

We quickly became friends with the parents of the children in the kindergarten group — a diverse mix of Danes, Americans, Spaniards, Mexicans, Swedes, and Italians. Together, we enjoyed hikes, excursions, holiday celebrations, and even yoga sessions. I even taught yoga for a time, back when it was still relatively uncommon in Tbilisi.

I must admit that on the way to my discovery of Tbilisi, I was pursued by many temptations:

"One of my greatest discoveries has been the Georgian cuisine, which easily rivals anything I've tasted in Georgian restaurants abroad. The pastries and mchadi (cornbread) are incredibly delicious and utterly tempting! The sight of the

Mchadi is a maize bread baked in clay pans called *ketsi*. It is eaten with cheese. In restaurants, it is served together with *pkhali* — vegetables seasoned with walnuts and spices. *Mchadi* and *pkhali* are popular Georgian dishes.

delicate cheeses and dairy products is enough to make my stomach rumble. The spices and herbs are truly remarkable, their flavors unlike any others in the world. I could happily eat spinach and beetroot pkhali and eggplant with walnut paste every single day!"

One of Tbilisi's most appealing aspects for me is the ease with which we can escape to the countryside. My first trip to the Manglisi resort solidified this feeling, revealing that life in Tbilisi offers a sense of perpetual vacation. The ability to readily exchange the city's bustle for the tranquility of forests and mountains is a true privilege—and one not afforded to many residents of large metropolitan areas.

> Manglisi is a popular resort in the suburbs of Tbilisi, at an altitude of 1200 meters above sea level. It borders the Algeti National Park.

My breath was taken on my first visit to Manglisi:

"As we ascended, magnificent mountain panoramas unfolded before me – a tapestry of mountains, hills, and expansive meadows. The sensation was akin to flying, as if a magician had transported me to a truly enchanted land. Was this real? I stopped the car at a bend to fully absorb the awe-inspiring scenery. Climbing a nearby hill and descending its other side, I found myself at the edge of a precipice. The view was simply stunning. A wave of déjà vu washed over me: I felt transported to... Spain, a country I adore! Then it struck me: Spain would have to wait. My focus now was on exploring Georgia."

I must confess, hand on heart, that everything I've described about my initial experiences in Tbilisi still holds true today. Over the fourteen plus years I've lived here, my love for the city and country has been tested many times. Yet, through every challenge, my affection for Tbilisi has not only endured, it has grown even stronger.

Tbilisi, 11th July 2024

Important Notes

The self-name of the inhabitants of this country is *Kartveli*, the language is *Kartuli*, and they call their country "the country of Kartveli," i.e. *Sakartvelo*. Toponyms in the book are presented using standard English transliteration. In the excerpts I have cited from historical books of the Russian Imperial period, I have kept the Russian transliteration of city names.

Gvara Fortress in Machakhela Gorge, Adjara

Part One.
Western Georgia:
The Legacy of Ancient Colchis

Georgia is truly a sacred land. Its sacred power is based, among other things, on the fact that this land is blessed in every way, because Georgia was one of the first Christian countries in the world. Saint Nino brought the faith in Jesus Christ here from Cappadocia in the 3rd century, and, in the 4th century, King Mirian III and his wife Queen Nana officially introduced Christianity as the state religion. Pilgrimage tours to Georgia are very popular, as many early Christian and Medieval churches have been preserved here.

However, the history of the Georgian state predates the arrival of Christianity. The existence of powerful state formations on Georgian soil throughout various centuries, which played a significant role in the history of the ancient world, makes Georgia one of the most historically remarkable countries among ancient civilizations.

Western Georgia is an extremely interesting place: a land associated with Ancient Colchis, which most people know about only from Ancient Greek myths. But can anyone give an exact answer to the question, where exactly did the formidable King Aeëtes, his sorceress sister Circe (Circea), and his daughter Medea the Enchantress live? Where did the Argonauts come for the Golden Fleece? To which mountains was the titan Prometheus chained? These are just some of the many secrets that Georgia holds within. This country is as much a gold mine for archeologists and historians trying to unravel the mysteries of the past as it is for history lovers in general.

As the reader will discover in the following chapters, all these mythical (and perhaps even historical) figures are deeply connected to Ancient Colchis, the land that corresponds to present-day Western Georgia.

Ancient Colchis is a state that existed from the 8th century BC. to the 1st century AD. It was located on the territory of today's Adjara, Guria, Imereti, Samegrelo, Abkhazia, Svaneti, Racha and Lechkhumi.

> The Colchis Kingdom was succeeded by the state of Egrisi, and the toponym "Colchis" (Kolkha, Colchis in Georgian) is still widely used in science and literature.

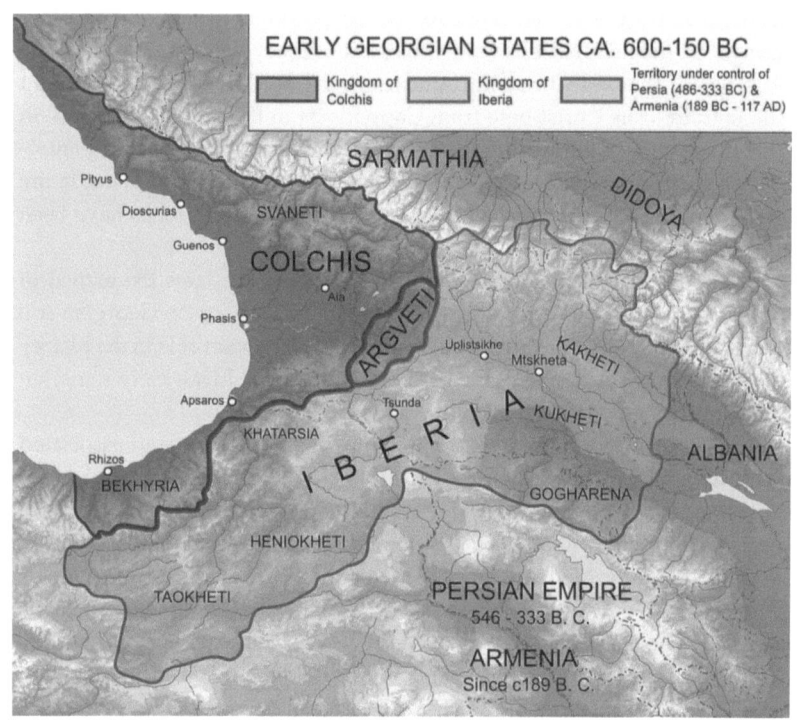

*Map of the early Georgian states, Colchis and Iberia. Map by Deu, World
History Encyclopedia (http://www.worldhistory.org), licensed under CC
BY-SA 4.0, https://creativecommons.org/licenses/by-sa/4.0/*

Chapter 1.
Colchis — A Mystery of Legends and Gold

It was interesting for me to learn about the history of Ancient Colchis and its inhabitants from the book 'Batum and its Neighborhood' published in 1906 in Russian.

"The oldest population of the country was made up of the Colchians, Geniochians, Chaldeans, Meschians and Tubals. These peoples had their own culture and were at a high stage of commercial and industrial development. They traded with the Phoenicians, sending them slaves and copper utensils, processed flax on the Egyptian model, on which, among other things, Herodotus bases his assumption about the origin of the Colchians from the Egyptians, not from the Greeks. They were engaged in cattle breeding, were able to make leather, and sold timber for ships.

"These peoples had their own beautifully armed army, were skilful in warfare and brave in campaigns, and in their private lives, they loved fun (...). It is not surprising, therefore, that all the great conquerors of ancient times were rulers of this beautiful country, described in the folk art of the Ancient Greeks as a source of gold, wealth, and, consequently, of people's happiness."

Much of our knowledge of the history of ancient Georgia we owe to archeological discoveries.

Archeological excavations of Colchian and Greek settlements began in Western Georgia only 60 years ago. All of the projects are connected to the history of the oldest state on the territory of Georgia — Colchis.

Such a journey was made by the famous British scientist and traveler Tim Severin. Having created a replica of an ancient Greek ship in 1984, he traveled along the supposed route of Jason and the Argonauts, and trod in the footsteps of Odysseus, who visited the island of the sorceress Circea - the sister of King Aeëtes.

The ancient Greeks saw Colchis as a mythical kingdom- exotic, rich, mysterious, inaccessible, and ruled by the formidable and severe King Aeëtes, son of the sun god Helios.

The historian Strabo reports that, *"In their country, it is said, the mountain streams bring gold, and the barbarians catch it with gratings and braided skins. Hence, they say, arose the myth of the golden fleece"* (Strabo. Geography. Book XI, II, 19).

The regions of Western Georgia - Racha, Lechkhumi, Svaneti, Samegrelo, Guria, Imereti, Adjara, Abkhazia, as well as the lands that are now part of the Russian Federation (Sochi and Tuapse district) and Turkey (Lazica, Ardakhani, Artvini, Rize, etc.), constituted in ancient times the Kingdom of Colchis, known to the world from the legend of Jason, the Argonauts and the golden fleece.

The legendary Argonauts famously sailed to Colchis in search of that very Golden Fleece. According to the 'Caucasian Calendar' of 1846, this expedition took place around 1250 BC. However, the myth of the Argonauts likely originated from historical accounts of Greek seafarers' raids on ancient states along the Black Sea coast.

I believe that the rich history of Colchis alone could make Georgia a pilgrimage site for ancient history enthusiasts from around the globe. Who wouldn't be drawn to walk in the footsteps of the Argonauts? And even if the Golden Fleece remains elusive, who knows what invaluable, intangible treasures such a visit might yield?

Prometheus vs Amirani

Another world-famous legend is tied to Colchis, which tells of the hero Prometheus being chained to one of the Caucasus mountains in Colchis as punishment for his selfless service to humanity. A prototype of Prometheus is also found in Georgian mythology: Amirani, one of the main, sacred characters of the ancient Georgian, pre-Christian religion.

Images of Amirani can be found in many archeological monuments of Georgia, most of which date back to the 3rd millennium BC. Tales about Amirani are recorded in all Kartvelian languages (Georgian, Svan, Mingrelian, Laz), and their dialects, which testifies to the formation of the image at a very early stage of the ethnogenesis of the Georgian people.

Heinrich Schliemann and the
Palace of King Aeëtes

Due to historical, political and economic circumstances, the history of Ancient Colchis remains insufficiently studied. It is known, for example, that German amateur archeologist Heinrich Schliemann, who discovered Troy despite the limits of science, following this sensational discovery, sought to dig up the palace of Colchian King Aeëtes. Yet he did not receive permission from the Russian tsar to do so. I will tell you more about that later. But just imagine how the course of history could have turned if Schliemann had managed to excavate the palace before the Russian Revolution of 1917!

What Archeologists Know about Colchis

To delve deeper into the history of Ancient Colchis, I visited the Batumi Archeological Museum. Its extensive collection showcases artifacts discovered in towns and villages throughout Adjara, all connected to the region's ancient past. The highlight of the museum is undoubtedly its Golden Fund, a dazzling display of Colchian gold jewelry — necklaces, earrings, clothing ornaments — along with ancient coins dating as far back as the 7th century BC.

After the tour, I spoke with the museum's director, scientist Emzar Kakhidze. He told me that the first Georgian proto-state formation existed in the Chorokhi river basin as early as the Late Bronze Age, in the 13th-9th centuries BC:

"For the first time, Assyrians and Urartu inhabitants started talking about Colchis," he says. *"The Assyrians mentioned Dayani, and this most likely corresponds to the historical Tao (now part of Turkey). Xenophontes also mentioned the Taokh tribe. And in the historical part of Southern Georgia was located this very Dayani. Some scholars, including myself, believe that the archaic form of Colchis, Aia-Colchis, where Aeëtes reigned, corresponds to Tao, and Colchis itself, or Kulha, which is mentioned from the 9th or 8th century BC in Urartian sources and corresponds to southern Colchis. We have an idea that Colchis is the basin of the Rioni River, the ancient Phasis River. But, according to archeological data and other sources, we come to the conclusion that Colchis began to form somewhat further south, in the basin of the Chorokhi River, and the Urartians, on reaching*

> The inhabitants of Colchis were called *Kolkhi*. *Kolkhi*, or *Kulkhi*, was the name of the people in neighboring Urartu, which is close to the sound of the Akkadian *Kilhi*. From Akkadian, the word passed into Ancient Greek as Κολχίς, and the Romans came to know this state as Colchis.

this country, found themselves exactly in the area of the Chorokhi River." (Note: The Chorokhi River still flows into the Black Sea near the city of Batumi).

The Apsar Fortress in Gonio

This was also the time when the settlement of Apsar was established. According to Stephen of Byzantium, Artemidorus of Ephesus, Arian, and Procopius of Caesarea, the emergence of the Apsar fortress is connected with the Argonauts' campaign to Aia Colchis. Legend has it that when Jason's detachment, with the help of Medea, managed to steal the Golden Fleece and, together with Medea, set a course for Hellas, King Aeëtes, son of the god Helios, sent after him his fleet, commanded by the heir to the throne Apsyrtes. The Colchis caught up with Argo's ship at the mouth of the river. On Medea's advice, Jason invited Apsyrtes onto his ship, where he brutally massacred him. The Argonauts hoisted the sails, and to delay the pursuers, began to throw parts of Apsyrtus' body off the ship. The Colchis are said to have collected the parts of Apsyrtus' body, brought them to land, and buried them where the Apsar fortress now stands.

What were the Argonauts looking for in the mysterious land? This question does not cause any doubt among archeologists: Emzar Kakhidze firmly states that the ancient Greeks were likely looking for the methods of gold production, or gold itself.

"Already in the third millennium BC, if not earlier, there was an advanced civilization in Colchis, where people knew how to cultivate the land, how to mine metal, and how to sell it afterwards," he tells me.

A Little Excursion into Mythology

Jason gathered a crew and commissioned the architect Argos to build their ship, which was then named in his honor. Interestingly, Argos had a direct connection to Colchis: he was the son of Phrixus and Chalciope. As children, Phrixus and his twin sister, Helle, faced mortal danger. Their mother, the cloud goddess Nephele, sent a golden ram to carry them across the sea to Colchis. During their flight, Helle fell and drowned, giving her name to the strait connecting the Aegean and Marmara Seas (the Hellespont, now known as the Dardanelles). Phrixus reached Colchis, where he sacrificed the ram in gratitude for his rescue, dedicating its fleece to a local temple. He then lived among King Aeëte's children—Medea, Chalciope, and Apsyrtus—and later married Chalciope. Their son was named Argos. Notably, in the Laz language, the toponym *Egrisi/Colchida* is written as *Argo*. Could it be that Argos was named after the land that saved his father and which was his mother's homeland? It is certainly a possibility.

Thus, a myth was formed about a kingdom rich in gold, and King Aeëtes reigned over this kingdom. After the coming of the Argonauts, the center of statehood and culture moved to the north, to the region of the Rioni River. And there the Colchis we know was formed.

Closer to the Mystery:
in the Footsteps of the Ancient Myths

What caused the Colchians to move north of their original lands? The answer lies in the invasion of the Scythians and Cimmerians in the late 8th century BC, Emzar believes.

Hoping to get even closer to the mystery of Ancient Colchis, I went to visit Nino Sulava, an archeologist at the Janashia Georgian National Museum. Nino has participated in many archeological expeditions carried out in the Imeretian town of Vani, and throughout the Lechkhumi region. During the excavations, she worked directly on preparing the artifacts as they were unearthed.

28

Excavations in Vani have been ongoing since the late 1950s, and archeologists are still finding ancient temple buildings and interesting artifacts there, among them cult objects, figurines of Greek gods, gold and silver jewelry, dishes, and more.

"Vani is an archeologist's paradise! There's a lot of archeological material there, and it is very rare. It is unlikely that such material will be discovered anywhere else," Nino tells me excitedly.

She's been lucky enough to hold many priceless objects in her hands—gold jewelry, beads and pottery. Indeed, the scholar believes that Vani gold is in no way inferior to the gold of Troy in terms of artistry.

Nino tells me that a large number of copper-smelting centers have been found in Georgia.

"These finds are the basis for the assertion that there was copper and bronze metallurgy in Colchis, and this was the main prerequisite for the establishment of the state. In those times, having such metallurgy was like us having the atomic bomb today, in terms of who holds the power," she claims.

Scientific findings suggest the Argonauts' voyage to Colchis may have occurred after the Trojan War, a period that coincided with the flourishing of Colchian metallurgy, spanning from the 2nd millennium BC to the 2nd century AD. Crucially, artifacts began appearing in Colchis with direct parallels in Greece, notably the fibula (a type of clasp or clothes pin). These fibulae have been found in collective burials near Ureki (Guria region), where excavations have taken place, as well as in Abkhazia. Fibulae became widespread throughout Colchis, and indeed became a key element of Colchian culture. The subsequent local production of such fibulae further supports the presence of imported examples in Colchis, strongly suggesting the possibility of Greek Argonauts having reached these shores.

Excavations in Pichvnari

According to Emzar Kakhidze, Colchis as a civilization was a mixture of local customs and Greek influence. For many decades, archeological excavations have been conducted near Kobuleti in the Pichvnari pine forest. There are two sites there: A Greek burial ground and a Colchis settlement. Unfortunately, the Greek settlement has yet to be processed by scientists. The distance between the settlement and the burial ground is less than a kilometer.

Scientists work in the area every summer, facing great difficulties as they excavate.

"There is sand in the burial ground, and all the contours are clearly visible," Emzar tells me. *"But you have to work very slowly so as not to miss beads, gold*

jewelry, and other things. And where the settlement is, there are difficult conditions, and that is why we have not made as much progress there as in the burial ground: the settlement is located in a swampy area, and the ground water prevents us from excavating. If it rains, we have to stop working for a time. But where there is sand, we can continue right after rainfall."

At present, Pichvnari is the only monument from which Greek colonization in Colchis, today's Western Georgia, can be studied. The other sites have either not yet been discovered, or remain poorly studied.

The Rioni River was known to the Greeks as *Phasis*. The river was considered the natural boundary between Europe and Asia by Anaximander and Herodotus.

Phasis

According to ancient authors and modern scientists, the ancient city of Phasis was located on a triangular island, surrounded on one side by the sea, on the other by a lake, and on the third side by the River Phasis.

In 1961, archeologists discovered evidence of a settlement from the 2nd century AD at the bottom of Lake Paleostomi. This area is the possible location of the city of Phasis.

As regards the Port of Phasis, where the city of Poti now stands, scientists there face great difficulties in terms of relief and geology, with the water in the basin of the Rioni River and Lake Paleostomi making excavations extremely difficult.

Colchis Settlements in Abkhazia

Undoubtedly, one of the most important places where ancient monuments await further study is Abkhazia. However, according to Emzar, *"in Abkhazia, where Russian troops are now on guard, locals do not take proper care of or pay proper attention to ancient historical sites. The Greek colony of Dioscuria, aka late Roman Sebastopolis, and the Greek polis of Gienos* (today's Ochamchire), *and Pitsunda* (antique *Pitiunt*, in Georgian *Bichvinta*) – *these are very important centers of antiquity."*

The main studies of Ancient Colchis in the Soviet period were carried out by Academician Otar Lordkipanidze and his Georgian and Russian colleagues. Many monographs were published on the subject. However, due to the Abkhaz War in the 1990s, which resulted in the occupation of the region by the Russian army, for thirty years Georgian scientists have not had access to study and preserve the archeological and cultural monuments of the region.

The Role of Women in the Integration of Greeks and Colchians

How did the Greeks and the local population interact with each other? According to scholars, it was most likely a peaceful coexistence that featured both cultural and trade interaction. David Brond, author of the book 'Georgia in Antiquity. The History of Colchis and Transcaucasian Iberia from 550 BC to 562 AD,' writes that local women played a major role.

The marriage of Greeks to local girls was considered the norm. The myth of the arrival of the Greek Phrixus in Colchis is a good example of this. The rescued Phrixus was given shelter, grew up in the court of the king, and later married the king's daughter. The Greeks regarded dynastic marriages as a transfer of land into Greek possession.

The Greeks brought with them religious cults that influenced local rituals. Emzar told me that the local population in Pichvnari adopted the Greek tradition of orienting the graves of the dead towards the east, placing the head of the deceased pointing eastwards. He also mentions the transition from collective burials to individual, and the introduction of the ritual called "agapos," what we call the "wake," as such a custom was not encountered in Colchis before that time: it appeared in the 5th century BC, precisely in Pichvnari, in coastal Colchis.

However, the influence of the Greeks was not one-sided, as the Greeks also learnt something from the Colchians. Greek burial sites provide ample evidence of contact with the Colchians, among which are Colchian vessels. The Greeks were obviously delighted with Colchis gold necklaces, which were made with such skill and with such a technique that today they can be proudly shown to the world as masterpieces of ancient Georgian jewelers. The rich collection of such items comes not only from Pichvnari, but also from other places, such as Vani.

The close relations between the Greeks and the Colchians continued into Hellenistic times. The Greeks buried their people separately from the Colchians in the 5th-4th centuries BC, but from the end of the 4th to the beginning of the 3rd century, united burial grounds began to be seen. It turns out that the intensity of relations between the Colchians and Greeks led to a mixed Colkh-Hellenistic settlement in Pichvnari, where people were together both during life and after death.

The Civilizational Choice of Ancient Georgia

The main conclusion drawn by the director of the Archeological Museum in Batumi about the interaction between ancient civilizations and Ancient

Colchis is as follows: *"The Classical period, the Hellenistic period and the late Roman period led to Georgia becoming part of the ancient world, and this brought the country into the pan-Christian world. Those countries that remained under the influence of the Parthian kingdom and then Persia (Iran) moved into the Eastern cultures and then into the Islamic world. The Roman in-*

Christianity was brought to Western Georgia by Apostle Andrew the First-Called, who traveled along the shores of the Black Sea. Apostles Simon the Canaanite (Zealot) and Matthias, who took the place of Judas Iscariot, also preached in Georgia. The tomb of Apostle Matthias is located on the territory of the Gonio fortress near Batumi. The tomb of Apostle Simon the Canaanite is on the territory of occupied Abkhazia.

fluence on Colchis was superficial if you compare it to their influence on Asia Minor. But the fact that we were under the influence of the Roman Empire led to the appearance of apostles in Colchis. Colchis' relationship with the ancient world was not just a relationship: it was her civilizational choice."

It would have been a missed opportunity not to ask Emzar what he knew about Heinrich Schliemann's intentions in Georgia.

"Schliemann applied to the Russian Academy of Sciences and asked for permission to excavate in the Batumi district. But he was refused," Emzar tells me. *"No official reason was given for the refusal. One of the possible reasons, though, according to some sources, could have been Schliemann's bigamy. The fact is that, while being married in Russia, he entered into a second marriage in Greece, which under Russian law was considered bigamy and was prosecuted by law."*

As we can see, Schliemann considered the territory of Colchis as a potentially rich place for archeological research. It is interesting to speculate what would have happened if he had managed to find the palace of Aeëtes or other monuments of Colchian material culture:

"Of course, Schliemann, in discovering Troy, made a landmark discovery, but he also damaged the site, so that it is now difficult to identify any archeological layers there. I don't know what would have become of his excavations of Colchis. Maybe there wouldn't have been half the artifacts left there had they agreed to it," the scientist responded.

In a 1974 issue of the Soviet travel magazine 'Around the World' (Russian: *Vokrug sveta*), it was suggested that the famous gold of Troy might have originated from Colchis. I asked Emzar about it.

"It's not out of the question," he says. *"We have data from archeological excavations that speak of southwestern modern Georgia as one of the main centers of ancient metallurgy. From the 3rd millennium BC, the Khats, aka proto-Hittites, who lived in Anatolia before the Indo-Europeans came there, were interested in the region. We have some evidence that they imported metal from this region (Note: from Colchis). We have Hittite ceramic finds, archeological layers that are saturated with them. There is evidence that bronze and iron metallurgy was also formed*

in this region. The oldest iron furnaces have been discovered in modern Adjara and Guria."

Traveling in the Footsteps of the Argonauts

Which exact places would the Argonauts have passed through? This question does not cause my respondents any difficulties. Here, for example, is what Nino Sulava had to say:

"For those interested in exploring Colchian history, several sites are worth visiting. In the village of Gonio, you can see the Roman fortress of Apsaros. Batumi also offers several relevant museums, including archeological and historical ones. A key destination is the town of Vani in Imereti, where you can explore excavation sites and a new archeological museum. Poti is believed to be the site of ancient Phasis, and boasts a museum with a rich collection of Greek and Colchian artifacts. A visit to Kutaisi and the village of Martvili is a must, as is the fortress of Noka-lakevi, where there is an excellent archeological museum. Via Khoni, you can go through Lechkhumi to Khvamli mountain, to which, according to legend, Prometheus was chained, and see the museum there. There is a new open-air museum in the village of Dekhviri in Lechkhumi, where materials from ancient Colchian burials and settlements are kept. And at the end, from Tsageri, you can head to Ushguli, and you will find yourself in Svaneti."

Doesn't it sound tempting?

Tbilisi—Gonio—Batumi—Kobuleti, April 2021

Tower of the Apsar Fortress in Gonio

*Family in Tskarota village,
in the Adjaran mountains*

*Mikho Kokoladze, from the
village Kokoleti in
Machakhela Gorge, loves
his small homeland*

*92-year-old Fati from Khulo
honoring guests staying in her house*

Chapter 2.
Adjara: A Historical, Ethnographical and Religious Puzzle

The Georgian Black Sea region of Adjara is directly related to the semi-mythical Colchis, the land of King Aeëtes and his daughter Medea.

Adjara is like a jigsaw puzzle, with all the pieces barely possible to put together, but we know the region was once part of Ancient Colchis and that great empires have fought over it, each leaving its mark on the cultural and historical heritage of the place.

However, Adjara's conquerors did not always bring with them death, misery and destruction. On the contrary, many great achievements, improvements and discoveries were connected with the endless competition between different powers. Otherwise, would the bridges of Queen Tamar (named King, or *mepe*, in Georgian) be scattered all over mountainous Adjara? These bridges, once part of the main trade routes, were built in the Middle Ages using ancient Roman technology, despite the times of Roman domination being long gone. They were named "the bridges of Queen Tamar" out of love for this revered ruler.

Or take another example. The city of Batumi, known in ancient times as Bathys, or "deep harbor," once lay in an unsightly swampy area which left almost no escape from malarial mosquitoes. Conquerors, seeking to use the port for strategic and trading purposes, drained the swamps and beautified the area.

In the 1st century AD, Apostle Andrew the First-Called preached in the mountains of Adjara, while Simon the Canaanite went to Abkhazia. The Apostle Matthew, one of the twelve apostles of Jesus Christ who replaced Judas Iscariot in the circle of Christ's disciples, is buried on the grounds of the Gonio fortress in Georgia. (Note: He should not be confused with the Evangelist Matthew, the author of one of the Gospels. Although both are important figures in Christianity, they are different people). As such, it is clear that the ancestors of today's Georgians associated themselves with the Christian faith long before Christianity was officially proclaimed the state religion in the 4th century.

Much later, in the Middle Ages, the Ottoman Empire, whose policy was to Islamize the local population, set the tone in the region. Georgians who converted to Islam risked losing their national identity. Nevertheless, the Adjarians managed to find their own middle way. Temur Tunadze, a historian from Batumi, told me about it:

"In Georgia, nationality and religion have become so intertwined that it is hard to imagine them as separate entities. However, the spread of Islam in Adjara has made this distinction less prominent today. As people converted to Islam, whether willingly or by force, they were among the first to recognize that their faith differed and should not be confused with their nationality. They did not want to lose their national identity. The Adjarians disrupted the symbiosis of faith and nationality."

Matters of Faith

In Adjara, there is great tolerance in matters of religion. During my journey through the region, I gradually realized that faith in Christ is in the genes of the people of Adjara. Almost all my respondents, when asked what religion they practise, answered something like this: *"First, of course, we are Christians, but then, you know, the Turks came here, and we...."*

An acquaintance told me that her grandmother and great-grandmother, who were Muslims, when baking *mchadi* in clay pans, *ketsi*, marked a cross in the middle of it, because that's how their distant ancestors had always done it.

At different times, Adjarians have experienced completely different vicissitudes: Christianization, Islamization, Soviet-style atheism, re-Islamization and, finally, re-Christianization. In matters of faith, the Soviet period was perhaps the most ruthless. The Soviet authorities were even less tolerant towards Muslims than towards Christians, although they were particularly vigilant in monitoring both those who attended mosques and those who attended churches.

An acquaintance of mine from Khulo is a Muslim called Jacob, a name which tends to be more popular in Christian countries. As it turned out, his

Crosses are also made in corn bread, *mchadi*, in Laz villages in Turkey. The inhabitants of Georgian villages profess Islam but remember that their grandmothers and great-grandmothers were Christians.

father was an active Muslim believer but chose to give his son a name that was "not too suspicious."

"We have always believed in God," Jacob tells me. *"All old people prayed, but the children were not allowed to. We have a mosque in Khulo now, where in Soviet times there was a warehouse, and we all prayed there without anyone noticing. Even funerals according to Muslim rites were not allowed here, so we buried our dead at night. If someone found out that you were burying your dead according to Muslim rites, you could quickly lose your job."*

It seems to me that the influence of the Orthodox Church in Adjara is increasing these days. But in Khulo of the 1990s, local Muslims clashed quite aggressively with Orthodox priests who went there to preach.

In reality, in today's Adjara, people of any religion can feel comfortable. The Gomarduli Zen Garden, which opened in 2022 near the village of Shuakhevi, and which looks very much like a Buddhist retreat, is perfect proof of this. On my way to Gomarduli, I was preoccupied with the question: How does "Zen" fit into the Muslim reality of this remote corner of paradise? Ukrainian citizen Yevgeniy, the owner, explained to me the attitude of the locals to his institution: *"My hotel fits into the local reality pretty well, because I am not propagandizing my views here. Of course, purely from an aesthetic point of view, my place looks something like a Buddhist monastery, a kind of kaizen, on land that has long been Muslim. But in reality, a lot of people here go simultaneously to mosque and to church, and they are generally not particularly religious. All this is to our advantage, because religion doesn't stand between us, and we can communicate just as people. Here, we have simple communication between humans, and humanistic treatment – things that are respected all over the world, regardless of religion or race."*

In the village of Kvirike, Kobuleti municipality, I visited an ancient wooden mosque, a marvelous work created by Laz masters. Its Khoja, Aslan Abashidze, gave us a short tour, during which he lamented that his fellow villagers are not very choosy when it comes to matters of faith: *"They believe in this and that* (Note: they are Christians and Muslims at the same time). *But this is wrong. When a person has several faiths, it is not right. I have relatives who converted to Christianity. Why? I don't know! Many people wear crosses and think that's the end of it. It's not the end of anything: faith should be carried in the heart and not on the body."*

A Melting Pot of Nations

It is still not entirely clear where the Adjarians came from. According to one theory, it is not a tribe, but a toponym which came from the name of the river Adjaristsqali, and that, by origin, Adjarians are mostly Gurians, as well as Mingrelians and Laz. But there is another opinion: Adjarians are a sub-ethnos of the Georgian people, like the Gurians, Mingrelians and Imeretians. It is not easy to say which of the two is closer to the truth.

Lazica

The Roman province of Lazica encompassed present-day Adjara. But what exactly was Lazica, and who were its inhabitants? The Laz people were renowned for their daring and bravery, inspiring numerous legends.

The 19th-century French scholar Marie Brosset, who conducted extensive research on Georgia, expressed surprise at the limited attention Lazica had received from Georgian historians. He even noted the inaccuracies and confusion present in the accounts of the ancient Greeks, who fought many battles in the region.

The historical lands of Georgia have been divided many times. And they were divided once again under the Soviet regime.

Following the Russian Revolution, Georgia declared its independence. However, in 1921, the Red Army invaded. It was a campaign facilitated, in part, by internal dissent within Georgia. The ensuing brutal battles against the occupying forces culminated in the defeat of the Georgian Democratic Republic, marking its end.

A year after the occupation of Georgia, the territory of Lazica was divided between Soviet Russia and Kemalist Turkey. Thus, many Laz people, together with their land, became part of a foreign state overnight. A demarcation line was drawn through their villages, and the inhabitants of those Georgian villages woke up to find themselves in a foreign state.

> The Greeks and Romans knew the Kingdom of Egrisi (the Kingdom of Colchis) by the name Lazica. The Persians used the toponym Lazistan. After the Georgian provinces became part of the Russian Empire, a part of Lazica, together with the Laz inhabitants, became part of the Ottoman Empire - now Turkey.

According to various sources, from 120,000 to 1.5 million Lazs live in Turkey today. A very small number of them remain in the region of Adjara, more precisely in Sarpi, near the Georgian-Turkish border. Lazs also live in Kvariati, Gonio and Makho, and in Batumi, Kobuleti, Zugdidi and Abkhazia. On Turkish territory, the Laz people live in three districts of Rize province — Hopa, Arkaba and Borchkhi.

Many authors, including Procopius of Caesarea, stated a belief that the Lazs were Colchians. He mentioned the Chans, a people related to the Laz, but in Procopius' time, the Chans did not live by the sea. Now this difference, if there was one, has been erased. Lazs and Chans are considered synonyms and are used to describe the same people — Georgians from Western Georgia.

Interestingly, on the territory of modern Turkey, there are several other sub-ethnic groups that were historically part of the Georgian nation.

The Chveneburi (Georgian ჩვენებურნი, lit. "our own," "one of ours," Turkish *Çveneburi*), like the Lazs, were Muslims, which distanced them from Christian Georgians. In addition, unlike the Lazs, the Chveneburi were resettled in Turkey relatively recently, from the late 19th century. They preserved the Georgian language and culture, but do not live as compactly as the Lazs, often intermarrying, which is leading to their gradual assimilation. This is especially noticeable among young people, who have adopted the Turkish language. The bulk of the Chveneburi live in the cities of Trabzon, Rize, Ordu, Sinop, Bursa and Istanbul.

Imerkhevians and Shavshets are two closely related ethnographic groups of Georgians who live in the historical region of Shavsheti, now located in northeastern Turkey. This is an ethnographic group of Georgians professing the Muslim religion. They call themselves the *Imerkheveli*, and they number several tens of thousands. Almost all of them are bilingual, speaking the Imerkhevi dialect of Georgian, and Turkish. The Imerkhevi dialect (*Imerkheuli*) has many common features with the neighboring Ajarian dialect. In terms of traditional culture, the Imerkheuli are close to the population of Western and Southern Georgia. Most of them

> While the citizenship of the Lazs has changed depending on political events, the Lazs have retained their language. They speak the Laz language, which is related to Mingrelian. And together, Laz and Mingrelian are part of the Mingrelo-Chan language group of the Kartvelian language family. The Lazs of Turkey speak Laz and Turkish.

live compactly in Artvin, mainly in the highland part of the historical Shavsheti-Imerkhevi.

Close to the Imerkhevians are the Klardjians (of historical Tao Klarjeti) and Machakhelians (of historical Machakhela), living in the north of Artvin.

The number of Georgian-Muslims (Imerkhevians, Adjarians, Chveneburi) in Turkey is estimated at 300,000.

We now know the Adjarians as a warm, friendly and hospitable people. However, their description of a century ago could instil fear in any traveler. This is an excerpt from the 1886 edition of the book 'Noteworthy Corners of the Caucasus. Batumi district, Svaneti,' published in Tbilisi in Russian:

"According to stories and very limited personal observations, we can only notice that the inhabitants of the district are wild, extremely passionate and mobile, giving in to the first impulse without analysis and reasoning. Although, on the face of it, in petty relations, they appear to be very restrained and able to control themselves, they are terrible fanatics, especially in the ceremonial aspects of religion, and they strongly hate Russians (...).

"Blood feuds are practiced throughout the district, and it's said that the accounts regarding this matter are so complex and tangled among the residents that few of them will venture out at night if a blood debt is owed, not by them, but by any of their relatives, and blood feudists find it most convenient to carry out their duties at night. During the day, however, they very much enjoy strolling aimlessly from village to village, and while doing so, they take pleasure in firing their guns into the air."

The "saber-rattling" in the mountains of Adjara has some historical logic: Adjarians are proud of their signature hand-made flintlock rifle, the Machakhela, which was once supplied far beyond the borders of Georgia.

Discoveries in Khulo

Thank God, I did not hear any gunshots on my way over the Goderji Pass to Khulo, the district center of mountainous Adjara. On the contrary, it seemed to me that it is in the mountains of Adjara that you can make friends with almost every local resident.

When I was looking for information about the local ethnographic museum in Khulo, a kind-hearted taxi driver, Jacob, offered to help me. Having learnt about the purpose of my visit, he not only took me to the home of the museum guide, but also organized a meeting with a relative of his, a historian by training. After that, Jacob solemnly announced to me that his daughter was waiting for us at home with dinner, where local specialities had been prepared for me. But before that, of course, we went to see one of the bridges of Queen Tamar, an indispensable attribute of the region. The historian Jemal proudly informed me that the Golden Age of Georgian history, i.e. the reign of Queen Tamar and the work of the immortal poet Shota Rustaveli, had happened a whole century earlier than the European Renaissance.

At Jacob's home, his daughter and mother, 92-year-old Fati, were waiting for me. They had prepared a table of local specialities: *sinori*, a local lasagne, *burano*- mashed potato with cheese and melted butter, and a very peculiar dry braided cheese called *chinchili*. A few more relatives soon joined our feast, which Jacob brightened up with lavish toasts, accordion playing and singing. We talked about life now and then, about the rich traditions and customs of the local area, and about family matters.

I was most impressed by Fati, a mother of seven children and grandmother of seventeen grandchildren. This quiet woman, with her discerning eyes, watched over our meal until it was done. It was noticeable how proud Jacob was of his mother, who, he said, never leaves the table before the guests.

It was impossible not to ask Fati when she considered her life better: before, or now. I confess that I expected to hear the typical answer I get from older people: that everything used to be much better, tastier, and more beautiful. Fati's answer surprised me: *"Before, when we were young, we had a very hard time. We worked hard, but we lived very poorly. We didn't have much corn. We didn't have bread, either, so we had to eat even corn husks to survive. But now look at us: we have everything on the table, and we always have bread too. Of course, I was happiest when I had children and when my now deceased husband was still around. The whole family helped us to raise the children- the old people used to live together with the young."*

Jacob's family history is surely typical of the inhabitants of these places:

"My father was born in 1910, and he was always a healthy man. He walked a lot. My father was a Khoja, and he was never afraid to pray. Our mosque in Khulo was not working, so my father would go to the mosque in Batumi. But the KGB was always watching the believers, and that's why they started to create problems for my brother, who worked in Khulo as an investigator in those years. When he was to be appointed a judge in our town, my brother was told that since his father was a Muslim and prayed, if he wanted to become a judge, he should tell his father to shave off his beard and stop praying. But my father had always been a Muslim, and he would not hear of such a thing. So, my brother was not made a judge, and he had to go and work in Batumi."

Times have changed, and now Jacob's family is partly Christian: his daughter married an Imeretian, a man from Kutaisi, and changed her faith. His sister also became a Christian, as she was offered a job at a Christian college in Khulo, where the main requirement for employment was conversion to Orthodoxy. Jacob is not particularly worried about the Christianization of part of his family: *"to each their own,"* he says.

Women in Adjara

During the meal, I noticed that the local women did not touch any alcohol. However, for some reason, this did not apply to me: as a guest, I was constantly being served wine, and they regularly tried to make me drain my glass. *"Since you are a Christian, you must drink it,"* was the verdict of my new friends. The only thing that saved me was that I was driving. At Jacob's house, I had to defend my right to be on an equal footing with the non-drinking Adjarian women!

Interesting information about the status of women in 19th century Adjara society can be found in the book by traveler Igor Kanevsky,

'Noteworthy corners of the Caucasus. Batumi district. Svaneti, Tiflis' (1886). In it, he wrote the following:

"The attitude of men towards women in some details is very strange; it is a mixture of ardent southern jealousy, nourished by religious regulations, and not a kind of chivalry, not a kind of nastiness and disdain (...). They are locked up and wrapped up in the most intensified way, almost hermetic, and let out from behind bars only for field work, and that on condition that the wrongful eye of a giaour could not admire a wrapped-up figure with a hoe in their hands from dozens of fathoms away (...).

"How wild, timid and limited these unfortunate women are, hidden by nature in deep inaccessible gorges, and locked up in harems by harsh customs – it is hard to imagine."

(Note: The term *giaour* was used mainly by Muslims for those who didn't belong to their religion).

At the ethnographic museum in Khulo, the local guide, Nana Shantadze, told me curious stories about the emancipation of Adjarian women during the Soviet era. Women began to be employed in the local theater, in the song and dance ensemble. They were also accepted for various public positions. Nevertheless, despite the emancipatory trends of the 20th – 21st centuries, in my opinion, Adjarian women are still half a step below men in the social hierarchy.

A Special Kind of Hospitality

I was invited to stay the night in Jacob's hospitable home, but I had to refuse and instead stayed at the guesthouse that he had helped me to find.

"Well, if you don't feel comfortable, go to them yourself and warn them. I won't go there with you, or they'll be angry with me for stealing their guest!" Jacob said.

Hospitality is deeply ingrained in Adjarian and Georgian culture. Georgians consider a guest a messenger of God. Guest rooms are typically more elaborately furnished than the hosts' own living quarters, and are meticulously maintained, always ready for unexpected arrivals. At the ethnographic museums in Khulo and Batumi, I learned that in traditional Adjarian houses, guest rooms were invariably located on the first floor, with a separate entrance.

Tskarota: In Jesus's Pocket

Hospitality is a phenomenon embedded in the ethnopsychology of Georgians in general, and Adjarians in particular. I soon became convinced of this when I accidentally came across the village of Tskarota. A random passerby named Zurab realized that I was lost and suggested that I go to his house. Or rather, he said "to his family." It was a great temptation for me – to find out how people live in highland traditional villages, of which there are only a few in modern Europe. I took the risk of accepting the invitation, and soon saw that life in these villages still flows in the same way it did a hundred, two hundred and three hundred years ago.

Zurab, 36, is the head of the family, with a beautiful young wife, a black-clad grandmother-widow, and three cheeky sons. The family is completely self-sufficient, despite the fact that Zurab has many professions bringing in an income, among them as an economist and accountant: they have cattle and rabbits, a large garden, and a vegetable garden where everything grows in abundance. They also grow tobacco and make fruit vodka.

The large house on stilts, made entirely of chestnut, smelt cozy, warm and comfortable. The view from the balcony over the neighboring villages and mountains was such that I felt as if eternity was opening its arms to me. Yevgeniy, the owner of Gomarduli Zen Garden, made a similar observation later on, noting: *"People in these parts live as if they are going to live forever."*

After a spontaneous feast filled with toasts and laughter, Zurab and I took a stroll through his native village, which he described with evident affection. He then showed me some of the village's highlights: another Tamar bridge, cascading waterfalls on a mountain stream (a welcome respite from the sweltering heat), and ancient water mills.

It seems to me that even after an extended stay in the Adjarian mountains, one could never tire of their natural splendor: the countless diverse waterfalls, the rushing mountain rivers, the secluded lakes, the rich vegetation of these lush, forested areas, and the breathtaking vistas that unfold at every turn.

Machakhela

There are four national parks in Adjara: Kobuleti, Mtirala, Kintrishi and Machakhela, and each of them is valuable and remarkable in its own way.

The rapid development of tourism has quickly re-oriented the local economy. New hotels have sprung up in almost every village, and crafts have been given a much-needed boost. In addition, locals have developed a keen interest in discovering new places and routes near their villages to share with travelers. Sulkhan Nizharadze, a local historian from Kobuleti, was with me when we bumped into one such enthusiast, Mikho

Kokoladze, by chance, when we were looking for the mysterious twin waterfalls, which Sulkhan had previously known about only from hearsay.

Gustave Eiffel's atelier also designed a viaduct in Tsemi on the Borjomi-Bakuriani narrow-gauge railway line. In 1902, the components of the bridge were delivered from France, and were assembled under the supervision of the famous Georgian engineer and aviator, Vissarion Keburia.

The village of Kokoleti was reached by a narrow, steep road, which we traveled up by car, seemingly up into the sky. At the end of the village, there was a house, near which we stopped to ask a local how to find the waterfalls. Mikho came to our rescue, immediately announcing his willingness to help us in our search: *"You're lucky! I recently discovered these waterfalls by chance! If you want, I'll show you the way."*

A fifteen-minute drive further on, and we climbed out to walk along a path that Mikho and his fellow villagers had cleared and fitted with wooden steps and railings.

The sound of the waterfalls could be heard from afar, but to get close to them, we had to several times cross the turbulent mountain river, climbing over huge, mossy and slippery boulders. And then we came to the foot of the waterfalls.

In a mighty torrent of myriad splashes, the two unruly mountain rivers rushed downwards, forming a triangle and merging with a furious roar right at our feet. The noise was so loud that we could hardly hear each other speaking. On the road, we had dreamed of throwing ourselves headlong into these mountain torrents. However, it was already evening, and the cool splashes quickly soaked us through, so much so that we were soon freezing. Needless to say, we decided to abandon the idea of swimming in the waterfall!

We sat down on the cozy benches the villagers had installed. On the wooden table, we found two antique green glasses. *"These shot glasses are mine,"* Mikho announced proudly. *"I left them here on purpose for guests. And now, wait, there will be some vodka for you!"* And Mikho ran off, jumped deftly into the almost knee-deep water, and retrieved his trophy: a bottle of ice-cold honey vodka: *"I keep it in the river, in the cold, to make it nicer to drink. It's my own- homemade! Gagimarjos, megobrebo!"* (Note: Georgian for "Cheers, my friends!").

The Machakhela Gorge is full of wonders: waterfalls, fortresses, mosques, Tamar bridges and iron suspension bridges designed by Eiffel's atelier.

However, it is not only fantastic nature and architectural monuments that make these places unforgettable: people like Mikho Kokoladze can be considered another priceless asset of this region.

Before the collapse of the Soviet Union, Mikho worked in the merchant naval fleet: he was a sailor, a canteen boy, a cook, and a motor mechanic. Over eleven years, he traveled the world. *"While at sea, I longed to return to my native village, even for a single day, to play Joker with my friends in the evening and then set sail once more. The sea, I tell you, can be incredibly tiring. A ship is, in many ways, a floating prison – a confined space shared with the same faces for months, with no sight of land. This sense of confinement is amplified during the night watch, when time seems to stretch on endlessly."*

Mikho became more than just our guide: after the tour, he invited us to his home, introduced us to his wife, and treated us to honey, coffee, vodka and fresh homemade bread before we went on our way. Mikho Kokoladze now hosts guests in his family guesthouse, makes honey in his apiary, and distils mead. His house overlooks the entire Machakhela Gorge.

> Joker (painted poker) is a card game for four players. This game is popular in Georgia. You can buy the game as a set, with a pack of cards, a notepad and a pen.

"I've done my time," Mikho says with a sigh of relief. *"The earth, my friends, is round, and this is how I came back home. I guess I deserved it. That's why I'm satisfied and happy. Whenever I visit a large city, I find it difficult to sleep; I'm bothered by the noise and the stifling air. I struggle to understand how anyone can live in an apartment, so disconnected from nature. For me, life in the countryside feels more authentic, and the food is certainly fresher. While rural life requires hard work, it also offers opportunities for rest and a healthier, more balanced lifestyle."*

To be honest, we did not want to leave Mikho's beautiful house at the end of the world. However, our next hosts were waiting for us in another great little village close to Batumi.

Zarzma — Goderdzi — Khulo — Tskarota — Kokoleti — Tbilisi,
July - August 2020

Adjarian historian Sulkhan Nizharadze in Petra Fortress

Two Greeks from Adjara: Misha Puturidi on the left

Tea plantation in Guria, western Georgia

Chapter 3.
The Black Sea Riviera

The Black Sea Riviera of Georgia is not only a divine combination of sun, sea, beaches, luxurious nature and magnificent views, it is also made up of a multitude of significant places and personalities, as well as historical events that have influenced the course of world history. Among those personalities, events and places are the ancient Egyptians, Greeks, Persians, Byzantines; the fight for the coast by ancient empires, the legendary fortress of Gonio, where the relics of Apostle Matthew rest, the Batumi oil port founded by the Nobel brothers, the first tea plantations, and — imagine! — the beginning of Joseph Stalin's revolutionary activity! Added to this is a unique climate and numerous other curiosities of history, geography, anthropology and ethnography.

The Nobel Brothers Technological Museum was established in 2007. It is located in the building of the former office of the Nobel Brothers Oil Production Partnership in Batumi. In the mid-2000s, the personal archive of the Nobel brothers was discovered in Kutaisi, consisting of photographs, written documents, oil samples in bottles with the Nobel family's name branding, and other materials. This archive was added to the museum collection.

Tsikhisdziri and Petra Fortress

Without knowledge of ancient history, it is almost impossible to understand and get a real sense of the Black Sea coast. That is why the first thing I did with Sulkhan was go to Petra, one of the most remarkable fortresses on the coast, set on a high sea cliff, from which the whole of Batumi can be seen, as if it is sitting in the palm of your hand.

One day, my friends and I went to Petra at sunset. The sun's disc had almost sunk into the sea and was beginning to change the color of everything around it, plunging the outlines of the coast into a translucent evening haze. Admiring the disappearing views of the Kobuleti-Batumi coastline, it was easy to be transported back in time, and to feel a sense of awe for the place. Since then, Petra Fortress has been like a time machine for me.

"Petra was built in 529-538 AD, on the order of Emperor Justinian the First," Sulkhan tells me. *"In those times, the Kingdom of Egrisi (Colchis) was under the influence of Byzantium. The place where Petra Fortress stands was considered strategically important due to the important trade routes that passed*

by it. After completion of the fortress, a war broke out between Persia and Byzantium which lasted from 542 to 562 AD. The Kingdom of Egrisi fought on the side of Byzantium, but the Persian Shah, Khosrov Anushirvan, attacked Petra and held it for nine years. The fortress was periodically destroyed by enemies, but the Georgians rebuilt it."

In the 18th century, bloody battles of the Russian-Turkish War took place here. A Turkish division of 30,000 men was stationed in Petra Fortress. The Russian army tried to take the fortress, but British ships came to the aid of the Turks, and only when the Turks surrendered Adjara was Petra also surrendered.

Sulkhan and I visited on a rainy July morning, and the wind was whipping our clothes this way and that. I was saved from the weather by my hooded mackintosh, but Sulkhan, dressed in a thin, short-sleeved summer shirt, seemed immune to the rain. He claimed that he had got used to the rain in his childhood, and didn't even think to hide under an umbrella. *"The Chakvi-Tsikhisdziri area was considered the area with the highest annual rainfall in the entire USSR,"* Sulkhan explains.

The abundant local rain has one lovely side effect: all year round, everything around here is a lush emerald green.

Near the fortress, Sulkhan told me, they had filmed scenes of the Estonian-Georgian military drama 'Tangerines,' which takes place in Abkhazia in the 1990s. A number of scenes of other famous Georgian films have been shot on the territory of Petra, among them 'An Extraordinary Exhibition,' directed by Rezo Gabriadze.

Standing in the fortress, Sulkhan and I looked down at the raging Black Sea, which on that day was truly black, roaring with a beastly, long howl.

Why doesn't Petra have a fortress wall on the seaside? I asked him.

"When, in 1881, they started to build the Baku-Batumi railway, the wall was dismantled, and all the bridges from here to Batumi, as well as the entire Batumi port and the villa of engineer Skarjinsky, under the beautiful name 'Castello Mare' were built from its stones," my companion replied.

The Black Sea Imperial Villas — Shrouded in Historical Mystery

On that day, Sulkhan told me an intriguing story that left me speechless.

It turns out that after Adjara was liberated from Turkish rule, the lands near Batumi began to be called "the Russian Riviera." Literary sources from the turn of the 19th-20th centuries testify to the fact that Russian emperors had great hopes for the Batumi region. Immediately after the conquest of this land from the Turks, the Russian authorities sent expeditions there, the purpose of which was to familiarize themselves with the newly conquered lands in detail, as well as to describe their history, condition, and the economic, strategic, therapeutic and recreational potential of the area.

Here is an extract from the book 'Batumi Coast. Russian Tropics,' edited by S.A. Anisimov in 1911:

"The Batumi region has a unique climate of its own; a climate that no other state in Europe possesses, the likes of which we can only look for in distant overseas countries.

"In the climatic regard, the Batumi coastal strip, belonging to the belt of grapes and laurel cherry, is characterized by the possibility to grow rice, by the ripening of lemons and oranges under the open sky, by the presence of laurel in forests, and in gardens – lush camellias, magnolias, dracaenas, palms, and, in general, various representatives of the subtropical zone, tea and mandarins inclusive.

"The greenery here does not disappear throughout the year, and in January, many plants are in bloom. In December, there are often a number of warm, sunny days; violets and roses bloom, and the inhabitants of the north are particularly struck by the contrast between the poor north and the lush tropical nature here."

In the above-mentioned book, researchers wrote about the Batumi climate especially in connection to its benefits for people with incipient pulmonary tuberculosis:

"Compared to Sochi, Sukhum, Yalta, according to Dr Triantafyllidis, Batum has the following advantages:

- *Batum's average annual temperature (about 15 degrees Celsius) is higher than in these resorts.*
- *Winter and autumn are warmer (autumn 16.5°C, winter 7.5°C).*
- *The temperature is more even and does not present sharp fluctuations.*
- *There are twice as many quiet days as in Sukhum and Sochi, and the average strength of the winds is half as high."*

Dr Frenkel, in his 'Essays on Batum,' wrote the following about its climate:
"In summer, the air resembles that artificially maintained in greenhouses: a person arriving here at the beginning of August from Tiflis, after a hot summer spent there, feels a pleasant languor, a desire for tenderness; thirst, dry mouth, perspiration are sharply reduced; urination is greatly increased; bowel movements

and sleep are improved. If the visitor is possessed by dry bronchitis, coughing and expectoration of sputum are relieved remarkably quickly.

"The summer is hot; the rest of the year is quite pleasant. There is almost no winter; spring starts in February, and the water in the sea is already so warm that locals and many visitors start swimming from halfway through February, without any harm to their health, although in March there are sometimes cold days. After January, the trees start to blossom, as in February there are days when it is 15-16 degrees Celsius in the shade.

"Observations on the temperature of Batum show that it, as a winter and autumn (climatic) station, has undoubted advantages compared to Sukhum, Sochi, Yalta and, in its warmer and more uniform climate, it is closer to Nice than other stations."

The Russian emperors, on finally getting their own Cote d'Azur, began to distribute the land to the Russian nobility, as well as to generals, officers, doctors, engineers and other high-ranking officials. Plots from Batumi to Makhinjauri were allocated to the most noble persons of the empire; plots from Tsikhisdziri to Chakvi were given to generals who had participated in the war; while the area around Kobuleti was given to less noble persons- doctors, prosecutors, officials, etc.

In this area, there were many pompous summer houses, each more beautiful than the last. In 1905, the cottage of the engineer Skarjinsky, known as *Castello Mare*, was built, where the hotel of the same name is now located. In 1910, the owner lost the house to the winemaker Ananov. After the revolution, health resort Nauka was located there, with a tourist center situated nearby. Before the revolution, the house of the tourist resort belonged to Baroness von Tiesenhausen, great-granddaughter of Field Marshal Kutuzov, hero of the Patriotic War of 1812. Sulkhan's grandfather was the director of this health resort for twenty years, and Sulkhan himself spent his youth there. What a lucky man!

In 1888, the Russian imperial family came to Batumi for the first time: Alexander III, his wife Maria, and heir to the throne Nicholas, together with Italian King Vittorio Emanuele. There, they laid the foundation stone for the Church of St Alexander Nevsky, which was later destroyed by the Soviet authorities. That same year, a park near Lake Nurigela was opened (now it is the Central Batumi Park).

It was on that first visit of the imperial couple to Batumi that the heir to the throne's chief nanny, Countess Maria Fesenkova, noted how much she liked Makhinjauri. In appreciation, Nicholas gave her land there. A project for a three-storey villa built in the Moorish style was begun by a Georgian architect, although it was completed by Russian architects. Soon after the October Revolution, in 1918, Maria Fesenkova was murdered by her own servant. During the Second World War, the palace housed a military hospital. Later, the authorities gave the Countess' house to an orphanage. After the collapse of the USSR, the palace was occupied by forced migrants from Abkhazia. Now, the palace is abandoned, although it is included in the list of Monuments of Cultural Heritage of Georgia.

It took us quite a long time to find Fesenkova's summer house in Makhinjauri. The locals knew nothing about the countess, and the estate was known to them only as a former orphanage.

A narrow gravel road led us along a stream through a subtropical forest of eucalyptus, oleander and other strange plants. We ventured into the Countess' house, full of mystery and ghosts, though it was not entirely safe. We were rewarded, though, for the risk of wandering through the rooms, along balconies, and for climbing the broken staircase to the very roof, by the sense of the palace still seeming to breathe the air of bygone eras; by the panoramic views of the neighboring villages slumbering serenely on the green hills, and by the vast expanse of the sea. Later, I learned that artists like to sneak into this estate and paint one sketch after another, because such motifs for painting are not easy to find even on this gorgeous coast.

After that, Sulkhan showed us another summer estate in Tsikhisdziri, one which once belonged to General Zalensky. The General's closest neighbors were representatives of the Russian nobility: the Golitsyns and the Tolstoys, the Maryanovs and the Shendrikovskys. The manor house, with its portico and Greek columns, also built in the once fashionable Moorish style, sits high on a hill above the sea in a lush tropical park with banana palms and oleanders. At present, this house, too, is abandoned. But even in its state of decay, it is beautiful, and provides a rich ground for fantasizing about the lives of local nobility at the end of the *Belle Époque*.

A Lyrical Digression

During one of my trips to Batumi, I met an elder, very sociable lady named Elena. During our conversation, I mentioned that Sulkhan and I had been exploring the Batumi coast. She then told me the story of her acquaintance with the Shendrikovskys' summer house in Tsikhisdziri. Here is her story:

"At school, I sat at the same desk with Ludmila Shendrikovskaya. She was the granddaughter of an officer in the Tsarist army. Once, I spent the summer at their dacha (Note: summer house). *Luda's grandfather had already died, and her grandmother was left alone. She was an aristocrat who spoke perfect French. Ludmila, by the way, also knew it perfectly. I enjoyed talking to this lady. I don't remember her name, but she was a fabulous woman! They had a magnificent*

portrait of her sitting in an armchair, and her grandfather, a royal officer, standing beside her with all the regalia. The land around the dacha was magnificent. True, it was very high above the sea. The air was the freshest, but it took a long time to get down to the sea, and then it was difficult to climb back up. Every evening, we ran to the health resort 'Nauka' to dance. Those were the serene days of our youth, when we still had our whole lives ahead of us!"

Georgian Tea

Batumi historian Temur Tunadze invited me to Chakvi to see another beautiful villa. It had belonged to Lau John Jau, the founder of the tea industry in Georgia, an agronomist and planter from China.

Judging by the location of the house, right by the sea, one can understand how important this man was to the Russian Empire. The Lau John Jau estate was built in the Chinese traditional style. Now, it is in disrepair, although it has the status of a historical monument.

Liu Junzhou (Lau John Jau) came to the Russian Empire in 1896 with his wife and five children and lived here for thirty years. He first produced tea under his own name, then went into the service of the Russian Imperial House and became the head of the Chakvin Tea Factory. After the Russian Revolution, the Chinese agronomist also worked for the Soviet authorities. He categorically refused to use machines to pick tea and recognized only

manual labor. This opposition led to his renunciation of Soviet citizenship and his departure from the USSR in 1926.

Lau John Jau returned to China with his family. He passed away in 1939, in Harbin. Lau John Jau's children—two sons and three daughters—were educated in Georgia and Russia. After returning to China, they taught Russian at Chinese universities.

One of Lau John Jau's sons was married to a Georgian woman, and they had a daughter, Mali Liu Kuangwen, born to them in Harbin. At the age of 22, she continued her studies at the Art Academy of Georgia. She married Georgian artist Givi Kandareli and stayed in Georgia.

Mali Kandareli, as she is known in Georgia, founded the Chair of Sinology in Tbilisi, and after that the Georgian-Chinese Friendship Society and the Georgian branch of the Confucius Institute.

After the collapse of the Soviet Union, the Chakvin Tea Factory ceased operations. In the 1990s, the factory was bought by the Turks. Why do you think? The answer is simple: Georgian tea could compete with Turkish tea, so they bought the factory to close it down. However, the competitors miscalculated, because Turkish tea is a mass product, while Georgian tea is an exquisite, elite drink.

The Georgian tea leaf is a subtropical *Tea Cammelia Sinensis*, which was brought to Georgia from China in 1847, where, unlike in Crimea, it took root perfectly well. This tea grew in Azerbaijan, Turkey, Persia, the Krasnodar region of Russia and Ukraine only following its acclimatization in Georgia. In 1900, tea from Chakvi, at the time named *Imperial Tea*, won the Gold Medal at the World Exhibition in Paris.

After the collapse of the USSR, the production of Georgian tea ceased, a fact which was to work to the advantage of the tea leaf: for thirty years, the land "rested," seeing some of the old plantations becoming overgrown with forest. In this unusual way, one of the rarest, most expensive and useful types of tea appeared in Georgia—wild tea, the price of which can reach exorbitant heights on global markets. The area of wild tea plantations in Georgia is larger than that found in other tea-growing countries.

This and other fascinating stories about Georgian tea were told to me by Shota Bitadze, a wonderful tea enthusiast. His Tbilisi tea boutique is not only a shop, but also a museum with a library. I highly recommend a visit to his tea kingdom on Galaktion Tabidze Street in Tbilisi's Sololaki district.

Misha Puturidi and the Georgian Greeks

Another curious page of Adjara's history relates to the Greeks. I already mentioned at the very beginning that in Ancient Colchis, around the turn of the 8th century BC, there were quite a few Greek settlements. However, in the 6th-5th centuries BC, evidence of Greeks in these places was lost.

Much later, in the early 20th century, Greeks and Armenians fled from Ottoman Turkey, where massacres of "infidels" were held a number of times, to find a new homeland on the Black Sea coast of Georgia. Only after the collapse of the USSR did most of their descendants return to Greece.

The Greek villages of these regions—Kvirike, Dagva and Achkva—are no longer inhabited only by Greeks, yet the material monuments of their culture are still preserved. One of them is the "Palace of Culture" in the village of Dagva, the largest and most pompous of such palaces in the whole territory of Georgia, with an auditorium for 800 people, where concerts and film screenings were regularly held, and all kinds of hobby groups and workshops existed. Dagva was the richest village in the republic, an exemplary one that demonstrated the happy life of national minorities in the USSR. Such a palace could have been the jewel of even a large city; indeed, it was quite unexpected to see such monumental buildings in the countryside.

Later, in the Greek Orthodox Church of St Helen and St Constantine in the village of Kvirike, I met Misha Puturidi, the caretaker of the Greek churches in the area. A vivacious 67-year-old, jovial man, Misha is one of the few Georgian Greeks who did not move to Greece in the troubled 1990s. Misha claims to be on a mission to protect his ancestral heritage.

"One day, I was driving a car, and it flipped over. I was already dead. But then Saint Giorgi appeared to me—I am also Giorgi by baptism—and he said: 'Don't be afraid!' He saved me. What was it—a vision or salvation? I don't know, but it was Saint Giorgi who entrusted me with the task of looking after these churches, which I do now."

Misha used to be a successful mandarin seller, and says he was very far from God. Now, he considers himself a servant of God and studies the Creed in Greek and Old Slavonic. Almost all of his relatives now reside in Greece. How does it feel to be left alone in the village he grew up and spent his entire life in? Misha's response is simple: *"How can I be lonely when Christ is with me? My daughter is here too; she's married to a Georgian. With God by my side, how could I ever be bored or lonely? Yes, my wife is in Greece, but in her place, I have Jesus Christ and my savior, the Blessed Virgin Mary."*

Standing before the altar, Misha enthusiastically sang church hymns in Greek, Russian, and Georgian for me and Sulkhan. It was a deeply sincere and moving performance. Afterwards, he went to the open-air bell tower and rang the bells, their sound resonating throughout the neighborhood and echoing far across the green hills to the sea.

"I'll tell you something," Misha said, giving me a wink, his voice filled with inspiration. *"Sometimes, in the summer, it gets terribly hot here. So, I put a bench near the church by the bell tower, and the wind blows on me from both directions—from the sea and from the land. I sit there in this refreshing breeze, and it feels wonderful! How could I ever be bored when I, a servant of God, have been entrusted with the great task of serving this church, even though I'm not a priest?"*

Tbilisi—Kobuleti—Makhinjauri—Chakvi—Batumi,
August – September 2020

Villa of General Zalensky

Villa of Countess Fesenkova

Ancient lamp from one of the many hoards unearthed in Vani, western Georgia

Greek statuette of the Goddess Nika found in Vani

Chapter 4.
Vani: The Temple City of Ancient Colchis

Ancient Colchis is a land covered with a shroud of millennia-old secrets, the same age as Hellas, about which many legends have been formed over the centuries of the land of Homer. The wealth and power of this state caused the Greeks not only to respect it, but also grew in them a sacred fear on the verge of awe. It is known that in the literary tradition of Hellas, Colchis, along with Troy, occupied a leading place.

About a Book that Everyone Needs to Read

A real monument to Ancient Colchis was erected by the Georgian writer Otar Chiladze with his trilogy 'A Man Walked along the Road' (in Georgian გ ზა ზე ერთი კაცი მიდიოდა). In my opinion, this novel should be included in the list of must-read books for all lovers of Georgian history and culture.

There are many merits to Chiladze's novel, and one of them is the opportunity for us readers to realize the importance of the ground Georgia is built upon.

Colchis, so mysterious and inaccessible to us today, becomes vivid and tangible on the pages of his novel. This colorful, philosophical, and deeply psychological work, which presents a Georgian interpretation of the Argonaut legend, had a profound

> Otar Chiladze was a Georgian writer, poet and playwright. In 1998, he was nominated for the Nobel Prize for Literature, but the prize was awarded that year to José Saramago, a Portuguese author. Otar Chiladze died on 1 October 2009. He is buried in the Pantheon on Mount Mtatsminda in Tbilisi.

impact on my imagination. The living, breathing characters of Greek myth—Phrixus, arriving in King Aeëtes' Colchian kingdom on a golden ram, the formidable king himself, his daughters, Medea and Chalciope, and the Argonaut Jason—impressed me not simply as legendary heroes, but as complex figures. Through these ancient myths, the author explores the archetypes of the collective unconscious.

Chiladze's trilogy was the starting point for my personal study of the history of Ancient Colchis and its heritage. I was drawn most strongly, of course, to the town of Vani! And as it turned out, it did not happen for nothing and not by chance.

The Mystery of Vani

Modern Vani is a small city of regional importance in Western Georgia, located 24 km from Samtredia station, in a picturesque gorge of the Sulori River, a left tributary of the Rioni River.

According to Otar Chiladze, Vani was the main city of the Colchian civilization, where the palace of the formidable King Aeëtes was located. Vani was also the place where the Golden Fleece was kept. According to the writer, during the reign of Aeëtes, the Black Sea reached the city, and then gradually receded from it as punishment for human sins.

This, as well as a number of other colorful details, is a figment of the author's imagination. In fact, the seacoast is up to 100 kilometers away! Scientists have claimed that the sea once really did reach the place where the city would have been, but this was in prehistoric times, while the march of the Argonauts to Colchis, according to historians, took place around the 13th century BC. It is also not clear whether Vani was a royal residence or not, because the exact location of the palace of King Aeëtes has yet to be established.

In fact, the royal seat of the Colchian kingdom was in the city of Kut-Aia (according to different sources Aia, Kutaia, Koitaia, Kotiaion, or Kvatatisi). The modern name is Kutaisi. It is one of the most ancient cities, the most important historical and economic center of Western Georgia, and the administrative center of the modern Imereti region. The documentary history of Kutaisi begins in the 3rd century BC, when Apollonius of Rhodes described the capital of Colchis in his work 'Argonautica':

> Ufimererei is the Greek or Latin variant of the Georgian name for the fortress of Ukimerioni, which has long been within the Kutaisi city limits, and borders Bagrati Cathedral.

"From the mountains of Amaranth, far away across the plain of Kirksey.
"Phasis, the turbulent Phasis, carries the wide waters of the sea.
"To the mouth of this river, you can see the city of Cythea."

Byzantine historian Procopius of Caesarea (6th century), in the book 'War with the Goths' (Book 4, section 14), so describes Kutaisi:

"There are many crowded settlements in this region. Of all the lands of Colchis, it is the best. Wine is made here, and many good fruits grow here which are not found anywhere in the rest of Lazika. A river named Rioni flows through this country. In ancient times, the Colchians built a fortification here, the greater part of which they themselves later ruined to the ground, as it was situated on a plain and, in their opinion, gave easy access and an opportunity to be conquered. At that time, this fortification in Greek was called Kotiaion; now the Lazs call it Kutaisi (...)."

Hardly anyone would deny that Vani, along with the famous Colchian cities—Phasis, Dioscuria, Gianos, Apsaros—was the main religious and cult city of Colchis.

This summer, I finally had the opportunity to pay the once glorious and legendary, but nowadays somewhat sleepy, town a visit. No, no, don't think these are words of disparagement! On the contrary! I am more than sure that in the near future, Vani's fame will be quite different. Important historical and archeological conferences and symposiums are often held there, largely thanks to the fact that the local archeological museum was reopened last year after a thorough modernization.

In May 2023, at the European Museum of the Year Award in Barcelona, 47 countries voted unanimously to award The Silletto to the Vani Archeological Museum. It is now rightly recognized as one of the best museums in the world.

The Treasures of Ancient Colchis

When and why did the world learn about the legendary treasures of Colchis, many of which were found in Vani? It all started when, at the end of the 18th century, the Akhvlediani family settled on a hill in mountainous Imereti, a region forgotten by God and people, and a whole village grew around them. It was then that miracles began to happen in this place, a fact which dumbfounded the locals: After every rain, the Vani soil gave birth to treasures- jewelry, gold and silver ornaments, beads, rings, bronze figurines and other ancient things washed out of the belly of the earth. It is said that the women of Vani, when they went out for a walk after the rain, felt as if they were enjoying harvest time: in the hems of their dresses, they gathered one jewel after another! Can you imagine how many treasures in this way disappeared without a trace?

The tale of this bizarre place quickly spread throughout Georgia. The *Droeba* newspaper, for example, wrote about it in 1876. The first scientific study of Akhvlediani Hill was conducted in the early 20th century by the Georgian scientist Ekvtime Takaishvili. He wrote about how many jewels had already been found in Vani, and described them in detail. But all of them, according to the archeologist, had disappeared.

Fundamental archeological excavations began in 1947, but were soon interrupted, only to be resumed in the 1960s. The leading archeologists in these works were Nino Khoshtaria and Otar Lordkipanidze. In those years, several rich burial sites of wealthy citizens and religious servants were found, indicating that Colchian ruling nobles and priests had been buried in the town.

The 5th-century treasures found in Vani impressed the world for the extraordinary sophistication of jewelry craftsmanship, elegance of form, and incredible ideological content. A detailed description and analysis of the Vani burial sites, and their contents are given by a scientist in the book 'Ancient Colchis. Myth and Archeology,' published in Tbilisi in 1979.

Ekvtime Takaishvili was a Georgian scientist, historian, archeologist and politician. On 26 May, 1918, he signed the Declaration of Independence of Georgia, and he was also one of the founders of Tbilisi State University. After the Sovietization of Georgia, he lost the right to scientific activity and teaching, and went into exile in France with the government of Noe Jordania. In emigration, the scientist was the custodian of the treasury and all monuments of material culture until the return of the heritage to Soviet Georgia in 1944. Upon returning to Georgia, Takaishvili again took up scientific studies, but was kept under house arrest until his death in 1953, after which he was canonized by the Georgian Orthodox Church.

Otar Lordkipanidze claimed that Ancient Colchis' gold and silver items, made with the finest graining and filigree, belonged to a single highly artistic and original school of goldsmithing located in Vani. This school applied the most complex technical methods of forging, chasing and embossing, casting, overlaying grain and filigree. On this basis, he concluded that among the supposed centers of goldsmithing in the Middle East (Achaemenid Persia, Midia, Cyprus, Lydia, Egypt, Armenia, Bactria) in the 6th – 5th centuries BC, Colchis should be included with good reason.

Colchis is mentioned in Ancient Greek literature as being "rich in gold," the same epithet given to the powerful and famous-for-their-wealth cities of Mycenae, Sardes and Babylon. However, I will not bore the reader with long quotations and descriptions. Instead, I suggest that you take a trip to the Museum of Vani and see for yourself the treasures stored there.

The Most Exciting Museum in Georgia

The provincial town of Vani, with its rolling hills and terraced landscape, is charming and picturesque, offering a truly romantic panorama of its surroundings. However, Vani is situated far from major transportation routes, making direct access to the coast impossible due to the intervening mountains. Many other charming and comfortable towns like Vani dot the Georgian landscape. As such, it is primarily the town's remarkable museum that draws visitors to come.

The Vani Archeological Museum is named after Otar Lordkipanidze. It is a modern building equipped with the latest technology, with interactive components, video presentations and professionally made exhibit illumination. We were lucky: we arrived at the museum when the exhibition 'Life and Death. The Glory of Pompeii' was on. It is not surprising that the museum in Vani was chosen for this exhibition: in the 1st century AD, the Italian city of Pompeii was wiped out by the eruption of the volcano Vesuvius. The town of Vani was also destroyed in the 1st century BC, but not by the elements: at the hands of enemies. Thus, Vani and Pompeii are cities that represent two once powerful civilizations that vanished.

On the ground floor of the museum are treasures that were found in 28 burial sites. Half of these were looted in ancient times. Several large, semi-dark rooms invite the visitor to travel back there as if in a time machine.

The illumination of the exhibits dispels the darkness, highlighting the exhibits, emphasizing that each of them is unique and should be remembered at all costs. Here, you'll find that famous bronze figure of a *tamada* (toastmaster), with a drinking horn in his hand, that dates back to the 8th-7th centuries BC, personifying a local deity. Near him are chased bronze belt buckles with geometric ornaments of the 8th century BC, and the well-known Colchis bronze axes with two riders on the handle — charioteers of the Mother Goddess.

Vani's Treasures

After the first tour, we decided to take a breather and settle our emotions — our brains no longer able to tell past from present. We walked to the terraces where the remains of religious buildings had been found. There is a round temple there, a 12-stage altar, a temple with a mosaic floor, and various other altars.

The upper terrace offered a magnificent view of the hills, the museum and important archeological sites of the town, but due to the sticky humidity and incessant attacks from local mosquitoes, our walk did not last long, and we quickly took refuge again in the coolness of the cherished museum.

The director of the museum, Manana Vashakmadze, an art historian with 36 years' experience, took us to the first floor.

She asked if we had enjoyed the previous exhibition. In response to our enthusiasm, she proudly declared: *"Well, now you can be convinced that 'gold-rich Colchis' is not a myth! Colchis gold, the Colchis school of gold processing — there is nothing like it anywhere in the world! For example, in a grave discovered in 1966, which is considered the richest in our country, almost 1700 gold items were found, among them a necklace of turtles weighing 1 kg, bracelets weighing 300 grams, many different headdresses, temple pendants and diadems,*

and a variety of buttons, gold nails and even gold thread. All this shows that, in Colchis, gold was not only mined, but also skilfully processed."

To prove her words, Manana brings us to a video presentation, which tells us about an experiment recently conducted by scientist Ermile Magradze. Magradze proved in practice the knowledge that the masters of Ancient Colchis had possessed: with the help of an iron cone-shaped mold with holes, the scientist recreated the method of achieving the highest possible temperature of metal smelting, which the people of Ancient Colchis kept in great secrecy. With the help of this mold, he poured molten copper into clay molds, thus obtaining figures and objects of various shapes, which were then decorated with gold plating: all-in-all a rather complicated technique!

Magradze's experiment proves that Vani was not only a religious center, but also a hotbed of knowledge. Both bronze and gold were made here, as were molds for casting, and there were numerous workshops here as well.

At this point, I'll quote that renowned academician, Otar Lordkipanidze:

"In an anonymous mythographic treatise of the 2nd century, an interesting message is preserved, dating back, it is supposed, to the Euhemerist of the 4th century BC Palephanthus: 'The fleece kept by the Colchians was not really a golden fleece, but a book written on skins, which contained a description of how gold could be extracted through chemistry.' (...) It can be said that it was not so much the gold-bearing rivers as the numerous gold items that made Colchis famous as a country rich in gold."

The fate of the sacred ram that saved Phrixus and became the magical artifact that Jason was after is interesting. Phrixus' mother, the goddess Nephela, in order to avoid mortals' claims to the ram's golden fleece, placed it in the sky. It is now the constellation of Aries.

In Otar Chiladze's trilogy, the ram that brought the Greek Phrixus across the Black Sea to Colchis walks peacefully through the streets of Vani, becoming day by day covered with a patina of gold dust. What an interesting interpretation of the origin of the Golden Fleece!

I also want to share some lines from that beautiful novel by Otar Chiladze, where he describes the goldsmithing district of the city of Vani:

"Every visiting stranger, before leaving Vani, had to walk through this quarter. From morning till evening came from the goldsmiths' quarter the tapping of small hammers, the singing of grinding wheels and the creaking of chisels; from morning till evening, gold plates were forged, chased, covered with carvings; from morning till evening, the noble metal, like a ripe, blossoming girl, jingled and laughed, becoming flesh and blood. This end of the city was also called the quarter of magicians – and indeed, there was something mysterious, fascinating in the slyly squinted eyes of yet another goldsmith, in the discreet smile playing on his lips. At the entrance to the quarter were installed huge mirrors – such that they could fit a rider with his horse. And who would not be attracted by such a mirror, who would not look into it, when everyone knew that any passer-by who turned into this quarter would come out of it golden. Others couldn't tear themselves away from their seats, reaching out to touch the gleaming surface with their hands and smiling uncertainly, much like the golden figure gazing out from the mirror.

"(...) Everyone was astonished and timid before the incomprehensible and unsolved sight. And yet there was nothing to solve: all these workshops, huddled together, emitted so much gold dust that a herd of elephants, walking along the street, between them would have been gilded from head to toe" (Otar Chiladze, A Man Walked along the Road).

Vani – Tbilisi, August – September 2021

View from Dekhviri Fortress, Lechkhumi

Old wine vessels (qvevri) in Dekhuiri Fortress

Chapter 5.
Lechkhumi:
The Gateway to Mountainous Colchis

The Lechkhumi region in north-west Georgia is known as one of the poorest in the country. In my opinion, this is extremely unfair, because Lechkhumi has many riches: it is famous for its fantastic landscapes, sleepy, picturesque villages, legends, delicious food and, of course, wine. It is in Lechkhumi that the most delicious but rare grape varieties — Usakhelauri and Tsolikouri — grow, the wines of which are exceptional in their flavors and bouquet.

> Usakhelauri is a grape variety used for the production of wine of the same name. The variety is autochthonous to Georgia. It is cultivated in the microzone near the villages of Zubi and Okureshi in the Tsageri municipality of the Racha-Lechkhumi and Lower Svaneti region. It is used for the production of the semi-sweet red wine Usakhelauri, through both the European and Georgian *qvevri* method. No more than 1000 bottles are produced in an average harvest year.
>
> Tsolikouri is a grape variety used for the production of high-quality white wines (Sviri, Tvishi, Tsolikauri). The variety is autochthonous. It is cultivated in the Imereti and Lechkhumi regions.

My next story will describe a journey from Lechkhumi to Upper Svaneti through the Zagaro Pass. After this, we drove along the Rioni River past the Khvamli mountain range, the calling card of Lechkhumi. According to legend, it was to this mountain that Prometheus was chained as punishment for serving humanity. Legends say that the caves of this mountain used to store the gold of the Georgian kings.

Last time, we drove through the village of Tvishi on the Alpana road. This time, we traveled along another road, no less picturesque, but much better organized.

From Tskhaltubo, the track, winding like a ribbon, took us higher and higher, from hill to hill. We were leaving Imereti. The road to Tsageri passed alongside the turbulent river Tskhenistskali (translated from Georgian as "Horse Water"). It is said that the Ancient Greeks had the same name for this river.

Tsageri is a city of fortresses. They can be seen from the road and are located in all the important strategic parts, high up in the mountains. Why there are so many citadels here, we will find out soon.

Mid-summer, the Tskhenistskali Valley is a large accumulation of boulders. There is little water in the river, but this does not weaken the turbulent current. We cross the bridge to the right bank of the river and follow the flow for a while. Then it's uphill. On the way, we pass village after village, all of them incredibly cute, with houses buried in greenery and covered with vines. Our path takes us past shady orchards and maize gardens.

The way up lies along another mountain stream. The views from the heights become more and more captivating. Tsageri is already visible. You want to stop again and again to admire the views, but we must go higher and higher, to the place where majestic age-old trees grow. In this grove is an old cemetery, and from it, the road slopes steeply downwards. A few more meters and we are there, in the village of Dekhviri.

Giorgi Gasviani, director of the Ethnographic-Archeological Open Air Museum, is waiting for us. Giorgi lives not far from the museum. He welcomes us with full hospitality, having promised to show us the territory of the ancient fortress and tell us about the most recent discoveries. Interestingly, for now, the museum is virtual: the territory is fenced, but the building itself has yet to be built. There is an amazingly fascinating story here, for which there is bound to be a sequel!

On the mountain to which Giorgi leads us, there is a 360-degree view.

"From here, you can see the Mingrelian mountains, the Greater Caucasus Range, Racha, and Imereti!" our guide proudly declares. *"Indeed, since ancient times, this place has been a kind of gateway to all the important regions of Georgia, the strategic importance of which cannot be overestimated. In the 18th century, Prince Vakhushti Bagrationi, Georgian historian and geographer, wrote that whoever owns the fortress of Dekhviri in Lechkhumi controls all roads leading to Svaneti, Racha, Imereti and Samegrelo."*

This land is a trove of priceless treasures for archeologists. Artifacts from the Late Bronze Age (a bronze Colchian engraved axe, a horse harness, a bull figurine and a Colchian settlement from the 8th to 5th centuries BC featuring beautiful Colchian pottery and a stone mold for casting thin plates for inlaying Colchian buckles and fibulae) have been discovered in and around the Dekhviri fortress. These findings have enabled scholars to argue that the territory of the fortress was important not only in the Middle Ages, as previously thought, but also in the Late Bronze Age.

Local people have long been finding hordes of treasure, as well as individual antiquities, throughout Lechkhumi. However, archeological excavations were first conducted in Dekhviri in 1961-1962, during which fifteen burial sites from the ancient era were found. Scientists discovered the above-mentioned 8th to 5th-century Colchian settlement in 1970-71.

In 2012, excavations were resumed once more, giving scientists the opportunity to discover 15 more burial sites, and in them utensils, tools and weapons, coins, jewelry (beads, earrings) and much more. According to scientists, the necropolis existed in Dekhviri from the 4th century BC to the 4th century AD. One of the most important finds of recent years is the grave of a Colchian warrior, dated to the 1st-3rd centuries AD. We saw the remains of the warrior with our own eyes when we visited the museum in Tsageri: he was buried lying on his right side, hands under his head, knees bent, with a spearhead and buckles beside him and a wine jug at his feet. This was the manner of burial in the pre-Christian period.

Scientists were able to establish that even in antiquity, this small region surrounded by mountains was connected to the big world! Proof of this is an entire set of beads found here which are known to have been popular throughout the Mediterranean region, a coin of Emperor Augustus, and gold earrings in the form of bunches of grapes, which were also common in the ancient world. You can see them for yourself at the Simon Janashia National History Museum in Tbilisi.

Giorgi climbs with us up the hill of the main fortress of Dekhviri, on the slopes of which *pithos*, ancient vessels for wine and water, were recently found, and tells us about plans to preserve this place by covering it with glass. Not far from here, scientists have discovered the foundations of an ancient church. There is a well in what was once the fortress, whose water has a unique composition, as witnessed by several experts who tried it. At sunset, we sit on a bench under an ancient linden tree and drink that outlandish water, the composition of which is truly something special.

Giorgi is a visionary: he is convinced he lives in a place that is extremely important for world history and archeology, as well as for geology and tourism.

Later, back in Tbilisi, Nino Sulava, the head of the archeological expedition in Dekhviri, tells me that all the artifacts found in the fortress itself and in its vicinity show that, since ancient times, this place has been of great importance for the whole region. And its most important finds are most likely still lurking underground! According to the scientist, the ancient inhabitants of the nearby settlement were engaged not only in agriculture, but also in metallurgy, as remains of ancient metallurgical centers where copper was smelted were found not far from Dekhviri— dating to the 9th-8th centuries BC.

Nino is one of those scholars who shares the conviction that the Greek Argonauts did not make their difficult journey to the kingdom of the fearsome Aeëtes in order to claim the skin of a golden ram: most likely, they were looking for the secret knowledge, which was not available to the Greeks, which the Colchians possessed — the secret of metal smelting.

The Greco-Roman historian and geographer Strabo noted that: *"The richness of this country (Colchis) in gold, silver, iron and copper, provides a sure pretext for the Argonauts' campaign. The first trip for this purpose was organized by Phrixus..."* (The Geography of Strabo, text taken from the Bell Edition of 1903, now in the public domain, The Geography of Strabo [Harvard/Heinemann 1924], digitized by the Perseus Project).

This quote is cited by many scholars, as it describes the period of the Argonauts' voyage — the 14th to 13th centuries BC. Interest in Colchis came precisely due to the abundance of metals there.

There is a plan to create a large research and tourist complex in Dekhviri on the territory of the fortress, where scientists and students from all over the world will be able to come and study their subject in an applied way. Not only archeologists, but also ethnographers, anthropologists, geologists and geographers will find work in Dekhviri.

In the Tsageri Historical Museum, where all the historical epochs of Lechkhumi are represented, we found further confirmation that this region could be next on the priority list of development for the Georgian economy, science and tourism.

Sitting by a well under that old linden tree, Giorgi dreams of what the region might be like in 10 years. And these are not just the fantasies of a visionary: we know ourselves how quickly and successfully transformations took place in Svaneti, Kakheti and Adjara. Now it is Lechkhumi's turn.

Tsageri — Dekhviri — Tbilisi, August 2021

View of Tsageri, as seen from Dekhviri Fortress

Grave of a Colchian warrior in the Varlam Makharoblidze Tsageri Historical Museum, 1 century AD

Harvest season in a Tvishi guesthouse: persimmon being air-dried

Peasant from the Tvishi village harvesting corn,
one of the main staples in western Georgia

Chapter 6.
Traveling from Lechkhumi to Svaneti

My friends from Berlin, Yulia and Nika, asked me to show them Georgia: not the one already trampled by crowds of gawkers, but the mysterious Caucasian country and its hidden places and secrets. And so, the Lechkhumi region, north-west of Racha, came to mind.

For gourmands, of course, Racha is a top destination after the cradle of traditional winemaking in Kakheti. But Racha's neighbor Lechkhumi is known, perhaps, to only a few. What is this area famous for? First, the sacred mountain Khvamli. It is a mountain enveloped in legends about Prometheus and the treasures of Queen Tamar hidden there. There are also many unrivalled gorges, high rocks and cliffs, waterfalls, picturesque mountain passes and fortresses too.

Together with Theo, my nine-year-old son, I traveled from Tbilisi to Kutaisi to pick up Nika and Yulia, who had flown in from Berlin to visit us. We took our guests for lunch at a restaurant in the city center, had coffee with them, and then hurried them up, reminding them we had to get on the road. Yulia and Nika, people of the arts, were not happy about the rush: *"Why rush in Georgia? We want to enjoy ourselves and relish every moment! After all, that's what we came here for."*

Our first destination is Tvishi, a legendary Lechkhumi village in which we plan to stay overnight. From Kutaisi, we drive north, along the full-flowing Rioni River, directly to Tvishi. Here, the semi-sweet wine of the

> Tvishi is a village in Tsageri municipality, in the Racha-Lechkhumi and Lower Svaneti region of Georgia.
>
> Tvishi is known for being the registered name — appellation — of the local white, semi-sweet wine of the same name.

same name is produced from the locally grown Tsolikouri grape. The dirt road Kutaisi — Tvishi — Alpana is probably one of the worst roads in this area. But it is fabulously beautiful!

Along the way, we stop often to admire the mountains rising straight up into the sky and the river rushing through the gorge. We make a nerve-jangling crossing on a narrow suspension bridge hanging over the turbulent Rioni, stretch our bones on the other bank, breathe in the invigorating freshness of the evening river air, then continue our journey with renewed vigor.

Tvishi and its Wine

We climb up the narrow, steep dirt road to the village of Tvishi in the dark. There is not a single streetlight here, and we feel completely lost: for some reason, we can't get in touch with the owner of the guesthouse. There is tremendous tension in my head and hands. I am trying hard not to drive off the road and end us up in a ditch. Nick is tormenting Google maps. The Google location confirms that the village of Tvishi is indeed nearby....

Suddenly, we come across an old woman carrying the weight of her years along with a bundle of brushwood. Apparently, she knows this path like the back of her hand; she is fearless as she walks alone in the dark.

The woman explains to us in Georgian that we will now have to take an old, concrete road and then turn left and go downhill. We drive slowly along the bumpy village roads for some time, until at last fate sends us the owner of our guesthouse, Giorgi, who had driven out to meet us and was already searching for us through the dark streets of his village.

Bone-tired and famished, we made our way into a dimly lit courtyard, where a grand old house, covered in lush greenery, loomed before us.

No sooner are we seated in the cozy living room, than a sumptuous dinner is brought out. Our hosts, Giorgi and his mother, treat us to local delicacies, including hot *lobio* (boiled beans seasoned with spices) and huge slices of warm *lori* (the famous Lechkhumi ham). Every twenty minutes, the owner of the house, Giorgi's mother, brings out new dishes. There seems to be no end to this feast!

We have not seen Nika and Yulia for several years. That is why we celebrate this long-awaited meeting on Georgian soil almost until dawn. Two liters of Tsolikouri for three people—is it a lot, or not enough? The question is rhetorical if you do not know the taste of this drink: moderately light, crispy, fruity, harmonious, and with its own special character—this wine is enchanting, and so two liters for three people is not really too much for such a divine drink!

Having talked ourselves out for the time being, we decide to turn in for the night. Only then do we realize that our hosts, the modest and taciturn but hospitable mother and son, have been waiting all this time for the stormy feast to end! It turns out that they were waiting for the right moment to clear the table in the living room so as to prepare the table for our breakfast!

When Theo and I wake up late morning and walk out onto a terrace lit by the sun, we are knocked speechless, for the darkness of yesterday had prevented us from getting a good look at the place where we were stationed: vineyards blanket the hills, sheaves of corn stand taller than a man, trees are lavished with persimmons and pomegranates, and somewhere in the lowlands, the noisy Rioni can be heard in the grip of green mountains.

We learnt about Tvishi wine yesterday; now it's a good time to get to know the village of Tvishi itself. The owner explains that if you get closer to the river, you'll get even better views, so we follow his advice and start exploring.

The rich vegetation reminds us that we are in the subtropics. As we descend to the water, we find a viewing platform with a large cross attached to it. From here, we get an incredible 360-degree panorama of the surrounding area. The mere sight of the sleeping miracle dragon, the 2000-meter-high Khvamli Mountain, its ridge stretching on over four kilometers, makes the journey worth it!

After a hearty breakfast, we are again drawn to rest, and have to force ourselves not to waste time and to continue our adventure by taking a walk to the Sairme Pillars, which are located near the village of Sairme. These rocks are said to resemble a man-made creation, but in fact are just tall, beautiful columns of natural formation.

We leave the car on the side of the road and walk along a dirt track. The three kilometers of serpentine road take a good hour and a bit: the ascent is steep and the weather is hot, not at all typical for mid-autumn. The higher we get, the more beautiful the panoramas of villages are, stretching along the mountain slopes.

A Pause with the Restorers

High above the road, the village of Sairme is a hidden paradise. Its houses, with beautiful shady balconies, are hidden away in the depths of rich gardens, many of which are set behind picturesque hedges. The highlights of the village are the 800-year-old lime tree and the old church, which is currently under renovation.

We meet the restorers at the temple. They tell us that we would not be able to reach the cliffs of Sairme today, because it is about to get dark. It turns out that we should have traveled directly to the village by car and then walked to the rocks.

As compensation for the loss of time, the masters invite us to visit them. The new acquaintances warn us that since there are no shops in the village, the treats will be modest: sandwiches with sausage, *churchkhela* and local *chacha*. Yulia and Nika rejoice at this unexpected hospitality. They've got the hang of it, and now they are interested in every tiny detail of the portrait called "Georgia!"

A seasoned traveler knows that the destination of the journey is secondary to the experience on the way to it. Georgia has a magnificent gift to teach the traveler just this: to forget about the destination, instead engaging all the senses, plunging into the moment and living minute by minute, here and now! I would call this "Georgian Zen."

And although we have no idea where we'll be spending the next night, there's really no hurry.

Georgia should be explored with calmness, patience, and ease, occasionally accepting that things may not always align with our expectations. The joy of discovery will only come if you embrace the details — regional history, local life, cuisine, and the unique characteristics and worldview of its people. On arrival in Georgia, leave your plans to the higher powers and enjoy the adventure. If such thinking is alien to you, you should really look for other places to holiday.

Tsageri

After Sairme, we lean over a map of the area and decide to drive straight to the center of Lechkhumi, the town of Tsageri.

The picturesque winding track hardly resembles any other road in Georgia, passing as it does through narrow rocky gorges along the course of the Lajanuri River. The nature becomes more and more rugged and mighty, the villages more and more spartan. We wonder what awaits us on the other side of the pass.

Pausing at the top, we admire the view of Tsageri, a town built along the Tskhenistskali River; its ghostly lights spread across the wide valley. On the mountain, a little away from the road, we see the ruins of the fortress of Muri. It is said that this fortress, like many others, used to protect the neighboring Lower Svaneti from enemies. According to legend, once, the Turks reached this very place but were stopped: the fortress successfully fulfilled its defensive task and prevented the enemy from advancing further.

The capital of Lechkhumi is a small, sleepy town with one main street. Especially in late autumn, the town of Tsageri seems a harsh and not particularly friendly place. Nonetheless, we stop there for the night.

Legends of Mount Khvamli

The hotelier offered to organize a day trip to Mount Khvamli, which we had already admired from afar. It takes time to explore Khvamli, and you should not go there without a good guide. There are many legends about Khvamli, a mountain range of limestone origin. One of them says that the Argonauts came to Colchis not for the Golden Fleece, but to find rich deposits of iron ore which are located in the mountains of Rachi and Lechkhumi.

Another tale claims that Prometheus was chained to Khvamli with iron chains as punishment for "stealing fire from the gods."

Researchers link the legend of Prometheus to an epic from Georgian mythology. Amirani, son of the goddess Dali, was washed in a magic spring as a baby and became equal to the gods. He taught mortals how to make fire and work metals. Amirani refused to obey the gods, for which he was chained to Khvamli. An eagle constantly flew to him and pecked at his liver. According to legend, Amirani will come back to the people once again.

Yet another legend is from the Middle Ages. In the ancient Georgian chronicle 'Life of Kartli,' Khvamli is described as a place where *"Kartvelian kings hid their treasures, and is a land thanks to which Sakartvelo will one day be saved."*

During the Soviet era, Stalin sent two expeditions to this mountain to search for treasure—in 1939 and 1945. Both ventures were unsuccessful: the caves where the treasure was said to be stored turned out to have been either already looted or buried beneath the rocks.

The next morning, the hotel owner cancelled our trip at the last moment on some dubious pretext. And then, at breakfast, it dawned on us that we could go straight to Svaneti! We had learned from the locals that it was only five hours from Tsageri to Ushguli, and they said my toy SUV could easily handle the road.

Traveling along the Tsageri-Lentekhi-Ushguli highway, the so called South Svaneti road, has been a long-time dream of mine. And here it was, my chance!

Tbilisi, November 2019

Mountain view of the South Svanetian Road

Hospitable Zurab from Lower Svaneti inviting us to a spontaneous wine and honey tasting

Zagaro Pass in autumn

Chapter 7.
South Svaneti Route:
From Lower to Upper Svaneti

The South Svaneti Highway is considered the most difficult road in Svaneti, although it is also the shortest route up and the most memorable. It was once a good asphalt road, but now there is no trace of it left. That is why we were quite sceptical about the information we received from Mestia about the length of the road from Tsageri to Ushguli. But the allure of these places, abandoned by both God and man, makes the heart of any adventurer race with excitement, and so we decided to go for it! (Note: since penning this story, the road was reconstructed, and the drive on it is now a great pleasure, a fact we experienced in the summer of 2024).

Our food supply was meager: we had managed to buy only *khachapuri* and lobiani from a local shop, and from Kutaisi we had brought some smoked cheese, a couple of eggs, and cucumbers. Hoping that these products would be enough to get us to Ushguli, we set off.

Most of the way lies in a colorful mountain gorge along the Tskhenistskali River. In the 19th century, Russian traveler Igor Kanevsky made the same journey. Later, he wrote:

"...the road turned into the gorge of the Tskhenistskali River, striking for the wild beauty of its anteroom. A gigantic grey rock cut in two, barely giving passage to the frenzied river, rushing against the stone walls with a deafening roar and rumble. Soon, the sullen gate leading into the gorge was left behind. Tskhenistskali means horse-water or horse-river in Georgian. There are historical indications that this river was called this by the Ancient Greeks for the swiftness of its flow. (...) with thunder and rumbling, high splashes and foam, it jumps over the boulders sharpened by it, blocking its way, or with a deafening roar, compressed into a narrow stream, it passes between them, as if trying to separate these dead, immobile masses. Sometimes, through the roar and noise of the water, one can hear huge stones scraping against each other: the river turns them and drags them to the bottom, cluttering its path and thus sometimes blocking its own way" (Igor Kanevsky, Noteworthy Corners of the Caucasus).

Soon, the town of Lentekhi, the capital of Lower Svaneti, opened out before us. Once, Lower Svaneti was called the land of Dadiani, because it was ruled by Dadiani princes, while Upper Svaneti had no rulers at all.

From Lentekhi to Ushguli is only 55 kilometers. But how long would it take to cover the distance?

The mountain slopes are covered with dense, mixed forest. The shades of autumn are still barely visible here, even though the mountain tops you can see in the distance are already covered in a veil of snow. From time to time, the gorge widens, giving way to meadows and pastures. The unhurried pace of local life and the tranquillity that reigns make you want to stay in one of these villages longer so as to better explore the area; to be able to soak up all its mysteries, and discover the many abandoned 8th and 9th century churches and ruins of fortresses.

One day, in the National Library of Tbilisi, I came across notes on trips to this region made by various travelers in the distant tsarist times. One of those books contained a detailed description of the temples of Lower and Upper Svaneti and the treasures stored in them: crosses, bibles, chalices, icons, etc. It is interesting that one can only read about these treasures. I wonder what of this long list of treasures can be seen with our own eyes today?

A Stop with Wine and Honey Tasting

We take a break in one of the picturesque villages situated in a sun-drenched meadow. Out of the blue, an elderly man comes rushing towards us. Smiling cordially, he introduces himself to us as Zurab, and invites us to rest and talk in his garden. Yulia and Nika look at me questioningly. They are both pleased and surprised by this situation, because, in Europe, hardly anyone gets such invitations without a serious reason. In principle, I do not mind sparing time to spend chatting with this nice man, but, on the other hand, we still have a long way to go, and it would be good to get to Upper Svaneti before dusk. Ahead is the crossing of Zagaro Pass (2623 m above sea level). We ask our new acquaintance how long he thinks our journey to Ushguli will take. He thinks for a moment and answers: *"At least five hours."* And so we have to decline his tempting invitation to visit.

"Wait a minute! I'll treat you to my homemade wine and honey!" he says, hurrying into the house and bringing out a bottle of red wine, a couple of glasses, a jar of honeycomb honey, as well as several plates with spoons. We taste the fragrant mountain honey, rich with the essence of the flowers of the region, and Yulia and Nika taste the semi-dry house wine. Reluctantly saying goodbye to Zurab, we thank him from the bottom of our hearts for his hospitality and generosity.

The sun is mild and not at all searing. After a while, we stop again to pick some apples and pears and walnuts in the garden of an abandoned house. Once again, we want to press pause as we bask in this sudden, seemingly unreasonable happiness. Our harvest is rich: we have enough apples, walnuts and pears even for the long trek we will soon undertake from Ushguli.

In the Mele settlement, the road deteriorates. The villages look like aged people. Little by little we are drifting away from civilization. From Makhashi village, the road resembles a forest path, and the ascent is still not visible. Are we really going in the right direction? Soon, the villages on the road disappear altogether, the gorge narrows, and we continue along the river through the forest. In some places, the road has been washed out by rain and we have to slow down to a crawl.

It's time for a snack. With great appetite, we eat all the food supplies we brought from Tsageri. Smoked *sulguni* cheese combined with wild fruits is a delicacy when adventuring! To brighten up the celebration of life even more, Yulia and Nika take out a bottle of Saperavi. But in these camping conditions, only one sip is allowed.

> Saperavi is a variety of black grape originating from the wine zone in the Kakheti region. It serves as a basis for table, dessert, fortified and mono-varietal wines. Outside Georgia, the variety is widely cultivated in the Russian Federation, Bulgaria, Armenia, Moldova, Romania, Ukraine and Azerbaijan. It is also found in Uzbekistan, Australia and the USA.

Before the village of Tsana, the road starts to climb. Now we see why all the guides recommend a good off-road vehicle for this road: if it starts to rain, the chances of surviving if you're behind the wheel of an ordinary city car will be reduced to all but zero.

Autumn is becoming more and more tangible with every meter. The mixed forests have acquired a yellow and scarlet patina, the air is getting cooler, and the mountain peaks are completely covered with a thin shroud of snow.

The Legend of Zeskho Village

Before the village of Tsana, there is a turn to Zeskho, four kilometers away. This is a fascinating place; one that, in better conditions, would be worth taking a day or two to explore.

According to legend, there was once a large village in the valley of the Zeskho River (former name Zeria), which was repeatedly invaded by foreigners. During one of these raids, the enemies burnt and destroyed the village, tore down its fortresses and towers, looted its wealth, and killed the locals. That is why it was called Zeskho, meaning "drowned in blood." Later, Svans from the Mulakhi community moved there. Today, however, this village, located at an altitude of 1800 meters above sea level, has once more been completely deserted. In the river valley, at 1850 meters above sea level, there is a mountaineering camp which was founded by the famous Georgian mountaineer Jokia Gugava. It is a popular place with extreme sports lovers. Around it there are dozens of peaks, from 3000 m to 5000 m high. On a hiking route from here, you can reach the foot of Mount Pasimta, the source of the Tskhenistskhali River.

The Zagaro Pass

There are several passes along the Svanetian mountain range which connect Lower Svaneti with Upper: Lasila (3086m), Atkver (or Zagaro) and Latpari (2830m).

We head towards the Zagaro Pass, passing the village of Tsana, where we unexpectedly find several guesthouses, though they are already closed for the winter. As we move higher and higher up the serpentine road, which starts in the village of Koruldashi, we occasionally cross mountain rivers.

Before the climb started, Nika had offered to take over driving, taking a big load off my shoulders, but now I find myself flinching whenever we hit a rock or pothole. I feel like this steep road leading to the sky will never end.

From time to time, we are taken into meadows with sun-scorched grass. A couple of times, we think we've reached the highest point. But no! The pass is still ahead, the sun is sinking lower and lower, and the chances of reaching Ushguli before dusk are shrinking by the minute.

Our path lies to the west. The parting rays of the sun blind Nika so that he can barely make out the way up. Yulia comes to his aid: she runs ahead of the car, telling us where to go next. Several times we have to stop to allow the overheated engine to cool down. It is so hot! But we can't stop for long: there is a risk that the night will catch us right on the pass.

And here it is, the long-awaited Zagaro! It doesn't look like a classic pass at all: it turns out to be a simple narrow spot on a mountain ridge where the two roads leading up and down meet.

In the glow of the orange sun, we see an alien spectacle: a giant, sun-scorched meadow bordered by snow-capped giant mountains that seem so easy to touch—just stretch out your hand!

The majestic Inguri Gorge is not visible from the Zagaro Pass, but here we are welcomed by a number of peaks that are magnificent in their grandeur, including Ailama (4546 m) and Tsurungali (4249 m).

This is what the Georgian scientist Dimitri Bakradze, who traveled to Svaneti in 1860, wrote about the passes of Svaneti:

"The passes reach 10,000 feet. Nothing can be more varied than these mountain climbs. The vegetation changes with every step you take. As you ascend,

you enter a belt covered with thick grass, and then you see before you only bare masses of granite rock. But now you reach the highest point of the pass. What a magnificent picture is presented to your eyes: deep valleys in all their beauty spread out before you, high ridges with all their branches clearly drawn. One day is enough to reach any of the passes of Svaneti, but access to them on horseback is possible only in June, July, August and the first half of September. At other times of the year, it is decisively impossible. Huge crevasses are filled with brittle snow, smoothing over all the chasms; gusty winds rage with terrible force and threaten you with serious danger. Cases of death are quite frequent. Only courageous Svans dare to walk here in winter, but only while wearing big wooden hilari on their feet and with a long pointed pole in hand- tools with which the Svan does not part, even inside Svaneti. But even with such precautions, he does not set out except on a clear day. The most accessible way runs from Ushkul to Lashkheti through the sources of Ingur and the upper reaches of Tskhenis-Tskali – the way known as Tyuberi, which makes a rather large detour. It has no passes and is covered with birch and pine forests. There is a cave half way; in it, or in the ruins of towers and churches of the long abandoned village of Tsena, which separates one branch of the road leading to the upper parts of the Racha district, Ghebi and Gloli, a traveler can find shelter. However, even here caution is required, because in winter on this road there are often snow blocks, which break off in huge masses and can bury a careless traveler under them. Even in summer, it is not always safe to move along the narrow Tskhenis-Tskal gorge, where, for more than 10 versts, the way runs along the bed of a troubled stream: here sometimes after half an hour of heavy rain, the mountain stream swells up and can threaten a careless traveler with death" (Dimitri Bakradze, Svaneti).

The only thing I have to say here is that this description is almost unarguably applicable to our time too. In my conversations with travelers who dared to walk this difficult, not yet completed section of the so-called Transcaucasian Trail leading from Upper Svaneti to the Racha region, and the Ghebi and Glola villages, I found many confirmations of the fact.

Tbilisi, November 2019

View of Ushguli community

Chapter 8.
Ushguli. Under the Sky of Svaneti

We descended to Ushguli feeling triumphant. What a great thing to descend and not ascend to this legendary village! We arrived at an altitude of 2200 meters above sea level, to a village that is one of the highest in Europe. Moreover, it is one of the most exotic and secluded havens in Georgia.

When I first came to Mestia, the capital of the Svaneti region, in 2012, the road from there to Ushguli was a difficult gravel track, and the journey from Mestia to Ushguli (47 km) was not only long, but also expensive to travel, meaning that only fit tourists tended to walk the road; a journey which took around four days. The road that ends near Ushguli was built only a few years ago, and this time, by the will of fate, I was lucky enough to reach Ushguli from above.

In the pink Svan twilight, the stark outlines of Ushguli, surrounded by mountains and numerous formidable towers, transported us to some kind of cosmic dimension. Something mystical opened before our eyes. And we, who are living in the 21st century, are not the only ones to have such impressions. Travelers in the 19th century also felt something similar.

In 1886, traveler-author Igor Kanevsky described Svan settlements in his book as follows:

"I have seen villages and buildings of all Caucasian tribes except Dagestan, but I have never seen anything like the Svan villages. From afar, a Svanetian settlement appears to be a solid stone town; a group of merging buildings, of which slender square white towers with a sloping double-pitched roof 8-10 fathoms high often rise. Up close, such a village turns out to be an incomprehensible chaos of stone buildings, with flat or sloping slate roofs and high walls, either well-built on cement, or laid with dry masonry and therefore often half-collapsed; small holes in the form of embrasures darken the outer walls of the buildings instead of windows; groups of buildings are separated by narrow crooked alleys, which one can hardly pass through; the actual dwellings are mostly on the first floors of the buildings, accessed by wooden stairs. At the corners of the walls, or adjacent to their middle, towers protrude, perfectly built on bases of huge hewn stones; the square of their base has a small embedding, so that to the top they slightly taper. Under the double-pitched slate roof at the very top, on each of the four sides of the tower, there are three hinged embrasures, covered from above by stone vaults protruding from the walls. These embrasures provide a field of fire down to the base of the tower;

additional narrow arrowslits are sometimes incorporated into the middle of the towers.

"Our guide from Kala to Mesti, a Svanet, told us that under many towers there are wells and ways to underground passages, and under houses there are deep cellars for bread supplies; if this is true, then indeed Svanet villages were once impregnable shelters and the Svanets could hide in them from their former enemies for a whole year. Only good artillery could defeat these strongholds, but the enemy tribes must not have had it in those times when the Svanet had to fight for independence" (Igor Kanevsky, Noteworthy Corners of the Caucasus).

On the other side of Ushguli is a completely different landscape. When the weather is good, the panorama of Georgia's highest mountain, Shkhara (5204 meters), opens up in the background of the village. When you contemplate the snow-covered massif of this mountain from the village, it is easy to think that Shkhara is only a couple of hundred meters away. However, this is a gross misconception, and our hike to the foot of the mountain the next day confirmed it.

Here, under the very skies of Svaneti, it becomes obvious why Upper Svaneti has never been ruled by feudal lords: the inhabitants of this region valiantly defended their independence, and the harsh nature was their support. In such places, strength flows from above. That is one of the reasons why one should go to Svaneti for new energy and to reset!

One of the buildings by the road looks like a good enough hotel to rest our heads for the night. We don't want to be picky about finding a place to stay, besides, in the middle of October, there are not so many hotels open to guests. Now, we just need a quick refreshment and a walk around the village. The evening is very cold, and we put on all the warm clothes we have with us.

The Ushguli Community

The whole of Upper Svaneti is divided into communities. The Ushguli community consists of four villages: Zhibiani, Chvibiani, Chazhashi and Murkmeli. When walking through the upper villages of Ushguli, Zhibiani and Chvibiani, it is as if we are in the middle of a medieval film set. The houses, with their adjacent towers and surrounding walls of slate or rocks, speak of the constant danger that hung over the inhabitants of this area for centuries, like a Sword of Damocles.

There are no asphalt roads in the village. It is not difficult to imagine what it is like to try and move around here after rain or snowfall. The houses here vary greatly: from crumbling, rundown structures to grand, old, stone homes that still command respect with their strength, and new, modern buildings. However, the newer constructions often clash with the overall scenery. The plastic windows and doors of some homes are an eyesore, disrupting the aesthetic harmony. Sadly, the advancements of civilization don't always contribute to beauty.

Nearly every house bears a sign declaring it to be a hotel or guesthouse, as almost every family in the area is involved in hosting visitors.

There are only a few trees in this village. We are in a treeless area, above the limit of forest growth. We can only assume how meager the diet of the locals was in the old days. Apart from barley, practically nothing grew here. Even now, most of the foodstuffs are imported to Ushguli from outside. Therefore, one should not be surprised by the prices, which are often off the charts.

On our way, we meet riders on horseback, many of them teenagers. In the mountains, the upbringing of boys has always been taken very seriously, and boys become men early. According to the traditions of the highlanders, men are the wealth, adornment and continuation of the family.

When we reach the highest point of the village, the ascetic Church of Our Lady, or St Lamaria, towering above the whole village, we realize that we have no time left for sightseeing: it is already dark. The church is located at the highest point of Ushguli and is dedicated to the Mother of God, whom the Svans honor on a par with Queen Tamar.

Georgian archeologist Dimitri Bakradze, in his 1877 book 'Svaneti,' referring to the story of one of his companions, wrote:

"...they (the Svans) are convinced that they were converted to Orthodoxy by Jesus Christ himself, and that they have not changed their faith since. They do not remember anything about their former eristavs and rulers. They were Sakeisro, that is, they were part of Caesar's dominions; by this name they know the queen Tamar. Their folk tales preserve the image of this great woman alone among the Georgian kings. According to them, she lived in Georgia, but was especially fond of Svaneti, where she often spent her time, built churches, and supplied them with rich icons. She was a woman of striking beauty, and many sought her hand. But she chose an Ossetian, to whom she gave her heart. Queen Tamar is immortal, and her place of stay is in a dungeon in Ushkuli, under the Church of the Mother of God, where she rests in a clay vessel holding a candle in her hands. It cannot be opened, and if ever it is opened, they say Svaneti will be threatened with terrible disasters" (Dimitri Bakradze, Svaneti).

On the way back, we find a café located in a room resembling a grandiose barn. Georgian music flows out, very melodious, and we decide to stay for dinner. We need something warm to eat, because we are incredibly cold. In the café, which has several long tables with benches, we are almost the only guests. In the corner, a traveler is resting- a young man wrapped in a plaid with a book in his hand.

The small, nimble waitress invites us to sit close to the stove. We order vegetable soup, salad, cheese and *kubdari*, the famous Svan meat pie. The food in the café is both fresh and tasty, although we realize that after the journey we have made, we would be happy with anything! And then we try the *kubdari*.

The Svans have a special relationship not only with meat, but also with dough. I have never tasted bread tastier than Svan bread. And the cheese here is excellent, too, boasting an enormously rich flavor. Could cows grazing on the blessed Alpine meadows under the open sky ever give unpalatable milk?

During the meal, we are joined by the owner of the place, a thin man in his fifties, called Mirian. Throughout the evening, he talks to us about his beloved homeland, Svaneti's valiant past, and its mega-tourist future. Mirian built his café out of old material on the site of an old house, taking out a loan for the construction. This is what many Svanetians do nowadays: with the current tourist boom, it is always worth the gamble.

Mirian's unmarried sister runs the café, cooking the dishes and then serving them to the customers. A family business is a natural phenomenon for the Svans. In the past, it was hunting, cattle breeding and farming, but now it is tourism. Every year, the influx of those wishing to see the wonders and beauty of Svaneti grows exponentially. The infrastructure is changing accordingly: new hotels, cafés and guesthouses are built, and almost all the locals are involved in the business.

"In Soviet times, we lived here very modestly, and we didn't have many guests, except for mountaineers and a few hikers," Mirian tells us. *"But life was cheaper then than it is now. A guest in those days was indeed a gift from heaven for us. I remember one summer, some foreigners visited my parents' house. When, at the end of their visit, they wanted to thank us with money, my parents took offence: where is such a thing done, taking money for hospitality? But that's how we live now. It's very sad."*

Mirian offers us some wine he brought from Kakheti. We choose a wine that is thick, tart, and too cold to really please our taste buds. Mirian drinks vodka, occasionally topping it up for Nika and Yulia. Soon another group joins us- three Germans from East Germany, who Mirian had met earlier. We all sit at the same table.

Avalanches and Svan Women

I am curious to hear from the locals about wintertime in Ushguli. It is clear that Mestia has not been such a wilderness for a long time, as a good road from Zugdidi leads there. Ushguli is a different matter, though.

"Over-wintering in these parts must be a test!" I surmise.

"Oh, yeah! We have fun. And it's beautiful. You'll never see such scenery anywhere else in your life! Summer is nothing compared to winter. But if there's a lot of snow, you can't go down to Mestia and you have to stay here until the snowdrifts melt. That's why I will soon go to Tbilisi. I'm working on a construction site there."

"Do you get a lot of avalanches here?" I ask.

"Oh, yes! It happens! I remember one winter, it was 1987, it snowed non-stop for many days in a row, day and night. We knew we had to take urgent measures to avoid the risk of avalanches. After all, our village is in a valley between the mountains! We packed everything we needed, took a stock of food and water, and by evening had started to hide in our towers. Thank God we have these shelters, safe from any avalanche."

"Really? The towers can withstand that kind of pressure?" I wonder.

"Yes, they can! You have no idea how many lives these koshki (towers*) have saved over the centuries!"*

"And then what happened? How long were you in the towers?"

"All night we were there, burning fires. Of course, sleep was out of the question. And when we went outside in the morning, we saw that the snowfall had stopped, the sky was clear, the weather was sunny, but suddenly — some terrible muffled scream! It was a cry for help."

"Who was it?"

"For a long time, we couldn't understand where the sounds were coming from, because the echoes confused us. It was difficult to move around the village because everything was covered in snow; drifts several meters high, and the roads had to be cleared again. Later, when we sorted it out, we realized that one of the houses had been covered by an avalanche."

A shiver ran down my spine at his words.

"Were the people saved?" I ask.

"No. It's almost impossible to save people who've been buried in an avalanche. They were in a simple house, not a tower, and they died. It was that year that another village, Murkmeli, was destroyed by an avalanche. The survivors were later resettled in the Kvemo Kartli region. Now there is a whole Svan village there called Udabno, not far from the David Gareji monastery."

After this story, we remain silent for a while, digesting the terrible tale. Mirian makes another toast, this time to the deceased.

After a while, two of Mirian's cousins, who were until now at work on one of the many construction sites in the village, join us. After a few shots of vodka, our host becomes unusually sentimental. I say "unusually," because mountaineers are usually considered extremely averse to a display of emotions. And then Mirian tells the story of his love for a Russian-German who he met while working in Russia.

"She was nine years older than me! And she was a wonderful person," Mirian says dreamily. *"I brought her here to us, and we lived here together for a while. But everyone realized that there was no future with her for me, because she was too old (she was 32 at the time), a whole nine years. So we had to break up."*

Mirian took a moment to catch his breath, indulging in the sweet memories of his youth, then he continued: *"That woman.... I still can't forget her."*

"What happened to her?" I ask.

"We fell out of touch. I have my own family now," Mirian replies. *"She went to Germany. I took her to Tbilisi myself, to the airport. I never heard from her again."*

To bring a more cheerful tone to the conversation, one of his cousins proposes a toast: *"Let's drink to our Mirian and his family! May God finally bless them with a son!"*

"How many children do you have?" I ask.

"Three," our new acquaintance replies. *"But, unfortunately, all of them are girls. It's not good. I urgently need an heir."*

Many local historians and travelers, including Prince Eristov and Dimitri Bakradze, mentioned the cruel custom of killing girls in Svaneti. More precisely, female infants. This allegedly happened if there were too many girls in a family and no son was born. However, the Svans themselves deny the existence of such a terrible tradition.

"But if your girls marry and have husbands, they will be like sons to you, and they can be considered heirs too, can't they?"

"No, nothing like that," Mirian says with a sad sigh. *"Girls are different, girls are not boys, and sons-in-law are not sons."*

Both cousins and Mirian's sister nod: Mirian urgently needs an heir, and if his wife can't bear a son, he urgently needs to find another woman.

The same ethnographers in their notes record that according to ancient tradition, if a married couple in Svaneti gave birth to only girls, the husband had the right to marry another woman to get himself a son. The "old" wife was thus deposed from the "throne," and the husband no longer had conjugal relations with her, although she was allowed to remain in his household.

We're at a loss: "And what will your first wife say if you do this?"

"She won't mind," Mirian replies, winking slyly. *"She realizes how important a son is to the family."*

Walking to the Shkhara Glacier

The next day, we set out for the foot of the Shkhara. And here we are again on our way up to the Lamaria Church.

Looking down on Ushguli, one can guess what qualities of character nature could have instilled in the inhabitants of this region. If one looks at the world from its very roof every day, wouldn't it be natural to become a great philosopher or poet? Nevertheless, the majority of Svanetians did not inherit these qualities. On the contrary, the inhabitants of Svaneti are known as rational, sober-minded people. Perhaps the point is that, in these lands, one cannot survive without daily hard labor. It sucks up all their free time — and this applies to both men and women.

In 1898, Prince Eristov described the everyday life of the Svans as follows:

"The husband and wife bear the labors of the house equally: the wife does the woman's work and the husband does the man's, and in some cases the wife also takes on the work that is the husband's responsibility (...)" (Prince Eristov, Notes on Svaneti).

Here's another excerpt from the same book:

"A Svanet without a wife is no man at all. This can be seen from the importance of a woman as a spouse and a worker. A woman in Svaneti is more than a right hand for her husband; she is everything in the household; she does everything directly, and in addition she works next to her husband. Here is the proof: the husband goes with a scythe to cut hay, the wife follows him with a rake, collects it and brings it home on oxen; the husband goes with a plow, and the wife follows him with a hoe; the husband cuts wood in the forest, and the wife brings it home; the wife reaps the field, and the husband knits sheaves. The grain they thresh together. And if there is a need to fight with the enemy, a Svanetka will not give up even here — she can handle weapons (...) A wife not only performs the same labor as her husband, but also deals with the household chores that are inaccessible to her husband or unpleasant for a man to do. For example, a woman here weaves canvas and cloth, sews linen, chokhas, sharovars, leggings, and hats; she knits stockings, socks; cleans the house; goes to the mill to grind wheat; brings home flour; bakes bread; drives the cattle out to pasture; brings them back; milks the cows; makes butter, cheese, etc., etc. Deprive a Svanet of all this, and you will see what his life will be like without a wife" (Prince Eristov, Notes on Svaneti).

We descend the hill on which the Lamaria church is located and follow the wide gorge. It's mid-October, but the sun is baking hot, as if it were the height of summer. We have a long walk, and it would be an easy one if not for the merciless sun, which makes us thirsty. When we run out of water brought from the village, we fill our bottles directly from the river. The turbulent and full-flowing Inguri River (*Enguri* in Georgian) flows out of the Shkhara, which in these places is like a brook. On the way, we meet other tourists — some in jeeps, some on horses.

The panorama of the majestic Shkhara, whose snow-white ridge shines in the sunlight, beckons us. We walk, mesmerized by its power, burning with impatience to get to the foot of it as soon as possible.

After seven kilometers, not far from the foothills, Theo and I say goodbye to Yulia and Nika, who have decided to stay in Ushguli longer. They want to walk more in the vicinity of Shkhara. After returning to the village, Theo and I plan to descend to Mestia, so we need to hurry.

After lunch in Mirian's café, we drive down. We don't want to leave these places at all. You should spend at least a few nights in Ushguli to leisurely explore the natural beauty, as well as ancient monuments, such as the Chazhash Castle, the residence of Queen Tamar, and the numerous small churches. There is a reason why this village is on the UNESCO list of cultural heritage.

There are many interesting places between Ushguli and Mestia, too, though. On our way, high in the mountains, lies one of the most famous ancient temples of Georgia — the Church of Saints Kvirike and Ivlita, or, as it is popularly called, Lagurka, built in the 10th - 11th centuries. Local people tell many legends about this shrine. On St Kvirike's Day, believers from all over the country come here to pray at one of the most powerful miracle-working icons in Georgia — *Shaliani.*

On the way, we admire this strange land from the car. The forest is already dressed up in autumn colors, and now, against the background of evergreen spruce trees, the oaks, aspens, maples, hailstones and beeches shine with picturesque purple, gold and ochre strokes. The road to the nearest community, Kala, leads through a beautiful but unsafe canyon. Further along the way are villages, each more interesting than the last, and all so different.

This is what happens to me in Georgia: when I visit a region, I am often left with a feeling of incompletion, and an irrepressible desire to head back to those places again. Nevertheless, we continue our journey onwards, happy in the knowledge that we may soon return to this cherished land.

Tbilisi, November 2019

Hiking to the Shkhara Glacier

View of Ushguli

Outlook from the Svanetian tower of the Margiani family in Mestia

Chapter 9.
Svaneti: The Heart of Traditions

Mountains and Gods

Mountains have always been inaccessible sanctuaries for the Svans. Mountaineer Garry Khergiani expresses it this way: *"For centuries, we have felt reverence, fear, and at the same time unspeakable tenderness towards our mountains. We consider mountains to be living creatures. You never conquer a mountain; you cannot step on them. About mountains we say: 'The mountain let me in' or 'This time the mountain did not accept me'."*

Who better to tell us about the mountains than Garry, the nephew of the courageous, legendary Svan mountaineer Mikheil Khergiani? In his time, this climber earned the nickname "the Tiger of the Rocks," and, unrivalled, young athletes still look up to him. I'm told one can even get addicted to mountains, and this is probably not only inherent in alpinists and climbers.

"When you get addicted to mountains, it becomes difficult to live without them for long," Garry once explained to me. *"Then it becomes almost impossible to get away from them. And some of us prefer not to part with them ever: they end up at rest there, in the high altitudes forever."*

A Treacherous Goddess

The Svans associate many pagan deities with certain mountain peaks. For example, the two-horned beauty Ushba is the abode of Dali, the goddess of hunting, about whom many legends have been written. The goddess used to captivate hunters with her golden mane, so that they would start dreaming of her. Sometimes, they even betrayed their loved ones for her.

Dali is the goddess of hunting in Georgian mythology. She can appear to a person in the form of an animal or a bird. Dali is the patroness of wild animals, and is usually depicted as a beautiful naked woman with golden hair and glowing skin. Dali is the mother of the god Amirani.

Svan ethnographer Madona Chamgeliani told me this: *"Our mountain rivers are made of the golden hair of the goddess Dali, to which various magical properties have been attributed. Dali is a symbol of wealth. Our people associate the character of Dali with the harsh laws of the mountains. It is said that many pagan deities were prototypes for Christian saints. But Dali, who knows neither forgiveness nor mercy, is by no means a prototype of Maria, mother of Jesus Christ; she is rather akin to Medea, the daughter of King Aeëtes of Colchis."*

If somebody decides to connect their life with the mountains, the mountains begin to educate them; to form the character of that person; to teach them responsiveness and dedication.

"In the mountains, you must rely not only on yourself, but also on your friend," Garry explains. *"You and your friend become one, because it would be almost impossible for you to survive without each other. That's why bad people rarely go to the mountains. The mountain will always point you to your place as a small man. You must always respect the mountain so that it accepts you."*

This perception sounds rather fascinating, doesn't it? When Garry talks about mountains, it is as if he is talking about great deities.

Who knows, maybe the Svans were the first mountaineers? It is said that it was they who invented the first rock climbing shoes, because long before the beginning of mountaineering, the inhabitants of Svaneti would go hunting in the mountains, fearlessly climbing the cliffs to find food for themselves. The mountains were their breadwinners, and the Svan people utilized many different tools to reach those heights.

In the memorial house-museum of Mikheil Khergiani, you can see unpretentious equipment of mountaineers of the mid-20th century. After seeing this, one begins to marvel at the resilience and courage of the people who managed to climb enormous peaks not with the help of today's technical tricks, but only thanks to the strength of their spirit, perseverance and aspiration.

Garry spent his childhood and youth in this house—among the mountaineers, friends of his uncle, listening to many exciting stories about climbing to the summits, about difficulties and hardships, and about gaining victory over oneself. Having absorbed numerous vivid impressions from those strong people, Garry could no longer imagine his life without mountaineering or without those brave noble folks with whom he wanted to work his way up. Garry is now 51 years old, and he says he will continue going up into the mountains as long as he lives.

I could talk endlessly about the beauty and majesty of the Greater Caucasus Range, one of the most powerful places on planet Earth, but Svaneti is not only a place of legendary mountains; it is also a place where ancient customs, beliefs, and patriarchal ways of life have been preserved, even though the Tsarist, Soviet, and sometimes even the Church authorities, have fought against it.

In Upper, or "Free" Svaneti, before the Russian Empire arrived there in the mid-19th century, feudal lords had never ruled. The tsarist viceroys, who did not know nor respect the culture and traditions of these proud mountain people, were met with unprecedented resistance.

The Land of a Thousand Towers

Svaneti was once called "the land of a thousand towers." During Soviet rule, when private property was forbidden, the "care" of public property was transferred to the competence of the state. The lack of state care resulted in many towers falling into disrepair, with their roofs becoming dilapidated and their once-imposing walls slowly cracking and crumbling. As a result, only around 300 towers remain standing today.

The capital of "Free" Svaneti is the town of Mestia. In one of its neighborhoods, Lanchvali, I stayed with my good friends, the Margiani family. In Svaneti, it has long been believed that the stronger and more powerful a family is, the more towers it has. The Margiani family has three towers, its own small church with a cemetery, and the Museum of Svan Life, where you can see how Svan families have lived for centuries.

The head of the Margiani family is Murad, a long-serving architect-restorer. Since 2006, he has been working on the preservation and conservation of the main cultural heritage of his small homeland, the Svan towers, which he calls "the eighth wonder of the world," referring to the unique architecture of these structures.

A Svan tower (Georgian: "svanuri koshki") is a fortress defense structure in the form of a four-sided tower, typical of Svaneti. Built in the 8th - 18th centuries, these ancestral structures were used simultaneously as dwellings, as an emergency way out of the home in case of avalanches in winter, and as guard posts to protect against frequent invasions. The towers have between 3 and 5 floors.

"In one village, we found a huge stone on one of the upper floors of the tower and weighed it," Murad says. *"Laboratory studies showed it was 3.5 tons! How could our ancestors lift such a huge stone to the top? With the help of what devices? What kind of civilization was this?"*

In his fifteen years of hard labor, Murad's hands have saved some 136 towers. To achieve this, the restorer uses ancient technologies, employing limestone as a binding material, which is continuously burnt together with grass for a week in special lime houses. It is a long and labor-intensive process, but the end result is worth it, as the property of lime sees it becoming stronger and stronger over the years. In addition, by trial and error, Murad invented a unique method of giving the lime screed the desired color, allowing it to be harmoniously combined with the ancient stones. He keeps this recipe a secret.

Murad told me that the towers we see now are from the 9th-12th centuries. Before that, towers of a different type were built in Svaneti, like those in Tusheti. They were called *tsikhesakhli*, or house-towers. People lived there and were able to protect themselves from enemies. The restorer believes that we still know too little about the history and architecture of Svaneti, that this land holds many mysteries that people have yet to discover.

A Blood Feud

Svan towers served people both for defense against enemies and for protecting the clan from internecine disputes, for example, during *litsvri* — a rite of blood feud. It turns out that each clan built a complex system of tunnels and labyrinths under its towers to bait and destroy enemies. The schemes of the tunnels were kept in strict secrecy, and were passed on only to the men of the clan. Women were not privy to such strategic secrets, not because women were not trusted, but because representatives of the female sex could marry again, or even several times: it was not proper for a woman to linger in the status of a widow, and that is why, after the death of her husband, she was given in marriage to another, although the relatives of the deceased man did not give their children to the new family. As such, in the course of internecine strife, a woman was often faced with a difficult choice: A new family or the children's family, as a result of which a woman might be inclined to disclose the secret of the family tunnels.

Murad told me with great affection about the rich heritage of his homeland: the ancient towers and churches, many of which, alas, have been destroyed. He lamented the modern trend to build new churches everywhere.

"Our ancestors didn't build churches everywhere. They were very pure, and their knowledge came from God; they talked to God themselves, directly. We have God very close to us here, and He showed them where the power gathers, where they should build a church. If you have money, I advise you to rebuild old destroyed churches, even those of which only the foundation is left, because such a place of worship will have more power than one built for vanity."

The Margiani family is a clear example of how history and modernity are inextricably linked in Svaneti.

Murad's youngest son, 24-year-old Murman, recently graduated with a bachelor's degree in architecture. He kept me company on the way back up from Tbilisi. I have known Murman's parents for over 10 years, and his late mother Larisa Margiani and I were friends. On the way to Mestia, Murman and I had a lot of time for a heart-to-heart, and I was struck time and again by the extraordinary maturity and wisdom of this young man.

In Lanchvali, Murman gave me a quick tour of a small family church built in the 17th century. Such churches here are considered to be newfangled, as there are no unique ancient frescoes of the Svan school in such churches. It turned out that this church stands on the site of an even older temple, which was previously covered by a landslide. Murad had managed to excavate the roof of the former church, the walls of which were painted with frescoes, but he did not dare to carry out further research, as the ancient building seemed too fragile. As a rule, the keys to such churches are kept with the families, because there are often treasures inside, such as icons and ancient books, unless, of course, these have been given to museums.

Holding in his hands an old prayer book of impressive size, written in the old Georgian alphabet, Murman confided to me that at such moments, he felt above all strength and pride. And then he said something which was, in my opinion, very important: *"I think that every person should know where he comes from and what path his ancestors have traveled before him. I think that in difficult life situations, we should remember where our roots are and where we come from. This is what gives us strength."*

The fact that Murman's words are not empty can be seen in practice: he helps his father and two brothers in the family business (café, hotel, museum) every day, honors the memory and precepts of his recently departed mother, and respects his elders and seeks to learn from them.

Murman often goes rock climbing with his friends, all of them first training themselves on towers using climbing equipment. *"You need to train regularly, because otherwise you get out of shape quickly,"* Murman tells me. The most important thing is technique, he says — the ability to control your body — and strong arms.

Avtandil Japaridze is the most experienced climber among Murman's peers, although he is only 21 years old. He has climbed the iconic Svan peaks more than once, with good preparation after countless hours of training. *"I like mountaineering because it is the most extreme of all extreme sports, and it also makes us human and teaches us about life,"* he tells me when I meet him.

There is no doubt that sports can teach you a lot. But still, a big part of our upbringing, no matter how you look at it, comes from the family. I asked Murad how he had brought up his sons- what did he teach them? How are children brought up in Svaneti?

"My teaching is simple," Murad answers me. *"It is to love your homeland, to work hard, and to know about the culture of behavior. We have such an old and respected clan that it should not be dishonored in any way. I always forbade my children to go hunting and kill mountain turs. This was forbidden to our family members despite the fact that hunting is one of the main types of economy in*

Svaneti. Also, in the family, it is obligatory to respect women and women's labor, as well as to honor and obey one's parents."

Family — Clan — Community

Vakhtang Pilpani is an engineer by education, but by vocation he is a musician and a master of making folk musical instruments *chinuri* and *changi*. Like his grandfather and later his father, Vakhtang leads the Svan folk ensemble 'Riho.' He is proud of the rich cultural heritage of his region. Who better than such an enthusiast to tell us about the customs of Svan antiquity?

"In the past, our people had a traditional large family, with twenty, thirty, forty people," Vakhtang tells me. *"We had no rulers, and each family defended itself. The more people there were in a family, the stronger it was, especially if there were many men in it. And in these families, there was no Internet, no social media, no TV, no radio, and everyone entertained themselves with songs and dances. And when someone in the family sang songs in the evening, it was automatically passed on to the young and the children. The traditions they created or preserved were both entertainment and spiritual food for them. And these traditions have come down to us. Traditions that people have lived for centuries."*

At funerals in Svaneti, men are obliged to sing the song 'Zari,' without which no ritual ceremony takes place. Traditional dance and song are also closely linked here. Each song speaks about some historical moment in the life of the region. Often, the songs are dedicated to religious themes, and some songs are reminiscent of prayers.

"As long as singers sing these songs, our traditions will live on. But we also have a problem: young people are gradually losing interest in our heritage," Vakhtang complains, and goes on to give me some examples. In every Svan settlement, there is one special place called a svip. Traditionally, it is located near a spring, from which mountain water flows continuously. Not only the family, but all villagers traditionally gather there to discuss the latest events, affairs and news. It is also where the cattle come for water.

"Do you know when the tradition of gathering at the 'svip' began to break down?" Vakhtang asks. *"When television appeared! And after work, people didn't go to the svip- they were much more interested in news, then sports or a film, and then TV gradually disappeared, and why? Because the Internet appeared, and everyone has their own screen, and we are all connected, and everyone is watching something different! We need to come up with something urgently, to create some interest among young people, maybe even material interest, so that we keep our traditions alive!"*

In Svaneti, and throughout Georgia, representatives of at least three generations still often live under one roof. In the family of Levan Nikoloziani, in the village of Lakhushdi, I met 81-year-old Darya Kvanchiani, Levan's mother. Darya lives in a large, spacious house, fringed with many flowers. With her live her son and daughter-in-law, two grandchildren, the wife of one of those grandchildren, and two great-grandchildren. Darya bought a small house when she was young, and then her children and grandchildren added on to it, expanding the original property.

The house is now so big that there is also enough space for a wonderful hostel, as Data, Darya's grandson, is involved in tourism with his wife and father.

It was hard not to notice how, playing in the yard with her great-grandchildren, Darya sparkled with happiness. *"Svaneti is my native land, where I was born and grew up,"* Darya says. *"Our life is very difficult, but we Svans are a hard-working people. We are happy to work. And I am grateful to God for my life. It was difficult, but happy."*

In the past, Darya was a mother of four, as well as a cultural worker and the first voice of the village. She lost her husband and one of her sons too early. Her hard work and caring for her children helped her to survive the losses.

"I no longer sing: my voice is not the same, but I continue to do needlework," she says. *"And the fact that I have lived to such an advanced age is God's grace. Now I enjoy my grandchildren and great-grandchildren, caring for them and supporting them."*

Lakhushdi, the Village of Song

In Svaneti, Lakhushdi is known as the village of song. This happened thanks to the efforts of Madona Chamgeliani and her sisters Eka and Ana.

Everyone in the Chamgeliani family sang, but Madona was not in a hurry to learn the traditional chants at first—instead, she dreamed of becoming a mathematician. During her childhood, the village had neither transport nor any decent supplies, and people survived as best they could. Civil wars were raging in the country; robbery and banditry were rampant. To make a living, people had to come down off the mountains and sell potatoes, one of the few products that grew in Svaneti, in Zugdidi, the capital of the neighboring Samegrelo region. It was not uncommon for heavily armed bandits to then take away their modest earnings on their way back up.

One day, Madona's father, a soloist in the local choir, became seriously ill. It was impossible to take him to Zugdidi. The girl spent long winter evenings together with her father, listening as he told her the legends of Svaneti, about the rich folk traditions, and explained to her the culture of Svan multi-voiced chanting. After her father passed away, Madona became seriously interested in Svaneti antiquity and decided to become an ethnographer. When she realized that the inhabitants of her village were gradually losing the musical traditions of their homeland, she became frightened: like her, the other young people had no interest in studying the heritage of their ancestors. Added to which the fact that after the collapse of the USSR, the revival of church life had begun: priests coming from other regions were wary of the ancient Svan semi-pagan traditions, and would not support them if someone started to follow them.

The turning point for the Chamgeliani family came when they met an amazing woman from Scotland, Madge Bray, who at the time was researching Georgian polyphony for therapeutic purposes. Madge, a psychologist by training, saw Georgian chanting as a means of harmonizing the human soul.

In 2015, I was lucky enough to chat with Madge, and even heard her perform one of the Svan songs. In Svaneti, Madge told me, she felt she had found the promised land: she had never dared to dream of such rich material to research, she said.

"Georgian chanting is a great treasure, recognized by UNESCO as an intangible heritage of humanity," Madge explained to me excitedly. *"This music is extraordinary, it has absolutely unimaginable dissonance, but in the end, this dissonance always ends up in unity. There is an incredible battle in the sounds the singers make, which always leads to harmony."*

With the support of the Chamgeliani family, Madge began to bring foreigners interested in Georgian folk music to Lakhushdi. The project to study Georgian polyphony was later supported by Frenchwoman Zoé Perret. A concertmaster and cellist, Zoé has lived in Georgia for fifteen years and regularly visits Lakhushdi with guests from abroad.

Recently, I was lucky enough to attend one of the workshops organized by Zoé under the guidance of the Chamgeliani sisters. On a clear August night, a fire was lit for us, a group of guests from France and the author of these lines, in a clear field near the village.

Sitting by the fire, Madona told us about the ancient Svan legends, on the theme of which the Svans have composed many songs. The central figure of the legends is the goddess Dali, both beautiful and powerful. Later, the participants of the masterclass led round dances, danced and sang songs- Svan, and those from other regions of Georgia. This incredible spectacle gave us an opportunity to be transported back to times when humanity lived in harmony with nature: This is exactly what the participants of the seminar from France had traveled such a long way for.

I asked Zoé why she was so attracted to Svaneti.

"I love the Chamgeliani sisters and this family, this nature. I love Lakhushdi!" she said. *"Lakhushdi is a special village. When I'm here, I feel like I'm in a different dimension. Everything here is connected to nature: people and nature are one, and these songs also belong to nature. Svaneti is rich in legends and folk tales. Svan mythology is incredibly powerful! Madona knows folk tales well, and it is a great pleasure to study the songs in this context."*

"I never intended to go into business," Madona tells me later. *"The most important thing for me was to preserve our culture and musical traditions. I don't like the word 'tourist' — guests are important to me, not tourists. Our guests don't come here to look at us or take pictures, but to study our culture. They stay with different families, and we give them masterclasses in Svan music, the music of other regions of the country; we organize traditional feasts, show them our customs, in which Christianity and paganism are intertwined. And it so happens that under the influence of interest from outside, our young people remembered the wealth of our ancestors and began to sing."*

The Chamgeliani sisters' project quickly gained popularity among both local and foreign guests. During the celebration, I met Christian from Toulouse. He told me that he had learned about this workshop from friends who had visited Lakhushdi the year before and returned filled with harmony and strength. *"My friend and I also decided to participate in this project. We were energized by the idea of returning to humanity's roots, to the olden days, to man's unity with the world, and his own nature. These traditions are not disappearing, because the Svans are trying hard to preserve them."*

Protoculture

A similar idea was voiced later by Ksenia Parjiani, a remarkable woman from Siberia, a mother of four children, each of whom she is bringing up in the Svaneti spirit. Ksenia and her husband have a large, successful business, which Ksenia believes she owes to her strong family, as well as to the powerful nature of Svaneti, which fills her with energy and helps her maintain focus.

"I believe the Svan and Georgian cultures were the progenitors of many European cultures. I want my children to absorb this proto-culture as well. Caucasian culture is a culture of peace, and it is boundless," she says.

Ksenia's family has been running a guest house in Latali village for many years, hosting tourists from all over the world. That is why her statements are not at all speculative: *"I can give you hundreds of examples of how people from all over the world have come here and felt at home in Svaneti. I can tell you about Australians, Germans, Chinese, Japanese, and Slavs. These are people who come here and feel as if this is their home and family. They confess that they feel like they are visiting their grandmother or great-grandmother. It's not by chance; it's not for nothing!"*

Indeed, I have spoken in Svaneti with numerous foreigners who have lived there for a long time or visit regularly. Their experience, as well as my own, confirms that Svaneti cannot fail to captivate, and yes, like the mountains, it does not let go for long. It is easy to fall ill with it: without these mountains, life becomes unthinkable.

Lakhushdi — Mestia — Lengeri — Tbilisi, August 2022

Svanetian architect Murad Margiani has restored 135 Svanetian towers

Murman Margiani visiting his family chapel in the Lanchvali district of Mestia

Daria Kvanchiani from Lakhushdi village with her great-grandson

View of Mamisoni Pass on the abandoned Ossetian Military Road

Chapter 10.
A Flight above Racha

Gosha from Ghebi

On one of my first visits to Racha in 2018, fate rewarded me with a meeting with Malgorzata. This fragile, middle-aged woman looks like a young, mischievous biker. Gosha, as Malgorzata is called by her close friends, long ago traded Poznan for the Georgian countryside, and for many years has been living in what I think is the most delightful part of Racha, in the village of Ghebi. Here, she has her own hostel, mini-farm, horses and ... patients. In her past life, Gosha was a doctor, and now she provides medical assistance to the locals when needed, and she does it completely free of charge, because "being a doctor is a vocation."

The village of Ghebi once belonged to Svaneti, and the Svaneti-like remains of an ancient church and tower are still preserved there. The very way of life in Ghebi, its cobblestone streets, broken by time, as well as the stern faces of its inhabitants, cannot but remind one of Svaneti. Even the climate here is similar to Svaneti, and it is not easy to survive in it. This is probably why most Racha residents of Ghebi only come here in the summer, and for the rest of the year prefer to live in the city.

For lovers of the authentic and genuine, this Rachan village is the best! Its pristine nature, air filled with happiness and freedom, rushing mountain rivers and mineral springs that drive away any illness, and, of course, the mountain ranges surrounding the village — mighty, impregnable, snow-capped — is this not what every soul seeking reunion with the divine is looking for? Are places like Ghebi not a direct confirmation of God's existence on earth?

Countess and archeologist Praskovya Sergeevna Uvarova visited Ghebi in the late 19th century as part of her research trip to the Caucasus. In her diary, she wrote:

"... We see before us the whole village of Ghebi, located on both sides of the very noisy and deep Rion, which has made its bed in the limestone formation of the gorge, in which, for the first time, we notice a significant presence of coarse-grained granite boulders. The settlement seems to close the gorge. The area it occupies is quite large, and forms a deepened space on both banks of the Rion, protected on all sides by mountains. Here, we are at an altitude of 4600 feet, and we are dealing with the terminus of Transcaucasia. If we understand the Caucasus, as many writers do, in the close sense of the main Caucasian ridge; from here, a day, and we are

in Balkaria, Svanetia or Ossetia, as desired. We are surrounded on all sides by snowy peaks, to which we are so close that they seem to us, in comparison with the mountains we have seen, not so significant as they really are; we forget that we have risen to a certain height, and only the cold (the thermometer drops to 3 degrees) reminds us of the reality. Around us are the peaks of Shota, Tsitlistavi, Notsaristsveri, and at a great distance, as if closing the gorge from the opposite side, Dolomistsveri. The following glaciers are not far from Ghebi: Kolcheidunsky, Rubodzalsky, Pasis-Mta, the last of which gives rise to the Rion. General Totleben's detachment sent by Catherine II to help Solomon I, the King of Imereti, passed through Ghebi to Digori in 1771" (Praskovya Sergeevna Uvarova, Caucasus. Racha, Gori district, Ossetian Mountains, Pshavia, Khevsuretia and Svanetia. Traveling Notes of Countess Uvarova, 1904).

Ghebi captivated, as we can see, not only us wanderers of the 21st century, but also Praskovya Sergeevna Uvarova at the end of the century before last. Saying goodbye to Ghebi, the Countess wrote, quoting lines by Mikhail Lermontov:

"The village, the gorge and the snowy peaks in the moonlight are beautiful, so beautiful that it is a pity to tear oneself away from the balcony; a pity to think of leaving and, perhaps, of an eternal farewell to Ghebi. It is so quiet and peaceful here, so far from the whole world, that more often than ever, the words of the poet come to mind:

Countess Praskovya Uvarova, née Princess Scherbatova, was a Russian scholar, historian and archeologist. Together with her husband, archeologist Alexei Uvarov, she was engaged in research and public activities. After Alexei's death, she became chairman of the Moscow Archeological Society, an honorary member of the Imperial Academy of Sciences, a professor at the universities of Dorpat, Kharkov, Kazan, and Moscow, St. Petersburg Archeological University and Lazarev Institute of Oriental Languages. For many years, she worked on the book 'Description of Miniatures of Georgian Gospels of the XV and XVI centuries.' She died in emigration.

A miserable man,
What is it he desires?
The sky is bright,
There's plenty of room for everyone below;
Yet evermore, and all in vain,
He's at war all by himself... what for?" (Praskovya Sergeevna Uvarova, Caucasus. Racha, Gori district, Ossetian Mountains, Pshavia, Khevsuretia and Svanetia. Traveling Notes of Countess Uvarova, 1904).

I had to wait three years for my next trip to Upper Racha. All that time, I had pictures of peaks and mountain paths I had not yet traveled dancing in my mind; tempting and enticing me to return.

The Rachan Mountains

Racha can be roughly divided into two parts: north and south. The south is the land of winemakers and farmers, gardens, orchards, vineyards, luxurious houses in the Rioni Valley, and romantic panoramas of the mountains. On the terraces of these houses, it is particularly nice to relax on a hammock under an ancient tree with a book in hand.

The north of Racha is a wild land of glaciers, rushing, stormy rivers, endless mountain massifs and rebellious nature, which, like a fairy tale, first generously bestows on the traveler over-the-top delight, then sets him harsh tests to challenge him.

Are not the mountains the finest embodiment of life's philosophy? It is only at such heights that one can truly grasp the duality of being, its completeness and multifaceted nature.

Mravaldzali

To see the Rachan mountains, it is a good idea to first climb up to a village with the magical name of Mravaldzali. In Georgian, it means "much strength." There, at an altitude of 1840 meters above sea level, and in good weather, amazing landscapes open up, after the contemplation of which a traveler can easily feel himself omnipotent. Indeed, how else could one name a place that harbors so much energy?

From the main road leading from Ambrolauri to Oni, we turn right, cross the bridge over the Rioni River, and start climbing. We pass one village after another drowning in lavish greenery, trying to see the houses behind the rich old gardens. Sixteen kilometers of serpentine fly by unnoticed. Mravaldzali village is located on the border of tree growth: There are few tall trees here, but the views are stunning, and even breathing is easier: where, down below, even near the river, it was stuffy and the thermometer showed us +38 degrees, here it is only +27.

Countess Uvarova once came to Mravaldzali from the village of Shkmeri, in honor of which one of the most famous Georgian dishes, *shkmeruli* (fried chicken, or chicken in savory garlic sauce), is named.

In notes about her travels, Praskovya Sergeevna Uvarova wrote:

"The way from Shkmeri to Mravaldzali runs along the tops of mountains. It seems that you have already climbed so high that the whole Caucasus is at your feet, but here again the ascent is difficult and unpleasant, as we have to climb up limestone ranges located across the road in the form of stone, and not always convenient, stairs. Around us there are bushes and small forests – birch, rowan, hazel, and among the forest there are glades covered with magnificent crocuses of a purple

and milky color. The sun is warming, the sky is bright and friendly, the mountain air is so clear, and the leaves yellowing in the sun are so clear and golden... A lovely picture of autumn, and all around, or, rather, at our feet, the loveliest horizon, the loveliest panorama of the mountains, of the entire lower Racha" (Praskovya Sergeevna Uvarova, Caucasus. Racha, Gori district, Ossetian Mountains, Pshavia, Khevsuretia and Svanetia. Traveling Notes of Countess Uvarova, 1904).

The main attraction of the village is the Church of St Giorgi, built in the 11th century. Thanks to numerous restorations, the church has been well preserved, so Countess Uvarova's descriptions are just as relevant to modern times as they were back when she saw the church with her own eyes:

"The ancient church in Mravaldzali, in the name of St Giorgius, is basilic in shape and has a gable roof, from under which the heads of animals stand out: on the western side the head of a calf, on the northern side a lion. The window and door on the western side are decorated with rather rough ornaments (...). The eastern window is decorated with two relief, full-body images of saints. The icons are all embossed, as usual, with popular images of Giorgius the Victorious and the Archangels. However, there is also a cross and a small icon of the Mother of God with an infant, of a very delicate style (...)" (Praskovya Sergeevna Uvarova, Caucasus. Racha, Gori district, Ossetian Mountains, Pshavia, Khevsuretia and Svanetia. Traveling Notes of Countess Uvarova, 1904).

As we walked up to the church late morning on a Sunday, we caught a sea of people near the temple who had come for the service and a wedding. It was an event they were filming with the help of a drone. I can hardly think of a better place to hold and film such an event!

Despite the beautiful old church, we still felt that Mravaldzali's main advantage was its location. There are such panoramas that a hundred of the best drones would not be enough to capture this wonder in all its splendor!

That's why, in the mountains, you should not rely on your camera or even your video camera, but more on your feet: there is truth in your feet! It is not for nothing that several hiking trails pass through this village. In order to understand and feel the terrain, especially in forest and mountainous areas, it is important to explore it on foot. Otherwise, you risk missing out on at least half of the precious experiences available to you.

Mamisoni Pass

Climbing to the highest heavens of Racha had long been in my plans. But I did not think or guess that this time I would be able to make the trek to the

Mamisoni Pass. My friends told me that from these heights, all the Rachan mountains, the view of which also opens from Mravaldzali, seem even more spectacular.

Countess Uvarova regularly mentioned the Mamisoni Pass in her books. It was once an important transport route—the Ossetian Military Road—connecting Georgia with the North Caucasus. However, when Russian troops invaded Georgia in August 2008, Russia took control of the pass, meaning that neither Georgian nor foreign citizens can use it.

That summer, David, an acquaintance of mine from Oni, invited me to gather information with him about a new hiking trail. For this purpose, he organized an off-road vehicle for us with a local driver.

From the village of Shovi, we had to go up to the first border post to get permission to drive on to the Mamisoni Pass. From the pass, it is easy to walk to the glaciers of Buba and Tbilisa.

I rejoiced! David's invitation is another confirmation that if you send your clearly defined requests to the Universe, your desires are sure to be fulfilled.

> Shovi is a balneological and climatic resort in Georgia, 30 km from Oni. It is famous for its carbonate, hydrocarbonate, calcium-sodium springs. Respiratory, digestive and nervous system diseases are treated here, and it is also a popular place for family holidays. In 2022, the rehabilitation of the resort was begun, but on 3 August 2023, a massive land slide descended on that resort, burying it in mud. People died, mostly children and women, and the infrastructure was destroyed.

Flying above Racha

Early in the morning, I left Ambrolauri for Shovi, a picturesque resort village famous for its therapeutic mineral springs. These days, however, it is not health resorts that are thriving in this area, but hostels hosting hikers, among whom Racha is increasingly popular.

David was waiting for me in the village of Glola. He spends every summer in his childhood home, the house his ancestors built. He has his own travel agency specializing in hiking. A great enthusiast, David never misses an opportunity to explore new routes.

David was waiting for me with Alexander, the driver of an ancient Pajero that seemed to be falling apart. I had to get into Alexander's SUV, because my toy SUV, it was explained to me, was unlikely to be able to cope with the difficult journey ahead.

When Alexander offered me a seat in front next to him, I had to think seriously for a few seconds: the windscreen of the car had so many impressive cracks that I was sure any bump would shatter the glass into thousands of pieces. Nevertheless, I ventured forward, and was richly rewarded with a direct view of the marvelous scenery.

The gravel road was in much better condition than we expected. Our driver, a large guy with laughing eyes, said that this was "a serious road, a real *autobahn*." The climb and the increasing speed made Alexander's adrenaline rush, and he rode with panache up the steep winding road. Several times, we had to wade through turbulent rivers, but, thankfully, there had been no heavy rains lately.

We climbed higher and higher, crossed another mountain, and after about an hour of traveling, reached the first border checkpoint. There, David and I had to get passes to enter the border area. One of the soldiers asked David to write two applications, one for himself and one for me, and provided a sample. The application had to include our coordinates, personal ID numbers, and the intended time and purpose of our visit.

The Ossetian Military Road (270 km) was constructed by the Russian Empire in the 19th century (specifically between 1854 and 1889). Its purpose was to provide a strategic route through the central Caucasus, connecting what is now North Ossetia-Alania in Russia with areas in Georgia, including Kutaisi. It crossed the Main Caucasus Range via the Mamisoni Pass (2,911 m), a high-altitude and challenging route. The road followed the valleys of the Rioni and Ardon rivers. It passed through very scenic mountainous areas.

This route is seldom used today, having been supplanted by the 1971-1981 construction of the Transcaucasian Highway, which crosses the Caucasus range via the Roki Tunnel. Alternative crossings include the Georgian Military Road, which crosses the Jvari Pass at 2,379 meters. The geopolitics of the region, particularly the situation in "South Ossetia," further complicate its use. Parts of the road exist as rough tracks, suitable mainly for hiking and off-road travel.

Sitting on a stump, David diligently wrote our "petitions" to see the landscapes of Upper Racha, while I, sitting under a tree on a bench near the cliff, began to examine the place of our dislocation.

Stratification of Reality

Verdant mountain slopes, lush with dense thickets, generously covered with forests and glades, warmly opened their embrace. We were at 1900 meters above sea level, and the view from this height was almost like that from a helicopter. The ridges of mountains, like giant dragons lying next to each other, opened like a fan, and new, ever more powerful peaks and ridges grew behind them. Somewhere in the distance, the Gurshevi Glacier was visible. Near the glacier, Alexander remembered, there had once been an Ossetian village where his grandmother used to go every summer. The places there were cooler, and the meadows were fragrant with all the splendor of mountain herbs – sheer grace!

Time passed. We waited. After a while, David became nervous. He argued with the border guards, heatedly pointing out to the military officers that our wait time was too long, and explaining again and again our planned route. The border guards tried to dissuade us from walking: it was too far. Besides, we had to be back strictly by 6pm, and it was already midday.

David shuffled impatiently from foot to foot; Alexander smoked one cigarette after another to pass the time. For me, the waiting time was like watching a film in a cinema, only, during my session, more or less the same scene was shown: the boundless expanse of emerald mountains, the infinite blue of the heavens with wisps of cloud drifting across. I could have gazed upon this landscape forever, feeling a sense of peace and cosmic serenity. Time had completely stopped. The flawless green mountains, shimmering with different shades, caressed my eyes and allowed my mind, soul and heart to rest.

The wait lasted two hours. As it turned out, the head of the border post, to whom our applications had been written, had only recently turned up for work. In my mind, I thanked the chief for those two hours in paradise, on the border between dream and reality.

Having finally received permission to drive on, we did. Forty minutes later, we got to the second border checkpoint, and the last. Further on – Mamisoni, and even further, Russia, but we are not allowed to go there: the border guards allowed us only to walk near the outpost to take some photos.

We found ourselves in a spacious mountain gorge filled with the sweet scent of blossoms. In the distance, we could see glacier massifs, easy for us to reach on foot. The pass was also within walking distance: two kilometers, not more. At the top there is a meteorological station manned by Russians. But we couldn't go there either.

Like giant fragments from some ancient explosion, huge boulders are scattered everywhere. There are also two small ponds covered with tall grass.

After savoring the scenery, we move on, first backwards, then upwards again. Everywhere there is nothing but mountains, their slopes, bottomless chasms and endless stunning views.

For my companions, reserved and taciturn in the Rachan way, my enthusiastic exclamations are like balm to their souls. After each of my exclamations, Alexander smiles like a little child. He drives skilfully and confidently, no easy task with the road being two deep ruts washed out by rains and overgrown with tall grass. Yet it seems that our driver knows every bush, pebble, and dip, driving next to the ruts so as not to damage the bottom of the car.

Rachan Zen

Suddenly, Alexander asks me to close my eyes for a few minutes. I feel like I'm in for a surprise, but it's hard to keep my eyes closed, because I don't want to inadvertently miss something special. "Well, wait a minute, just wait two minutes!" But my companion persistently urges me: *"I'm telling you, you won't regret it!"*

I do as I'm told, and when I open my eyes again, I can't believe what I see: a whole range of mountains and glaciers stretches out in front of us, and we, numb with awe, look down at them from above. These are Burdjula, Shoda and Tsikhvarka, as well as the glaciers of Buba and Tbilisa. At the bottom, there is a hint of Shovi, which is very far away in the gorge, and of the river valley winding in a thin ribbon. And all this splendor we contemplate from above!

Satisfied with himself, Alexander climbs back into the car to fetch a surprise picnic. *"Well, megobrebo, now we have a feast!"* he proclaims. (*megobrebo* is Georgian vocative for "friends").

"How can we have a feast when there is such a fairy tale around?!" I wonder.

"Where better for a feast if not here in paradise? Is there anywhere better?" he asks, pulling out one delight after another: *lavash*, Georgian pita bread, tomatoes, cucumbers, cheese and potato pies, sausage, Coca-Cola and *chacha*.

It's a favored habit for Georgians to combine the enjoyment of nature with feasting. Even during the most ordinary picnic, a Georgian is sure to raise his glass to the sky and thank the Lord for having had the opportunity to enjoy the beauty of the place and the chance to share joy and table with friends and family.

It is now too hot under the sun, so we hide in the shade of the car before we start our feast. Suddenly, the border guards turn up in their SUV. They have decided to accompany us on our journey. One of the soldiers goes to stand not far from us, takes out his binoculars, and begins to look into the distance in a businesslike manner.

As a sign of honor before the men with epaulettes, David opens a can of tuna and invites them to eat with us. Yet they refuse to participate in our celebration of life, claiming they must remain vigilant in their difficult task of watching over our safety. When I go down the cliff a little to take a picture of Shovi, the border guards call me back. What vigilance!

After talking to our border convoy, we learn that we have no time left to descend to the glaciers and will have to drive back.

Before we get to the first border checkpoint, we decide to go to the Gurshevi Glacier, where there was once an Ossetian village. *"Maybe this plan is even better than the first, because it is further from the Russian border, and they let'll us stay there until seven instead of six,"* David comforts me.

We take a slightly different route down. It doesn't feel like driving at all, but like sliding down the mountainside. There are no villages here, only a couple of summertime shepherd's huts. Several times, Alexander stops the car and invites me to collect alpine tea: there is enough St John's wort and oregano for the whole of Tbilisi. All the way back, we are accompanied by the aroma of herbs.

On the way, we meet some village guys on a haymaking trip. In one of the groups are Alexander's friends and David's acquaintances, who are having a party. We are invited to join the feast. The men are making lavish toasts, drinking wine and *chacha*, and, for lack of cups, they pour alcohol into halved plastic bottles. We are soon joined by the same border guards, but even at this celebration they refuse to drink.

What a shame: now it looks like we'll have to forget about going to the glacier! But with deft elegance, David extricates himself from the awkward situation, apologising for us and saying that we are in a hurry, although Alexander's eyes show that he is eager to continue the feast.

We continue on our way, passing back through the first border checkpoint. There, we say goodbye to the guards represented by those two responsible officials, and, a little while later, David and I get out of the car to head up to the glacier. Alexander promises to pick us up from the same place in two hours, and leaves.

We walk up a narrow, steep path through grass that reaches up to our shoulders, gaining altitude quickly. Old trees grow in a large clearing with the ruins of a building that looks like a church or tower. This is where the locals come for picnics: there are traces of a campfire, and wooden benches and a table await. The first border outpost can be seen in the distance.

Through a thicket of giant thorns, we make our way towards abandoned Ossetian houses, which were used as summer cottages by shepherds, but it is impossible to get close to them: everything is covered with tall grass and thistles. Indeed, it seems that no human foot has stepped there for a long time. It's not easy to get to the glacier either. Perhaps we could try from the other side of the river, where the grass is lower? Having failed to find a suitable path, we give up and return to the clearing with trees and the ruins of a church, where we spend the remaining half an hour in contemplation of nature at sunset.

On the way, I manage to pick a bunch of the last daisies of the year. After descending to the road, we have a little more time to refresh ourselves in the coolness of the turbulent mountain river called Chanchakhi.

Alexander comes to pick us up at the agreed time and tells us a secret: he called the border guards to ask them about us, and, as it turned out, they had been watching us with binoculars the whole time!

Despite the long day and our cheerful chatter, I feel like all those hours were one solid and very rewarding meditation session.

Shovi — Oni-Ambrolauri — Tbilisi, August – September 2021

Polish lady Malgorzata, or Gosha, chose the mountains of Upper Racha to make her home in

Hay harvest in Upper Racha

View of the miners' town: Chiatura

Chapter 11.
Chiatura: Time Traveling by Cable Car

I learnt about the existence of the town of Chiatura quite by accident. One day, on our way to Racha, we passed Tkibuli, which impressed us with its numerous pompous buildings in the style of Stalinist monumentalism. I hadn't expected to see examples of such architecture in Upper Imereti.

Later, I did a little research and learned that there are two important industrial towns in Georgia — Tkibuli and Chiatura. After looking at photos on the Internet, I was astonished: it turns out that Chiatura once had as many as sixty (!) cable cars! My curiosity was piqued, and I quickly persuaded one of my editors to let me do a report on this unusual place.

The road led me through the picturesque landscapes of Upper Imereti. Each new turn inspired a photo shoot. In the distance, the peaks of the Greater Caucasus Range were already covered with snow, and fat, happy cows grazed peacefully in front of my eyes, recalling in my mind delicious Imereti cheese and the unparalleled Imereti cuisine.

After descending into the valley, I found myself in a small town called Sachkhere, which, to my surprise, boasts many new or recently renovated buildings, modern shopping centers and even an impressive sports complex with a swimming pool! Outside the town, however, there are many abandoned, ugly buildings where the industrial life of the region had once boiled: the hulks of factories, workshops, warehouses and other industrial buildings stretch for fifteen kilometers.

And then I saw the cable cars!

Chiatura is an industrial town nestled in the foothills of Imereti. With a population of approximately 13,000 people, it is situated in the deep gorge of the Kvirila River.

The history of Chiatura is inextricably linked to the discovery of rich manganese deposits in the late 19th century. The town quickly transformed into a center of the mining industry, and the first and almost only proletariat in Georgia was formed there. After the establishment of Soviet power, the miners of Chiatura, known for their independent spirit, repeatedly tried to protest their rights, but their attempts were brutally suppressed. During the Soviet era, the town experienced a period of rapid industrialization. The picturesque gorge was built up with industrial facilities, which significantly changed its original appearance. Chiatura's hallmark is an extensive network of cable cars. Created in the Soviet era, they serve as the primary mode of public transport, connecting various parts of the town on the mountain slopes. This makes Chiatura truly unique, its cable cars even today playing a significant role in everyday life.

Yes, I was in Chiatura! In the town center, there are many buildings from the Stalin era, the main one being the Georgian Manganese Department, a yellow house with a turret and large balconies standing on the bank of the Kvirila River. This building is the holy of holies of the town, because the manganese mining and enrichment industry still feeds and nourishes the town and its inhabitants.

In the small but beautiful square in front of the town hall, I meet Marika. She is a specialist in the public relations department of the local municipality, and she has promised to introduce me to her town. When I meet her, Marika describes her town as the "Venice of the Air" — a name many know Chiatura by.

Visiting a Local Poet

I had asked Marika to introduce me to notable, distinctive citizens of the town who would help me get a sense of the spirit of the place, and we were quickly on our way to meet one of these people. In the town's children's club, we wait for an honorable Chiaturan citizen, Petre Djajanidze, who today teaches children the game of chess.

Petre's office is at the end of a long corridor. Batoni Petre, as he is respectfully addressed, is a large 69-year-old man with a broad smile on his face (the vocative form *batono* literally means "my lord" and is a term of respect. To address women politely, they say *kalbatono*). His students, two little boys, the older of whom is seven, have already arrived for class. Batoni Petre shows us how dashingly the boys move pieces around the chessboard: *"Strong, very strong, these boys! They don't make a single mistake!"* concludes the teacher proudly. Leaving the children to finish the chess game, Batoni Petre reads me his poems written about his native town, about his first love, about a Georgian feast. I find out he has published fifteen poetry collections, and one of his poems had become the anthem of the town of Chiatura!

Petre tells me that there is nowhere else in the world with such a composition as manganese, and proudly lists all the chemical components of the Chiatura manganese. Petre is an engineer, but has never worked in the mining industry: he is simply a fiery patriot who just loves everything about Chiatura.

Chiatura used to be considered a town of intellectuals, seeing innovative engineers, scientists, teachers, actors, etc. coming here from all over the USSR. A branch of the Tbilisi Polytechnic Institute worked here, and there were eleven schools!

118

The story of the discovery of manganese in Chiatura is connected to the name of poet Akaki Tsereteli, a native of the place. One day in the 1870s, Tsereteli discovered a strange black deposit on grains of local wheat. He took the wheat to St. Petersburg for examination, and discovered that it was manganese, otherwise known as "black gold," without which it is impossible to produce steel.

Batoni Petre lists one name after another, briefly describing the remarkable people he was fortunate enough to know personally. He notes one of them with special respect: the architect Giorgi Pantsulaia, who designed the first passenger cable car and became the godfather of "Venice of the Air." *"We had the first cable car in Europe! After that, Pantsulaia was invited to build cable cars everywhere – in Italy, France, Latvia,"* Batoni Petre tells me proudly.

With Chiatura's remarkable past so strongly linked to the Soviet era, I ask Batoni Petre about it. He says believes that people used to live much better than they do now: *"I was not a Communist, but I knew how to get along with Communists. Communists tried to raise people from the lowest to the middle stratum. Now those in power are making sure that all but a small handful of people are at the bottom, and that only a minority live well."*

Batoni Petre recalls that, in the past, people used to know how to give, share, and rejoice in it. *"There was a rich man, Vano Meshkharashvili. He never let any guest to the town leave without a feast. As soon as Vano learned there was a guest in town, he would invite him together with their family and friends to visit and dine with him, and only after would he let them go,"* Batoni Petre recalls. It is not for nothing that Imereti hospitality is famous throughout Georgia!

I'm interested to find out what the current status of manganese mining is. It turns out that after a break in the hysterical nineties, when the city was close to dying out, ore mining has slowly been restored. Now, 57 companies are engaged in this sphere, but only one of them, Georgian Manganese, has a licence to sell, so all the ore goes through this company. Batoni Petre laments that although the ore is being mined again, which is good, now they have switched to open-pit mining, which is spoiling the fertile land – and it will take decades for that land to recover. *"In 10 years, we will probably have no more manganese, and our city will remain like a beautiful woman who was used and abandoned,"* he laments.

Marika and I walk around the pretty town, crossing one bridge, then another. I feel like I have returned to my childhood: the streets and buildings of Chiatura remind me of the provincial town in Belarus where my grandparents lived. But in Chiatura there are mountains and cable cars, old and vintage, and they add to the coziness of the town. Everywhere there is brisk trade: shops and markets overflowing with fresh goods. Autumn in Georgia is a fertile time full of pleasure, fragrance and colors!

We pass the Palace of Culture, another monumental Stalinist building, the dimensions of which do not quite match the size of the town itself, which has only 13,000 inhabitants. Children's clubs still operate in the building.

Cherishing Traditions

And indeed, as we get closer, we hear children singing through the ground floor windows. They are rehearsing, learning a song about love for their native land. From far away comes rhythmic drum music and someone's cheerful commands. *"It's our kids doing Georgian dancing,"* Marika explains. I look at her pleadingly: "Can we pop in and watch? At least one peek? I love Georgian dancing!"

We go up to the third floor to a huge assembly hall where about a hundred kids in black are dancing. *"Stumrebi!"* I hear: "Guests!" To please us, the kids start dancing to live music and rhythmically clapping their hands. It brings goosebumps to my skin. I don't know what dances in the world can compare with Georgian dances in terms of energy and passion!

Nona Tutarashvili, head of the Chitatura-XXI ensemble, tells us that in her youth, she once danced for several years in the legendary Erisioni ensemble. Now, she is in charge of two hundred children, with whom she and her husband, also a former dancer, work six hours a week.

"Is it difficult to dance Georgian dances?" I ask.

"Very much so!" Nona informs me.

"What's the most important thing?"

"It's all about discipline and character. These children are still young, and we are helping them to develop character. It takes pride to show the Georgian soul in dance. You must be a Georgian woman or a Georgian man to show the Georgian soul properly," she reveals.

Riding a Cable Car with a True Chiatura Gentleman

Marika and I move on, hoping to find out which cable car we can ride. A French firm has recently taken on the task of repairing the town's cable cars, promising to completely rehabilitate and replace all the cars with new ones within a year, and that's why most of the lines aren't running when I visit. We find two that are open: one to the so-called Stalin mine, the other to the Akaki Tsereteli mine. Marika tells me that she's not coming with me.

"Is it dangerous?" I ask.

"*No*," Marika asserts. "*There have never been any accidents on the cable cars in the town yet.*" It turns out Marika is simply very afraid of heights.

Zurab Kapanadze ("a very interesting person," as Marika introduces him to me), will accompany me on the cable car instead. He is a neurologist, a Doctor of Sciences, who studied and lived in Moscow for a long time, but then returned to his beloved town to, as he puts it, "spend his last days in peace," though Zurab is clearly still a long way from death: he is simply a joker. Indeed, Imeretians are famous for their genuine humor and savory jokes. My companion gallantly invites me for a ride on a cable car with the words: "*When you have a gentleman with you, there is nothing to be afraid of.*"

Marika stays waiting at the bottom, and we get into a small and very old, only recently repainted in bright blue, carriage with small windows covered with netting instead of glass. In just a few minutes, the cable car has whisked us up to a height of 180 meters. The noise of the motor creates an appropriate, vintage atmosphere. It might scare some, but not me! On the way up, I manage to take a couple of funny pictures.

As we climb up the mountain, we admire the views. To my surprise, there are few high-rise buildings which you can see from above. Chiatura became a town under Soviet rule: most of the residential buildings, especially those on the mountainside, are private. The panorama is amazing!

"*Over there is our Palace of Culture, and down there is a very good theater. We have a glorious theater, with centuries-old traditions!*" Zurab proudly proclaims. Among the detached houses there are a few high-rise buildings, and there is a sign which reads: 'Chiatura is my pride.' Down below, you can see the railway that carries manganese straight to the ferroalloy plant in Zestafoni. Passenger trains also travel along this railway.

Zurab tells me that last year a famous Australian film director, Ariel Kleiman, came to Georgia and wanted to shoot for at least half an hour "somewhere very beautiful." They took him everywhere—to Batumi, to Kakheti, to different mountain regions. But every time he said that it did not suit him. By

> The movie "Partisan" by Ariel Kleiman (2015) was indeed partly filmed in Chiatura. It is a psychological drama about a man named Gregori (Vincent Cassel) who leads a secluded commune. The film explores themes of control, manipulation, and the struggle for independence.

chance, the film group was driving through Chiatura when the director, who had fallen asleep in the car, woke up as the car bumped across a pothole. He saw the beauty around him and froze in surprise. "*Where are we?*" he asked, and was told: "*It's the town of Chiatura.*" "*It's exactly what I'm looking for!*" he exclaimed, and went on to shoot an Australian film, with the lead role played by Vincent Cassel.

121

My companion is a treasure trove of lively stories. Here is a taster in his own words:

"We started mining manganese in the 1870s. At the time, we had many newcomers – Germans, French, Greeks, Poles, Russians and, of course, Ukrainians – who lived and worked here. Belgians also came here. Chiatura had the first tennis court in the country, where a Belgian, Jan Hummer, taught. And in 1926, the Soviet government granted a concession for the extraction of manganese to the American industrialist and diplomat William Harriman. This concession was cancelled in 1931, but Harriman was an influential diplomat, and he considered himself a friend of Stalin. In 1941, he received $4 million from the Soviet government in compensation for having his concession interrupted!"

> William Averell Harriman (1891 -1986) was an American businessman, diplomat, and politician. Harriman came from a wealthy family and was involved in various business ventures, including banking and railroads. He was a key figure in American foreign policy during the 20th century, particularly in relations with the Soviet Union. He served as the U.S. Ambassador to the Soviet Union during World War II, and played a significant role in post-war negotiations.

"Is the well-being of the town's inhabitants increasing because of the manganese mining?" I ask Zurab.

"Unfortunately, not," he answers. *"The law is such that there is not much money left for the town. We produce over a hundred million dollars' worth of manganese a year, and yet the town budget is only about 9 million GEL. It is a pittance in the budget. It is not the investor's fault, but the law. The state should change something in the legislation."*

I want to see the manganese mines with my own eyes. We pass several five-floor buildings where miners live, and I only have time to look through a barbed wire fence. The view of the neighborhood is depressing: the old infrastructure has not been updated since Soviet times. Apparently, no one has invested a single tetri here (a tetri is a Georgian coin. 100 tetri is 1 Georgian lari). We are not allowed into the mines without special permission.

Concerned about our long absence, Marika calls us: *"Where have you disappeared to?"* We head back down on the same cable car, Zurab drawing my attention to the pompous building of the cable station, on which there is a bas-relief with portraits of the old leaders Lenin and Stalin.

"So, the Soviet regime was good for the Chiaturians after all, since these bas-reliefs haven't been removed?" I wonder.

"On the one hand, it was easier to live under that government, but on the other, the ideology stank," Zurab replies. *"Nevertheless, we had social benefits: free medical treatment, free holidays, free education. That's why many people have nostalgia for those times."*

"And you personally?"

"I don't. I have two American sons-in-law. They told me that at the end of the year, I will be given a MAP (Membership Action Plan, which is issued for countries to join NATO). So sometime in February or March, I'll 'join NATO'," he says with a laugh.

During our walk together, Zurab advises me to see the town's famous theater: "When our theater was founded, there were only three or four theaters in Georgia. All the great actors came here to play on this stage. The greatest actor of the Soviet era, Alexander Imedishvili, wrote: 'I play Hamlet most inspiringly in Chiatura, because the audience culture in Chiatura is unique'."

Zurab reveals to Marika and I his dream: to create an open-air museum in the square in front of the theater, featuring statues of all the famous actors who have ever performed on the stage there. I notice that on the theater façade, there is another bas-relief of the "Leader of the Nations," and the inscription: 'Glory to the great Stalin.'

Georgia has been actively pursuing a MAP for over 15 years, with significant efforts made since the Bucharest Summit in 2008. However, in 2014, NATO officials announced that Georgia would not yet be invited to join the MAP process, but that NATO would implement a "substantive package" of cooperation measures with Georgia instead. While Georgia has made significant progress in its efforts to align with NATO standards and has been a valuable partner to the alliance, it has yet to be granted a MAP. Concerns about Russia's reaction and the need for further reforms within Georgia remain barriers. Georgia's ruling party's increasing authoritarianism and anti-Western shift have, since 2024, led to the collapse of its strategic partnerships with all major allies, including NATO.

"The National Movement (former Georgian President Mikheil Saakashvili's party) was going to remove it," Zurab informs us. "They said: 'Remove this Satan!' But we said: 'No, this is a monument of the Stalin era, a cultural monument, it will remain'."

After a walk around the town and a fun dinner with a local oligarch, we are welcomed to visit a Chiaturan family whose father and son work in the mines.

Meeting Miners

In the cozy, vine-covered courtyard of a small private house, we are greeted by Kakhaber and Eliso, their son Shalva, and Shalva's wife and daughter. We sit and admire the view and the lights of the city at night. Eliso treats us to coffee, sweets, young wine, and grapes.

Our conversation turns to the fact that, in recent years, Chiatura has experienced something of a second wind, seeing many of those who left the town beginning to return. During the years of civil war and devastation, Kakha worked in a bakery in Tbilisi, because nothing was happening in the mines. However, he felt uncomfortable in the capital because the people there were strangers and less cordial. Nine years ago, he returned to his hometown when a job was found for him. He says that while he earned more in Tbilisi, now he lives in his hometown, with his family: *"My neighborhood, my neighbors are here. We are like one big family. And everyone helps each other,"* he says. Kakha works as a driver on a cable car and transports up to three hundred wagons of manganese per day. He works 12 hours for two days in a row, followed by two days of rest.

Kakha speaks Russian well, having worked with both Russians and Ukrainians. He served in Sevastopol in the army, and has many friends there.

Kakha's 24-year-old son Shalva works at the mine as a mechanic. He doesn't understand Russian, so his father helps him with translation. Is his work in the mine difficult, risky? I wonder. *"Yes, risky, of course, but where can you go? This is the only job in Chiatura!"*

Both father and son hope that more people will learn about Chiatura and that not only industry but also tourism will develop there. *"You won't find such a good town as Chiatura in the whole of Georgia. Our views are beautiful, and our mountains are magical! There is not only manganese mining here. There are also caves, ancient churches and monasteries. We invite everyone to visit us! We are ready to show you it all! We'll grill Imeretian kebabs, drink wine and chacha. Just come visit us!"* Kakha says.

My first day in Chiatura was full of impressions, and, that evening, my mind was a merry-go-round of questions: Where is Chiatura now- in the past, or in the present with echoes of the past? Why is the mining industry, its breadwinner, not properly helping this town with its great potential and talented people? What is in store for the talented children of Chiatura, who love chess, dancing, music and singing so much?

Echoes of the Cultural Past

The next day, I walked around the town and looked into the reading room of the Central Library, and immediately felt like I was back in the distant past once more. There are a lot of old books there, even newspapers, the oldest of which is from 9 May 1945! There was even a book about Chiatura in Russian from 1978, where this pioneering town was predicted to have a bright future. New books, as I was told, are not available: they are too expensive, so there are only local newspapers, and they do not come out regularly.

"Not enough people read nowadays, they are all on the Internet!" complains the library director, 60-year-old Marina Gogshelidze. *"Times are dif-*

ferent now. Before, in the USSR, everything was different, especially in the cultural aspect. It was easy to live. We were young then, we had different evenings, we had resorts, it was easy to go on holiday; medicine and everything was free, but now it is different."

In Marina's opinion, it is wrong for her to complain, though, because 10 years ago, Chiatura was in total ruins; nothing worked, not even the electrics. Many people left the city at the time, she tells me—some heading to Tbilisi, some moving abroad. *"It's not easy to live now, either, but we have Georgian Manganese as the main motor of the town."*

I left Chiatura with mixed feelings, heading back to Tbilisi via Sachkhere, where everything was so modern. The people of Chiatura had explained to me the reason: the infamous billionaire Bidzina Ivanishvili was born in a village near Sachkhere, and chose to spend money specifically on improving his birth town. But who will help Chiatura? Maybe that Australian film director?

Tbilisi—Choporti, October 2015

Riding a Soviet cable car with Zurab, a true Chiatura gentleman

One of Chiatura's cable car stations

The unrecognized border between Georgia and so-called South Ossetia

Chapter 12.
Georgia's Pain: Abkhazia and Samachablo (South Ossetia)

While many of my stories about Georgia celebrate its beauty and charm, this one is different. It's a story of profound suffering; of a country ripped apart. It's about the agonizing pain of its people, the twisting of lives, the hardship, the horror, the atrocities, and the countless lives lost.

The stories of Georgian refugees from Abkhazia and the Tskhinvali region, the echoes of the 1990s conflicts as told by my friends, only began to reach me after my arrival in Georgia in 2010. Before then, my knowledge was scant. Sadly, such ignorance is widespread.

Each account from those who lived through the atrocities of the so-called Georgian-Abkhaz war (so-called because of the Russian involvement) is a heartbreaking lament in the modern history of the South Caucasus. I first saw the Russian-occupied town of Tskhinvali from afar, from the village of Khurvaleti, which has been divided into two between Georgia and so-called "South Ossetia." I was there in 2015, preparing a report on the aftermath of the 2008 war. Together with representatives of the European Monitoring Mission (EUMM), I was able to drive up to that village divided by barbed wire, and look at Tskhinvali from there. The creeping occupation continues in this region to this day, with barbed wire "eating up" more Georgian land practically by the week. The inhabitants of the surrounding villages are taken prisoner, beaten and sometimes even killed; returned to their families only for a ransom.

This is a story about my second visit to the area.

How to Turn Paradise into Hell:
A Story of the Unrecognized Border in the Tskhinvali Region

When I wrote this, it had been seven years since, on August 8th, the Russo-Georgian Blitzkrieg began, the terrible consequences of which now extend far beyond the borders of Georgia.

Since the end of that military conflict in 2008, the internationally unrecognized Georgian-South Ossetian border has gradually been shifted further south. Another shift of border markers took place in July this year along the administrative boundary line (ABL) between Georgia and its occupied Tskhinvali region ("South Ossetia"), in the villages of Orchosani and Tsitelubani.

In Georgia, South Ossetia is most commonly referred to as Samachablo, or the Tskhinvali region. Samachablo is a historical name, meaning "fiefdom of the Machabeli clan," a noble family that once controlled the area. The Tskhinvali region is part of Shida Kartli, which translates to "Inner Kartli," referring to that region's location within the larger historical province of Kartli. While the name "South Ossetia" is used in international contexts, these alternative names reflect Georgia's perspective on the region and its history.

Does the prospect exist that the Georgian territories will be returned, when the same atrocious snatching-of-land was seen in the following years in Crimea and Eastern Ukraine? Is any agreement with Russia possible? Or should Georgia be preparing for a new war? These questions are being asked more and more frequently in connection with the creeping land occupation.

Two years after my report from the Tskhinvali region, I once again went to that ABL, where all my Georgian friends refuse to go. Their fears are understandable: in this area, people are regularly arrested for alleged "illegal border crossing."

This time, I traveled to the "border" village of Ergneti to attend an extraordinary meeting of the 'Incident Prevention and Response Mechanism' (IPRM) group, which took place under the auspices of the European Union Monitoring Mission (EUMM), with the participation of Georgia, "South Ossetia," and Russia. These sporadic meetings focus on local conflicts in which the local population is directly involved, such as arrests for "illegal border crossing," disputes over farmers' access to their land, visits to churches and cemeteries, and visits to relatives living on both sides of the former administrative boundary, which has been secured with barbed wire and Russian patrols since 2008.

This time, I was invited by an EUMM spokesperson to that extraordinary meeting on one condition: I had to travel independently, i.e., not with the EUMM mission's transport, as the mission cannot assume responsibility for the safety of journalists. Consequently, I drove to Ergneti alone in my own car.

Ergneti is located about 30 kilometers from the city of Gori. The drive from Tbilisi there takes a little over an hour.

When I reached the end of the village, I came across a massive wall made of stacked car tires, secured in such a way that it constituted a real anti-tank barrier. Police officers and a convoy of vehicles from various international organizations had been parked on the side of the road.

Journalists were only allowed to participate in the opening and closing of the conflict resolution group meeting, so I decided not to wait until the end of the event: after a brief interview with the mission's spokesperson, I photographed the view of Tskhinvali, the capital of the breakaway region, which was only 1.5 kilometers from Ergneti, and the massive concrete walls, from which the "South Ossetian" and Russian flags were hoisted a hundred meters away. What I wanted, why I was there, was to learn how people live in a war-torn area, what they hope for, and if they are afraid.

I am already on my way to the center of the village. There is not a soul to be seen on the main street, so I turn right and drive deeper in on the unpaved road, hoping to spy a villager.

I am looking forward to conducting my conversation with the locals without witnesses. My questions are sensitive, and I fear that not everyone will want to talk with a stranger, because, while such a conversation is just another job for a journalist, for the people here in this the conflict region, it is about their entire existence, which has been crumpled and mutilated by war. I still remember that from last time: two years ago, none of the people I met in the Tskhinvali region, neither in the village of Ditsi nor in Khurvaleti, were willing to share their memories with me. And it was quite understandable: what would it bring them to stir up their old wounds, after all? I resolved this time to proceed extremely correctly and as unobtrusively as possible.

Ergneti is nestled among blooming gardens. At around midday, one can so beautifully enjoy the play of shadows cast by the large old trees everywhere—on the ground, on houses, and on fences. The shade of these trees provides a very pleasant coolness.

The road bends to the left, where an old, broken-down taxi blocks my way. Four middle-aged men are sitting on a bench in front of a house there, one of whom jumps up to make space for my car by moving his own. I nod my thanks and park my car next to another completely demolished vehicle, an old Zhiguli.

I get out, greet the men, and tell them who I am and the reason for my visit to their village. They invite me to sit next to them on the bench to chat.

"It's beautiful here with you!" I exclaim enthusiastically. "It's like paradise!"

"Is that so?" one asks, with obvious satisfaction, then tells me: *"Before the war, it was much more beautiful here. In 2008, everything was destroyed. People moved away because it became difficult to live here. Many young people left, and only the old ones stayed."*

My new acquaintances tell me that, in 2008, one hundred and fifty of the 200 village houses were destroyed. Not all buildings were destroyed during those official three days of war, though- most were burned down later, at the end of August, when the Ossetians shifted the ABL further south and Ergneti was for some time on the territory of the self-proclaimed Republic of South Ossetia. The village school remained undamaged, but it was looted: the computers were stolen, all the windows were broken. The school building still stands today, but there are almost no children left here to study there.

I ask how the people who stayed behind live. Nika, a slender man with deep-set eyes, replies: *"We still live on agriculture. But it's not easy. In 2006, even before the war, Russia waged a trade war against us: it imposed an embargo on our produce, after which the prices for agricultural products fell sharply. Further wars followed, political and economic ones: Russia cut off our gas and electricity. In the end, when they could achieve nothing, Moscow resorted to military force."*

"That trade embargo from 2006 was lifted, right?" I ask cautiously. "Why is it still difficult to make money with agricultural products?"

"The embargo was lifted, yes, but they are constantly giving us new obstacles, which are equivalent to an embargo, like tariffs, so that our goods become unprofitable for sale in Russia," he tells me.

I wonder that they aren't afraid to live here, so close to Tskhinvali and another potential "explosion."

Sighing heavily, Nika replies: *"I'm not afraid of that. What worries me is that so many people have been separated from each other. I had many Ossetian friends who I can no longer contact. Many of my Georgian relatives who lived in Tskhinvali and in the Georgian villages in the Tskhinvali district had to flee and are now scattered all over Georgia. Many connections have been broken. Life has become complicated."*

It turns out that Nika went to school in Tskhinvali, where he completed six grades. But then, during the civil wars in the 1990s, he had to go to school in Gori, which is 30 kilometers away. *"My schooling wasn't consistent. I didn't even graduate secondary school,"* he says, with a sigh of regret.

Malkhaz, Nika's cousin, who has been silently listening to our conversation, admits that living at the "border" unsettles him. *"War is a terrible thing, but people got used to it in the 1990s. Then they got used to peace again. God save us from a new war!"* he exclaims.

Previously, Malkhaz made his living by bringing old cars from America to Georgia. He is uncertain how he will earn a living now. If he were to grow fruit, like Nika, he would earn about 300-400 GEL per month, with seasonal income averaged over the year. That roughly 150 Euros is hardly enough to live on.

"Is that why many of your fellow villagers have left?" I put to Malkhaz, and ask if he plans to leave as well. He smiles, though I see bitterness in his eyes as he answers: *"No, I will not! Because this is my home."*

Malkhaz has quite a bit to share of his life story. He recently returned from Kiev. He was living in Ukraine for a long time, working in various cities, but life became difficult there as well. He came back to be useful in his homeland.

Many are afraid of a new war, especially after the Russian takeover of Crimea and Donbas.

"Maybe Georgia and Russia will reconcile one day?" I suggest.

"We can reconcile if Russia treats our country as a partner and not as a state that deserves constant punishment!" Nika puts in. *"A few years ago, we had a change of government* (Note: when the Georgian Dream party came to power in 2012), *and the new cabinet made many overtures towards Russia, but there have been no reciprocations from the Russian side. Moscow can only offer us one thing: 'You may be doing poorly, but if you don't obey us, it will get even worse for you.' They have nothing else they are willing to give."*

I voice the claim that Russia is angry with Georgia because it wants to join the EU and NATO.

"Georgia wouldn't have wanted to join NATO or the EU if there hadn't been conflicts in Abkhazia and the Tskhinvali region in the 1990s, which were instigated by Russia!" my conversation partners argue. *"But even after that, everything could have been resolved peacefully, by allowing the IDPs* (Note: internally displaced persons) *to go back home, and by restoring good relations over time. But Russia has taken no steps in this direction, and not a single IDP has been able to return. So, Georgia had no choice but to seek protection in the EU and NATO."*

I ask if I can find someone from the older generation of the village. Nika invites me to his house so that I can speak with his parents.

We walk past several neighboring houses that were destroyed and have not been rebuilt. Nika opens his garden gate and leads me down a narrow path, past a barn and an orchard with roses, expertly pruned shrubs, and peach trees heavy with fruit, to a small house that lies in front of a large, half-destroyed villa.

Nika explains to me that the old family home, which was built by his grandfather and had a huge balcony, was burned down during the war.

"I remember so well how we used to have such a beautiful garden with house-plants on our balcony. People on the street would deliberately pass by to admire it. And when my mother asked us children in the winter to carry all the plants into the house, my God, how I hated that day! But now I have incredibly warm memories of it!" Nika says, and then sighs sadly.

After the war, the UN High Commissioner for Refugees helped the Kasradze family build a small temporary studio house so they could continue to tend to their garden. Nika's family returned to this one-room house, where the kitchen and bedroom are one, and lived there for four years before managing to rebuild three of the eight rooms of the old villa. The garage where the bomb hit has yet to be repaired.

A nice, friendly woman, Madina, comes out of the large house to greet us. This is Nika's mother. His father, who we disturbed during his lunch, greets us politely, gets up, and leaves.

Nika's mother speaks Russian without an accent: she is a Tatar from Kazan who has lived in Georgia for over 40 years. Madina also speaks Georgian fluently.

"Do you feel at home here?" I ask her curiously.

"Yes, of course! My home is where my family lives," she says.

I ask her which the best years of her life were.

"The seventies and eighties," she replies. *"Even though we weren't rich back then, we lived peacefully, happily, and contentedly. In the nineties, everything fell apart."*

Madina has two daughters and this one son, Nika (*"who is a bachelor,"* Madina tells me with a sigh). Nika, not wanting to disturb our conversation, goes into the small house to make us coffee and pick fresh, aromatic peaches for us to have with the coffee.

We sit on a bench in front of the house, and I can't get enough of the lush garden, the well-tended shrubs, the colorful roses, the fruit-bearing peach and apple trees. Now I understand why this region is called the "orchard of Georgia."

"I feel like I'm in paradise here with you!" I exclaim, happily repeating my earlier compliment to her son and his friends.

Madina replies with a cheerful laugh: *"It really is beautiful here with us! And the land here is good too, but we need a lot of water to irrigate the garden and fields. After the war, the water canal on that side was blocked, and we had no water in the field. Then a new canal was built, but there still wasn't enough water for everyone. Foreign aid helped us get a motor that pumps the water from the river into the canal here so we can irrigate our gardens. This year we finally have enough water!"*

That lightning war with Russia, which began on August 8th, is not easy for Madina to forget.

"We couldn't step foot into the yard, the shooting was so intense!" she tells me. *"On the 5th of August, my grandchildren were still here, and we all slept upstairs, on the second floor, but then we moved to the first floor: we felt safer there. When the shooting started, my grandchildren covered themselves with a blanket so as not to hear anything. And when it was over, they lifted the blanket and crossed themselves: 'God protect Georgia!' said my grandson, who was five years old at the time. On August 3rd, there was crazy shooting here. I couldn't milk my cows in the yard. Those were eerie days! On August 7th, we moved away."*

Like many other houses, Nika's family's house was not heavily damaged in the midst of that war itself. But after the family left, shortly before the official start of the war, Russian troops, together with the Ossetians, entered the village and fired on the houses from their tanks.

"Our houses were only not completely burned down by chance," Madina marvels. *"The neighbor's house over there burned down completely during the shooting. Our house was set on fire by Ossetians on August 25th, when they passed through our village. When we returned, our grapes had been completely harvested. Only the walls of the house remained, and nothing else. We'd had two cows and a large pig- everything was gone, including the chickens, and they harvested our entire garden."*

"It was the Russians!" Nika exclaims, joining us. *"Even if it was the Ossetians carrying out their orders, it was the Russian soldiers who stood around and watched. What difference does it make who committed the crimes?"*

Madina says she doesn't want to talk about politics, and she sharply reprimands her son in Georgian when he speaks out against the Russians.

I wonder if my respondents know how the people live over there, beyond the unrecognized border, in Tskhinvali.

"How are we supposed to know?" Nika exclaims with passion. He admits they get the Tskhinvali television channels in the village, but says no one watches them. *"There's nothing but propaganda there – about how Putin's government is the best. In the years before the 2008 war, all topics about Georgia were banned there. Because Georgia at that time was developing too quickly and too successfully for the Russian taste, and they were choking with envy.*

"We don't know what's happening in Tskhinvali right now," he says. *"But I am sure that those who want to achieve something in their lives left Tskhinvali long ago. There will be plenty of people like us there: those who have nowhere else to go."*

"Has any good come from the EUMM?" I ask.

133

Nika grins at this. *"The international observers will certainly not fight for us if there's another war. But at least they'll document everything if something happens again. And that's already something good."*

It's time for me to say goodbye to my new acquaintances. Nika accompanies me to my car. On the way, we stop at an old mulberry tree, laden with huge, sweet white berries. With Nika's help, I pick some—they are delicious.

"How could this paradise have turned into hell so quickly back in 2008?!" I wonder.

On a bench in front of Malkhaz's house sits his elderly mother, who is Ossetian. The woman smiles at me, but does not want to talk to me. If I were in her place, I would probably behave the same way.

Detained

According to the head of the EUMM mission, Kęstutis Jankauskas, 150 arrests of locals by representatives of the Tskhinvali side were registered in 2014 at the administrative boundary line with so-called South Ossetia. They were detained during "illegal border crossings," for example, when visiting ABL-side cemeteries and churches, when searching for their stray livestock, and when gathering berries, mushrooms, and the popular edible tree blossoms called *jonjoli*. The detention period was a few days, while the fine for this "offense" was between 2,000 and 3,000 Russian rubles.

Tbilisi, July-August 2015

Unspoken Wounds:
Abkhazia's War through Survivor Accounts

Once, in a cozy Tbilisi restaurant filled with the warm atmosphere of true Caucasian hospitality, I stumbled upon some old photo albums. Their owners, hailing from sunny Sukhumi, the Abkhazian capital, had carefully preserved these treasures of memory. Flipping through the pages, I felt as if I were stepping into another world: before me unfolded the enchanting landscapes of Abkhazia—emerald lakes reflecting majestic mountain peaks, velvety slopes draped in lush greenery, and azure sea caressing golden beaches. In these photographs, Abkhazia appeared as a promised land, where nature had generously bestowed its beauty upon humankind. Looking at these images, I found it hard to believe that this region had been shaken by such tragic events, leaving deep wounds in people's hearts.

Unfortunately, due to various reasons, I have not yet had the opportunity to personally experience these amazing places. And since I have no firsthand experience of traveling in Abkhazia, in this narrative, I will rely on the memories of those who were forced to leave their homeland, as well as the testimonies of eyewitnesses to the tragic events. After all, when talking about Abkhazia, it is impossible to ignore the painful subject of the wars that so dramatically impacted Georgia in the 1990s and left an indelible mark on the history of this region.

The common saying is that war has "an unwomanly face." But in this case, it was the women who spoke to me about it. The men, regardless of their involvement in the Abkhazian conflict, largely chose silence. As a result, this collection focuses mainly on women's experiences. All names have been changed to ensure anonymity.

Marika

"I was 6 years old on the 2nd of September 1993. I keep in my memory bright and warm pictures of my childhood. I can see the Agudzera lighthouse as if it were right in front of me now. I was young, but I still have very vivid memories: the white lighthouse and white magnolias, their intoxicating smell. My father used to pluck the leaves and make me a 'native's skirt' out of them. I remember the sanatorium and the smell of eucalyptus, and the calm azure-colored sea.

"I also remember our flat in Agudzera, as well as our house in the village of Pshapi. I remember champagne apples in the courtyard, tangerines and feijoas that I ate with a spoon, a fluffy yellow mimosa at the gate.

"But then suddenly — corpses by the ditches that the pigs were feeding on. We lived in a basement because Georgians were looking for Russians, and Russians/Abkhazians/Cossacks/Syrians and others were looking for Georgians. And the ribbons on the doors were either green or red, depending on what the neighbors had said about the soldiers coming.

"I remember it was the end of 1992. My dad didn't come home from work. I remember hiding from tanks in Sukhumi with my grandmother in a bombed-out toilet. I had sweets in my hands, chocolate covered peanuts. The toilet smelled of shit and blood. My grandmother hid my face for some reason. I suspect the source of that bloody smell was the reason. I've hated chocolate-covered peanuts ever since.

"My grandmother and I stayed with some local Armenians; it's thanks to them that I survived. We hid together almost all night in a cornfield.

"I remember my father carrying me to the hospital in his arms, while bullets whizzed by and the Grad rockets lit up the sky."

(Note: 'Grad' is the name of a Soviet and Russian multiple launch rocket system, the BM-21 Grad. It was used in the conflict in Abkhazia (1992-1993), and its use resulted in significant civilian casualties).

"At the hospital, they could not bring my temperature down below 40. They tried to keep me away from the worst of the sights, but people's legs torn off their bodies, hanging arms, and heads without faces – I saw it all.

"On 27 September 1993, Sukhumi fell, and we fled. The tangerine grove was burning behind us. That was the last time I saw our house. After that I was afraid of the sound of aeroplanes for a long time, afraid of the sky."

Nona

"In summer, Sukhumi always smelled of magnolias and osmanthus (a subtropical tree or shrub whose flowers have a delicate, spicy fragrance). *Before the war, we lived amazingly well. Sukhumi was a warm, homely town. Everyone knew each other and had done so for generations.*

"We had our own traditions there, and no one was divided by nationality or religion. Greeks and Armenians, Russians and Estonians, Jews and Turks, Georgians and Abkhazians, and many other representatives of different nations all invested their souls in our small city. They laid the foundations of its uniqueness, they gave it strength, means, love: love was the first thing that motivated them. They created that little paradise all together – merchants, industrialists, bankers, princes (remember the Prince of Oldenburg, who built Gagra?), simple laborers – for their children and grandchildren, sincerely hoping that their efforts would not be wasted, that everyone, once in this enchanted world, would sigh with admiration and wish to stay there forever...."

Mariam

"One thing I can say that I remember from when I was a schoolgirl, something which has stuck with me all my life, something I often dream about at night: the aerodrome and the screaming of the mothers... God, why did we children run there?! Now I'm a mother myself. When I remember it, everything clenches inside me: that was the cry of mothers greeting the zinc coffins.

"I didn't know for a whole year whether my father was alive, whether Ochamchire was still there.... I remember how a Russian colonel gave up everything and joined the Georgian National Guard to defend what was so dear to him. I remember how long ago it was and how terrible it was, and still I shed tears.

"Abkhazia, we'll come back, I know it! I made a promise to my children that we would get everything back! And Samachablo, my grandfather's homeland, we will also return."

Ruso

"My memories are such a heavy cross to bear... I was eight years old. We lived in the Gulripsh district, in the village of Tsebelda. On New Year's Eve, my aunt, my dad's sister, left us to head home to Sukhumi. She was killed by a shell explosion together with her mother-in-law and father-in-law. She was torn to pieces, and her children saw it. We buried her, sewn together in pieces, with her face bandaged. I, then a child, as I looked at her in her coffin, wanted so much to believe that it was all a dream.

"Then came Svaneti. People fleeing the war, dying on the way from hunger and cold. The dead were buried in hand-dug graves. They closed my eyes so I wouldn't see it all. But I was already very well aware of what was happening. After we fled Abkhazia, we went to Ukraine, to Kiev. My two brothers and I went to school, studied at institutes there, and in 2014 — war again, then in 2022 — again. It's hard to believe that, at 37 years old, I've experienced so much pain from so many wars."

During the Georgian-Abkhaz war (1992-1993), Ukraine provided significant assistance to the civilian population by organizing the evacuation of refugees by sea and air. Ukrainian military pilots made numerous rescue flights by helicopter from Kutaisi to Svaneti, taking out tens of thousands of civilians from Abkhazia who were fleeing the war. Ukraine's contribution is highly valued in Georgia, and will forever remain in the memory of the Georgian people.

Nikoloz

"I was six years old when Abkhazians, Russians and Chechens entered Sukhumi. They killed my father and my seventeen-year-old brother, who were both fighting, and I was hit on the head with a rifle butt. They thought I was dead, and buried us in one common grave. But my mom didn't believe I was dead. At night, she came with her sister and dug the grave up with her hands. I was alive. I had a lapse in my memory, I couldn't remember anything, so I didn't start school until I was nine.

"In 1992, my mother and I went to live in Kobuleti (a town on the Black sea coast, in the Adjara region). *We were put up in a shack with only two beds and nothing else. Until I was fourteen, I worked secretly without my mother knowing, selling juices and sunflower seeds on the beach in summer. We lived in the shack until 2001, by which point we had managed to raise enough money to buy a flat. From 2002 to 2006, I studied at the Military Academy. In 2008, I fought in the Samachablo war and was wounded three times."*

Tinatin

"My father died during our escape from Abkhazia. He was 57. It was the 14th of October 1992. He had driven us to Psou on the border with Adler, Russia. There were floods of refugees going to Russia. My father said he was going back to get our dog, who we'd left at home. He said that a lot of neighbors, elderly people, were choosing to stay there, and he wanted to persuade them to leave because the situation was not going well. Dad reassured us that our neighbors were there, all our friends were there, and that nothing bad would happen to him. He took us to Adler and went back. We waited for him all night. Then my mom and aunt went looking for him, but he was already dead.

"Many years later, I met people who told me that my father had broken into their house, forced them into a car, and in doing so had saved their lives. He managed to do the same for a few other families, and then there was haphazard shooting right on the border; a unit broke through. It was complete chaos, and nobody understood who was shooting at whom. And right on the Psou bridge, he was hit by a tracer bullet, the kind which tears all soft tissues. If it had been a normal bullet, he would have had a simple shoulder wound and he would have survived, but as it was, he died on that bridge, and then my neighbors brought him to Adler.

"We were all in shock. At that time, against the background of my father's death, I lost interest in everything. I don't remember his funeral. Everyone was stressed. It was the first death we'd seen with our own eyes. I never watch or listen to programs about the victims of Abkhazia, because it affects me so much."

Irina

"I can't forget the 25th of September, 1993. Our neighborhood was empty, we and one other family were the only ones left. I have only fear, no-one is there, only machine guns and explosions. I ask my husband to get me and my daughter out. We quickly pack our things, essentials that will fit into a small bag. We drive out over the bridge. We are being shot at. We ducked down in the car, and in our heads, we thought: 'How can he go back there?' Thank God, he didn't: he put us on a boat, then went on foot through Svaneti. And the few neighbors who stayed behind — they were tortured for two days, and then their corpses were buried, presumably on the territory of the Infectious Diseases Hospital."

Natela

"We fled to Svaneti. All of us had frostbite, and there were many deaths on the way. We dug graves in the frozen ground with our bare hands. Hunger. Uncertainty.

"My mom hadn't heard from her mother for about six months. She knew they'd gone into the mountains, but nobody knew what had happened to them. Soon, word started to spread and people began looking for them.

"Shevardnadze is to blame for this tragedy, because the Georgians could have left quietly, could have taken their valuables and belongings. But that day, Shevardnadze, deceived by the Kremlin, brought all the Georgians back and promised peace. And then what happened was not peace, but a massacre, genocide. People were fleeing just to survive, many wearing only their slippers.

"I remember my aunts had their things packed. They were thinking of leaving for Tbilisi. More or less quietly, together with other people, to cross the Inguri. But Shevardnadze brought them all back.

"A little later, my parents and I traveled that road of death to Svaneti. It was scary, but war teaches you not to look back and not to tremble, you have to go – so you go. I cannot accuse my parents of recklessness. Mom wanted us to stick together. We walked from Agudzer to Pshapi.

"The last time I was in the courtyard of our house in Pshapi, I remember my grandfather crying, things scattered and some kind of horror. My mom was crying when she heard that her sisters had gone into the mountains. But the next day, we left too."

Nino

"I still have nightmares about what we went through. I can still see everything as if it were happening in front of my eyes now.

"I was born in Kakheti, but I got married in Abkhazia. I graduated from the Medical Institute, met my husband, and moved to Abkhazia to live with him. I was twenty years old. We lived in the village of Shroma in the Sukhumi district. It was a beautiful life…we built our own house. I did not even hunger for anything more, we were so happy there! Perhaps the only thing we lacked for happiness was our own boat.

"We had good relations with the Abkhazians. They are good people, Abkhazians; they are just like us. We were just played against each other.

"Then came the war. That war buried our whole life. The first time an aeroplane flew over our house, my son was seven years old. He witnessed bombs raining down from above. The first one struck our home, and it was engulfed in flames. My child's cries lasted for five days, and then he began to get up at night, wandering and talking in his sleep. Now, at 37, he still sleeps sitting up, forever in anticipation of something horrible.

"We stayed there for a year, until our village was completely overrun. No, I don't want to tell you what I saw, what I suffered. To this day, in my dreams, I am in Sukhumi, in my house.

"Chechen mercenaries were brutalized there. Our guys caught 10 Chechens in Ochamchire. They had the ears of the people they had killed hanging around their necks like jewelry. It pains me to talk about it. There was a woman who worked with me in the ambulance. Her thirteen-year-old daughter was raped in front of her, and then she, the mother, was killed.

"A year later, we boarded a boat and were taken to Batumi. Through Batumi we came here (to Tbilisi). *And don't think that we were welcomed here with open arms. They chased us as they wanted. 'Why did you come here? Why didn't you stay there?' That's what they asked us. After that war, all my teeth fell out within a month because of the stress.*

"Our children's generation is also threatened by this war, and this war is still going on!

"At one time I worked in Tbilisi at the Republican Hospital. But then I left that job. After the war, as soon as I see the color red, I think it is blood. I can't see red, and I don't wear light-colored clothes anymore. I wear black all the time..."

Mamuka Areshidze, a Georgian political scientist who worked as a journalist during the Abkhaz war, told me that the horrors of that war could be described as ethnic cleansing. According to him, "atrocities were committed both by Abkhazians and, above all, by those who came to fight alongside them from southern Russia: Cossacks and residents of the North Caucasus." The latter fought on the side of Abkhazia, seeking to seize other people's property, and they did not stop at murders, especially during the retreat of the Georgian troops. At the same time, however, there were cases when Abkhazians, defending their Georgian neighbors, died themselves.

According to Mamuka Areshidze, a political scientist and expert on the Abkhaz conflict, the official number of refugees from Abkhazia — 300,000 people — is significantly underestimated. The fact is that many fled the conflict region not only to Georgia, but also abroad, including to Russia. Thus, according to Mamuka, the number of refugees should be estimated at no less than half a million people, because among the refugees were not only Georgians, but also Armenians, Greeks, Russians, Jews, and others. The same applies to the number of deaths. Officially, 3,000 Abkhazians and 23,000 Georgians died in the Abkhaz war. In reality, Mamuka says, the number of victims on the Georgian side amounted to at least 40,000.

Dreams of Reconciliation

The war in Abkhazia, one of the first of the Kremlin's hybrid wars in the post-Soviet space, is narrated in the Estonian-Georgian film 'Tangerines' directed by Zaza Urushadze. The film is the most humane anti-war film of the last decades, presenting the horrors of war without directly showing the nightmares. In it, there is no division into "strangers" and "outsiders," but instead another, wiser, divide: between people who have humanity and those who do not know it. It is impossible to watch this film without shedding tears.

What really happened? Until recently, it was extremely difficult to believe eyewitness accounts of the rape of girls and children, of women having their breasts cut off, of men having their tongues and eyes ripped out, of the heads of those murdered being used in games of football. But after seeing the atrocities of the war in Ukraine, one can understand that the purported crimes against civilians in Abkhazia were real, it's just that the world didn't learn about them soon enough.

'Tangerines' (2013), directed by Zaza Urushadze, is a poignant drama set during the 1992 Georgian-Abkhaz war. The story takes place in an Abkhazian village inhabited by Estonian settlers. Most of them have left their homes due to the war, but two men, Ivo and Margus, remain. Ivo is an elderly carpenter, and Margus owns a tangerine plantation he wants to harvest. The war intrudes on their lives when wounded soldiers from opposing sides end up in their home: a Georgian named Nika and a Chechen named Ahmed, who fights on the Abkhazian side. Ivo, despite the danger, decides to help both wounded men, and enemies are forced to coexist under his roof.

How did it happen that blossoming Abkhazia, this most paradisiacal corner of Georgia, was turned into a field of bloody massacres against a background of inter-ethnic discord?

Recently, Andrey Kozyrev, the former Minister of Foreign Affairs in the government of Boris Yeltsin from 1990 to 1996, answered this question on Mikhail Zygar's TV program. He shared interesting details about how the separatist hotbed in Abkhazia was created in the early 1990s. He claimed that when the process of forming independent union republics began, the Central Committee and the KGB, in opposition, conceived the idea of "awakening the autonomous republics." It was a way to challenge the countries that had separated from the USSR by highlighting the loss of their autonomous territories. This is what happened with Georgia, Armenia, Azerbaijan, and with Moldova, Kozyrev said. The diplomat also remembered the leader of the separatist movement of Abkhazia in the early 1990s, Vladislav Ardzinba, and how the image of the Abkhaz politician was created in the Kremlin: *"Ardzinba was a Moscow guy. He and I spoke the same language, with the same Moscow accent."*

Mikhail Zygar is a Russian writer, journalist, and director. He is the former editor-in-chief of the Dozhd TV channel and is the author of the books 'All the Kremlin's Men,' 'The Empire Must Die,' 'Everyone is Free,' and 'War and Punishment.' He is currently working on his own projects, including those on his YouTube channel.

The former Minister also said that the decision to send Ardzinba to Abkhazia was made by the then Minister of Defense of the Russian Federation, Pavel Grachev. According to Kozyrev, he supplied weapons to Abkhazia in secret from the Minister of Foreign Affairs, and Yeltsin was aware of the scheme.

"At that time, separatists in Russia were perceived as allies," Kozyrev said, recalling how Russian peacekeepers disarmed both warring parties several times, after which, however, they secretly returned weapons to the fighters of the Abkhaz National Guard. In the end, this led to the defeat of the Georgian side.

According to the recollections of the commander of one of the Georgian army's reconnaissance companies, David Sh., which he shared in a conversation with me, *"Georgian troops were forced to defend themselves with automatic weapons against tanks and artillery."* In that war, he said, residents of Georgia of various nationalities fought for Georgia—Georgians, Armenians, Kurds, Azerbaijanis, as well as Ukrainian units of UNA-UNSO. All three ceasefires concluded in that war were violated by the Abkhaz side. After the first ceasefire, Gagra fell; after the third—Sukhumi.

In war, no one truly wins. The defeated and the victors alike are left with the same legacy of trauma. Each side is filled with victims; their destinies twisted; their psyches scarred. For everyone caught in the conflict, life becomes a matter of "what ifs" and "might have beens."

I would like to write a completely different story about Abkhazia or Samachablo, one full of wonder, with enriching acquaintances and treasures discovered. But I could only do this under two conditions: if those wars had not happened in Georgia, and if I had the opportunity to see with my own eyes what I have read about in history books and scholarly works, such as the material monuments of Antiquity and the Middle Ages.

Nevertheless, I was pleased to learn that contacts between Georgian and Abkhaz historians continue to this day, despite the political strife of recent decades. It turns out that Georgian and Abkhaz scientists meet in neutral territories—somewhere in Turkey or Europe—for symposia devoted to current problems in archeology.

One of my acquaintances, an archeologist from Tbilisi, told me about such meetings: *"During our symposia, my colleagues from Abkhazia and I try to avoid political topics as much as possible. As soon as one of us forgets this agreement, I, as a Palaeolithic specialist, immediately interrupt the disputants and remind them that we are all natives of Africa!"*

A trip to Abkhazia remains just a dream for me now. Linked to it is also the hope that the hundreds of thousands of people who lost their homeland 30 years ago will be given the opportunity to return. I also dream that Abkhazia's historical role as a peaceful mediator between cultures and peoples will be restored. After all, it was so once, in Ancient Colchis.

Tbilisi, June 2023 – February 2025

Men in the village of Ergneti, close to the occupied town of Tskhinvali, South Ossetia

Scenic view from Jvari (Cross) Monastery, overlooking Mzkheta, (the ancient capital of Iberia) and the spot where the Mtkvari and Aragvi rivers meet

Part Two.
The Caucasian Iberia

Dear reader, here we are at the end of the first half of my book. Together, we have travelled to many unique places in Western Georgia. And yet, this journey is far from complete. The other parts of Western Georgia—Guria, Samegrelo, Lazika and Tao Klarjeti (both the latter now part of Turkey)— while left out this time, are also well worth your energy exploring.

I find it hard to part with the mystery of Ancient Colchis, but as part of our journey, it's time for us to cross the Rikoti Pass, which geographically divides the country, and to start exploring central, southern and eastern Georgia. Mtianeti, Samtskhe-Javakheti, Tusheti, Khevsureti and Kakheti lie ahead on our adventure!

*The ancient rock-hewn town of Uplistsikhe (Lord's Fortress),
located about 10km from Gori, was inhabited from as early as the late Bronze
Age (around the 2nd millennium BC) all the way through to the Late Middle
Ages*

Chapter 13.
The Kingdom of Kartli, or "Caucasian Iberia"

Imagine, for a moment, a land brimming with hidden treasures. Knowing of their existence, would you find rest? What actions would you take? This is how I feel in Georgia. The mystery of its historical "treasures" haunts my thoughts.

I live on a veritable "volcano of ancient treasures," constantly drawn to explore the echoes of the past: how people lived here long ago, the legacy they left behind, and what fragments of their former grandeur endure. I'm fortunate to have access to the expertise of historians and archeologists. Conversations with them, along with the historical texts listed in this book's bibliography, reveal the immense potential for archeological work in Georgia.

The challenge is that archeology is not only a young science, but also a resource-intensive one, with discoveries often taking considerable time to make. Moreover, archeology is significantly impacted by political circumstances. As a result, despite Georgia's extraordinary potential, vast stretches of its history remain unexplored- lost, as yet, to the unknown. The desire to uncover this ancient history, however, persists.

The Two Iberias: Western and Eastern

To avoid confusion, I will begin by noting that in the history of the world, there have been two Iberias: the western, lying on the Iberian Peninsula, and the eastern, Caucasian, on the territory of modern Eastern Georgia. Many ancient historians — among them Apollodorus, Varron, Pliny, Strabo, Appian, Eusebius of Caesarea — said that the people inhabiting these two lands were in direct kinship. In the *History of Rome*, in the 2nd century BC, the chronicler Appian wrote: *"The Iberians in Asia are considered by some as ancestors, by others as colonists, of the European Iberians, and by others only as tribes of the same name."*

Renowned Georgian archeologist Otar Lordkipanidze cites the following fact: *"In the 10th century, the prominent cultural figure Ioane Mtatsmindeli (Atoneli) intended to go to Spain with his students to familiarize himself with the 'life of the Western Georgians'."* The scientist writes that in translated texts from Greek to Georgian in the Middle Ages, the name "Spanish Georgians" often appears. However, scientists have not yet been able to prove the direct kinship of the two Iberian nations, despite the fact that many interesting scientific works have been written on this subject, and the topic has been widely discussed over the centuries. In Lordkipanidze's opinion, if such a kinship does exist, its roots should be sought in the prehistoric, Neolithic or early Chalcolithic eras.

It is noteworthy that the name "Iberia" and "Iberians" did not exist in ancient Georgian texts in relation to the Eastern Georgian lands: it was used only in Greco-Roman and Byzantine documents. In Georgia, the toponym "Kartli" was used instead.

The Mythical Kartlos

The history of the Ancient Iberian Kingdom (that of Georgia) is divided into mythical and documentary parts. The mythical information about Iberia is connected with the time after the Great Flood, when Kartlos, an ancestor of Noah of the Old Testament, was given lands in the South Caucasus, where present-day Kartli is located. His other brothers received Armenia, Albania, the lands of Egrisi (Colchis), and present-day Dagestan, Chechnya and Circassia.

Kartlos established his capital near Mount Kartli, later called Armazi, or Armaztsikhe. Kartlos' son Mtskhetos founded the city of Mtskheta, the main city of Kartli (in Georgian *deda kalaki,* or "mother city"), until the capital was moved to Tbilisi at the end of the 5th and beginning of the 6th century.

The formation of the state of Iberia relates to the campaigns of Alexander the Great. Did this great commander himself pass through the territory of modern Georgia? Unfortunately, no such information has been found to suggest the fact in historical documents, but, in chronicles, it is said that a Macedonian commander named Azo settled on the territory of Kartli and began to rule the lands. He was overthrown by Farnavaz (or Parnavaz) at the beginning of the 3rd century BC, who became the founder of the Farnavaziani Dynasty. This king strengthened and expanded Iberia, formed an alliance with the Colchian ruler Kuji, restructured the social hierarchy, and implemented various administrative reforms.

Life in Ancient Iberia (Kartli)

In order to visualize life in Iberia in the times of antiquity, I suggest starting with Plato Ioselini's historical work 'Towns that Existed and Exist in Georgia' (Tiflis, 1850):

"Towns in Georgia emerged mainly on the key rivers of the region and their main tributaries. In this regard, the first city location is found on the Kura (Mtkvari), the main river of the Transcaucasus, the length of which contained the core of the Kartvels', or Georgians', nationality and citizenship, due to which fact it was mainly called Kartli or Kartalinia. Here, along the entire length of the long arc described by the course of the Kura, from its source to its confluence with the Ktsia and the Temple, both banks of the picturesque valley were strewn with towns (...)" (Plato Ioselini, Towns that Existed and Exist in Georgia).

In the scientific world, it is generally believed that even before the formation of the Iberian state, an urban explosion took place on the territory of Kartli. In particular, the warriors of Alexander the Great found many fortress towns here, among them Khertvisi, Tsunda, Urbnisi, Kaspi, Uplistsikhe, Mtskheta, Samshvilde, and Hunani. In the Geographical Treatise of Claudius Ptolemy, the large town of Dzalisa in the Mukhrani valley was mentioned. Then boasting a territory of 70 hectares, it is now a village of the same name, the town having been destroyed in the 4th century. There were also large towns on the territory of modern Kakheti, which was part of Kartli.

Dedoplis Mindori, or "Queen's Field"

Unfortunately, we know very little about the beliefs of the ancient Iberians. Both Greco-Roman sources and old Georgian chronicles mention the names of a number of pre-Christian deities or idols, yet more detailed data on the ancient cults is lacking.

In this light, I was struck by information provided to me by Yulon Gagoshidze, a professor of archeology respected far beyond the borders of Georgia. For 10 years, from 1972 to 1982, Professor Gagoshidze and his colleagues conducted excavations at Dedoplis Mindori ("Queen's Field"), in the Shida Kartli region, near the village of Aradeti. One of their most notable finds was a temple and palace complex dating from the 2nd to the 1st century BC, which was destroyed in the 1st century AD, apparently during a military conflict.

"The grandiose, truly 'Old Eastern' scale of the temple complex of Dedoplis Mindori, and its geographical position in the very center of ancient Iberia, point to the particular importance of this sanctuary and the deity worshipped there," says the scholar.

"The temples of Dedoplis Mindori were built on the territory of the royal domain 'in memory of the souls' of the reigning house of Kartli, in the name of the great gods, whose viceroys or personifications on earth were considered to be the Georgian king and queen," Yulon then tells me.

Temples in ancient Iberia were usually the centers around which a community, settlement, or town were formed. Therefore, in the center of almost every village or settlement of the ancient epoch studied in Georgia (Uplistsikhe, Urbnisi, Vani, Samadlo, Tsikhis-gora), there was a temple.

The size and location of the foundations of the eight pre-Christian temples discovered at Dedoplis Mindori indicate that this was the main religious center of ancient Iberia, presumably adjacent to the summer residence of the kings. According to scholars, this religious center was associated with Mazdeism, with the incorporation of local beliefs.

One of these temples, perhaps even the main temple, according to archeologists, was dedicated to a female fertility deity of the type Avestan Ardvi Sūrā Anāhita, the great goddess of water and fertility, of vegetation; an immaculate ruler and formidable, warlike goddess. Many of Ardvi Sūrā Anāhita's features date back to the beliefs of the peoples of West Asia, long before the arrival of the Iranians. This goddess was included in the Zoroastrian triad of gods (Ahura Mazda, Mitra, Anahita) in the time of Artaxerxes II (404-359 BC.).

I learned from Yulon that *"already in Achaemenid times, Ardvi Sūrā Anāhita was identified with various female fertility deities: with the Semitic Nanaya and Atargatis, with the Greek Aphrodite and Artemis, and with Asia Minor's Kibela. Her cult was widespread both in Iran and beyond its borders, in Central and Minor Asia, Armenia and, apparently, in Georgia, where there were all the prerequisites for this in the form of the ancient cult of the female fertility deity, the solar goddess, the 'Great Mother of the Gods'."*

Having studied the excavation site, Georgian scientists suggested that Dedoplis Mindori was in ancient times the domain of Georgian queens and, as such, a temple dedicated to Anahita, whose earthly personification was considered to be that of a queen (as believed in Persia), may have been built there. The word *dedopali* not only means "queen" in Georgian, but also "ruler" and "mistress," which is one of the epithets of the goddess Anahita. Anahita was associated with the water element, and in the center of Dedoplis Mindori, in the vicinity of the temple, a spring called Dedoplis Tskaro ("Queen's Spring") gushes out of the ground.

In 1926, a hoard of treasure was found at Dedoplis Mindori. Among the artifacts was a gold plaque with a high relief depiction of a female head with a diadem, earrings, a necklace, and a moon sickle in her hair. It is an almost exact illustration of the description of Anahita found in ancient Persian texts. In addition, during excavations, archeologists found more than a hundred skulls of wild animals — deer, wild boar and bezoar goat, which, apparently, were sacrificed to this goddess. And the ancient Georgian custom of bringing deer horns to the sanctuary still exists in Georgia today!

Goddess Anahita, like the Greek Artemis, was identified with the moon. In ancient Georgian beliefs, the deity of the moon, or the month, was male (later, this was replaced by the cult of St Giorgi), but there was also a female hypostasis of this: the Goddess of the Moon.

Based on this, scholars assume that in the late 2nd or early 1st century BC, under King Parnajom (2nd century BC), who, according to an ancient Georgian source, "loved the faith of the Persians," temples were built in the royal domain in the central part of today's Shida Kartli region. These temples, they say, were dedicated to the gods worshipped by the royal family, the earthly viceroys or personifications of whom the Iberian kings and queens considered themselves to be. Most likely, these were Iranian gods, largely mixed with local Georgian astral deities.

The temples of Dedoplis Mindori were maintained at the expense of the royal domain, and the erection of a grandiose temple complex in the center of a vast plain, according to Yulon, *"had the purpose of confirming the ancestral cult of the royal house, whose worship became obligatory for all inhabitants of Iberia."* Nevertheless, this cult was unable to rise to the level of state religion: when the Sassanids began to forcefully impose Orthodox Persian Zoroastrianism in the countries under their control, this ancient "Georgian version" of Mazdeism was not accepted- hence the systematic shift from Georgian paganism to the "Persian faith" which can be found in various written sources. In this regard, Yulon came to the conclusion that perhaps it was *"at this time that the temples of Dedoplis Mindori were burnt to the ground. However, before the fire, all the shrines and other more or less valuable objects were taken out of the temples, apparently by the temple keepers themselves."*

The temples were not restored after the fire, yet researchers say that local residents, apparently descendants of members of the temple community, preserved and brought almost to our days the memory of this sanctuary. For more than one and a half thousand years, the entire area of more than 20 hectares, where temples and auxiliary temple buildings were once located, was considered sacred. In the center of this area, on a small hill, directly above the altar of the main temple, a stele with the image of St. George was placed in the late Middle Ages, and folk festivals organized on Dedoplis Mindori were associated with his name.

This is the synergy of ancient and modern beliefs that can be observed in just one example of an archeological complex, Dedoplis Mindori, which archeologists claim is the most unique in the entire South Caucasus.

I learned from Yulon Gagoshidze that, in the 1980s, he and his fellow scientists were unable to obtain funds for either the conservation of the excavation site or for further research, much less for the opening of an archeological museum there. *"Therefore, we were forced to cover many of the finds with earth again, where they are still hidden, perhaps in the best way. Fortunately, the excavation site was transferred to the Ministry of Culture, and construction has since been banned. However, agricultural works are still carried out in the vicinity,"* he notes with regret.

Many scientific works have been written on this temple complex. Yulon is still working on the most extensive of them, and continues to hope that, one day, his "brainchild" will be given a worthy place in the history of the ancient world, at least as the largest pre-Christian cult complex in Georgia.

The Cities of Ancient Iberia

Archeological excavations along the Mtkvari River in different years and decades have repeatedly confirmed that trade and commodity exchange flourished in the towns of Kartli. The high-level skill of Iberian craftsmen was also mentioned in the descriptions of Greco-Roman historian Strabo, who visited these lands. He wrote about densely populated cities boasting beautiful houses with tiled roofs, markets, and all kinds of public facilities.

Iberian architects were undoubtedly familiar with the main principles of ancient architecture. The main temple of the Dedoplis Mindori complex traces the influence of Persian temple architecture of the Achaemenid era. The most beautiful buildings in the ancient Persian cities of Persepolis and Souza were built in the same style.

Nevertheless, Georgian scholars consider this temple to be a work of ancient Georgian architecture. *"The architect who created this masterpiece was an outstanding master who creatively approached the solution of construction problems that arose during the creation of this impressive project,"* Yulon Gagoshidze tells me. *"The strict symmetry of the whole complex, the proportionality of the whole and its individual parts, in compliance with the golden ratio, the accuracy of execution of the author's plan have no equal among similar monuments of the Hellenistic East known to us."*

The golden ratio, also known as the golden mean or golden section, is a special mathematical ratio. It's approximately equal to 1.6180339887... The golden ratio is often seen in geometric shapes, particularly the golden rectangle. A golden rectangle's sides are in the golden ratio, and it can be divided into a square and another golden rectangle. This process can be repeated infinitely, creating a spiral pattern. Many artists and architects throughout history have used the golden ratio in their works, believing it to be aesthetically pleasing. The idea is that these proportions resonate with a natural sense of balance and beauty. Historically, the golden ratio is believed to have influenced the design of iconic structures like the Parthenon in Athens and the Great Pyramid of Giza.

Archeologists were particularly impressed by the elaborate capitals of the temple columns, decorated with floral patterns and crafted with intricate carvings.

In other temples of this complex, Hellenistic influence can be seen, and it is apparent that the artistic design of buildings in Iberia was of great importance. In many places, including Dzalisa, scientists have found Roman thermae, as well as sewerage and water supply systems.

Iberia was famous for its pottery and jewelry art, which used the sophisticated method of polychromy, that is, the embedding of precious stones in jewelry.

Iberia was part of the international trade system. Archeologists have found coins — Roman, Parthian, etc., as well as Italian jugs, Syrian glass balsamaria, jewelry and precious stones from the East, Asia Minor stone beads, and Roman silver phials.

In 1850, Platon Ioselini described the city of Mtskheta as follows: "*The ancient capital of Kartalinia and all the Kartlosian tribes lies at the confluence of the Aragva and the Kur. The beginning and the name comes, according to legend, from Mtskhetos, the bravest and most powerful of the sons of Kartlos. However, is not the original population of the city, the 'Moschi' (or Moschoi), hidden in the name 'Mtskheta'? (...) For many centuries, it was the center of citizenship, developed by Kartlosians under many different influences and in many different forms (...). The Persian domination tamed the primitive savagery of manners, and introduced the religion of Zoroaster. Then the worship of Armaz (Ormuzd), Zaden, and other symbols and ideas of the East, took root in Mtskheta. The Greeks, attracted by trade from Phasis to Kur, brought their mythological concepts here, and, from them, images of Venus and Hercules appeared in Mtskheta*" (Platon Ioselini, description of Mtskheta).

The Languages of Ancient Iberia

Some scholars attribute the creation of the Georgian alphabet to King Farnavaz, yet there is no documented evidence of this. As recorded in the 'Life of Kartli,' before Farnavaz, different languages were spoken in Iberia: Georgian, Armenian, Khazar, Assyrian, Hebrew and Greek. It is believed that after Farnavaz, Georgian became the main language.

According to archeologist Yulon Gagoshidze, Greek and Aramaic writing was used in Iberia during the early period of Georgian statehood. More than 50 Aramean inscriptions were found on Georgian territory that date from the 1st century AD to the 4th century AD. Scientist Giorgi Tsereteli deciphered some of these inscriptions for the first time, and called it "Armazi writing," which was used until Georgia adopted Christianity in the early 4th century AD. From the 5th century onwards, mostly Georgian and also Greek inscriptions were seen.

Iberia's Relationship with Rome

In different centuries of antiquity, Iberia's relationship with Rome varied from vassal dependence to partnership; confrontation to complete independence. When Iberia became close to the Kingdom of Pontus and Armenia during their confrontation with Rome, Iberia was targeted by the Roman commander Pompey, in 65 BC, who conquered the state and made it his ally in his campaign against ancient Albania (here, we mean the Caucasian Albania).

In 1867, a tablet from the time of Roman Emperor Vespasian, signed in 75 AD, was found near Mtskheta during the construction of a railway line. It revealed that Vespasian had helped the "city of cities" Mtskheta to strengthen its walls. It must be understood that in the Ancient World, Iberia was considered a powerful force and a barrier protecting its southern neighbors from nomads from the north. You can find out more about this and the gate at Darial Gorge in my stories about Mtianeti and the Georgian Military Road.

Yulon tells me that, in those times, Iberia was subordinated to Rome as a vassal, and this dependence implied only one thing: that Iberians were not allowed to fight against the Romans.

The whole history of West Asia was colored by the confrontation between Persia and Rome. And in this confrontation, Iberia always took Rome's side, the scholar says.

"Our ancestors were certainly intelligent: Persia was always too close and could easily conquer and enslave. Rome, on the other hand, was far away. However, Rome's help was enough to stop Persia and save Iberia. To this day, Georgia needs Europe, just like in ancient times, because Russia ('Asia') is too close."

The Peak of Iberia's Power

The 1st – 2nd centuries AD saw Iberia at the height of its power. At the time, the strength of neighboring Armenia was weakening, and the Iberian rulers were able to put representatives of their dynasty on the Armenian throne, having successfully snatched that throne away from the Parthians, Rome's long-time rivals.

The legendary King Farsman II succeeded in making Iberia an equal partner of Rome. This is evidenced by the Roman annals, which tell of the king's visit to the city, where Emperor Antony Pius bestowed on the Iberian ruler a great honor allowed only to the most distinguished of guests: a sacrifice in the temple of Bellona. An equestrian statue was also erected in honor of Farsman II in Rome.

Unfortunately, for centuries, its geopolitical position made Iberia vulnerable to confrontation with its powerful neighbors. As old empires declined and died, new neighbors grew up in their place. In the Middle Ages, Iberia faced new challenges: confrontation with the Arabs and the Mongols.

The City and Fortress of Ujarma: A Living Witness to the History of Ancient Iberia

In antiquity, the fortress and town of Ujarma were important points of strategic, political and economic importance for Ancient Iberia. It is believed that they already existed in the 2nd to 1st centuries BC, and were built by King Aspagur or Varaz-Bacur.

Ujarma is also closely connected with another legendary figure in the history of Kartli: Vakhtang Gorgasali. This is where his summer residence was located, and where he died in the war against Persian invaders, although he was buried in Mtskheta.

Along with Farnavaz and Farsman II, Vakhtang Gorgasali is a legendary figure in Georgian history, one of the most important rulers in the founding of Georgian statehood. It is not for nothing that so many folk songs and legends have been written about Gorgasali: he secured the north of Iberia, pacified the mountaineers of the North Caucasus, strengthened the Iberian fortresses, raised the Georgian Orthodox Church to the rank of autocephaly and, it is said, it was he who moved the capital from Mtskheta to Tbilisi.

If you travel from Tbilisi to Kakheti through the Gombori Pass, you will inevitably pass the Ujarma Fortress. From the roadside, you might get the impression that only one tower has been saved, but this is a serious misconception! And that is why it is sad that, despite the signpost and the parking lot next to this wonderful historical place, most tourists pass by without seeing this amazing and very important citadel.

For a long time, this was my case, until my search for "living witnesses" of antiquity in Iberia led me to Ujarma. I corrected my mistake by arranging an exploration of the site with archeologist Arsen Khatiashvili.

When the scientist led me along the fortress wall to one of the entrances to the fortress, I was struck by the scale of the structure. The citadel consisted of upper, middle and lower fortresses, on a total area of about 1400 square meters. Most of the towers have survived to this day, although not all of them are in their original form.

Arsen told me why this particular location was chosen for the construction of this fortification: The fortress stands on an almost sheer cliff, high above the Iori River, which flows from the Borbalo Ridge. In ancient times, important trade routes passed through here, seeing caravans from Central Asia, Dagestan and Chechnya traveling through the Iori Gorge from the north. In Ujarma, they stopped, rested, and then continued on their way either to the west or to the south, heading to Armenia, Persia, and beyond. When there was a need to defend themselves against enemies, the rock on which the fortress was built made the perfect natural defense.

Arsen has been working in Ujarma for 10 years. He tells me that the first excavations of the fortress started in 1951-1952, with archeologists, students and professors clearing the territory of the upper citadel, which had become overgrown with bushes and trees, and excavating the royal chambers. The main part of the work was carried out under the supervision of Irakli Tsitsishvili and Professor Giorgi Lomtatidze.

Ujarma shattered another of my misconceptions: that only the fortress in Gonio (near Batumi) in Georgia was built according to Roman technology. It turns out that, in Ujarma, the architecture was also Roman, with the fortress and its towers built in quadrants. Buildings of the same culture can be found in Greece, Italy, Spain, and England, all very similar to one other. *"This masonry is undoubtedly very famous,"* Arsen explains. *"But our historians call it* [the style] *'Gorgasali Ujarma masonry.'"* On the plan of the fortress drawn up by Irakli Tsitsishvili in 1952, the Roman style is clear to see.

The Roman masonry in the lower part of the towers is very different from that of the medieval period, when they started to use lime mortar. The Roman arches are one of the most important elements of Ujarma architure, boasting red stones that testify to the fires that raged here.

In the Middle Ages, in the times when King Giorgi III, the father of Queen Tamar, ruled, some towers were converted to rounded towers. Each tower had three floors, and they were defended from the top floor: the recesses where wooden beams were built into the stones for the ceiling can still be seen today.

Located on the steepest, south-facing, impregnable cliff, one of the towers has very thick walls and two entrances. Scientists have suggested that this is where King Vakhtang's bedchamber was located. Not very far from it is an underground chamber, thought to have been a prison where the ruler's personal prisoners were kept. Later, food was stored there.

From that tower, Arsen and I cross a low section of the fortress wall and find ourselves on a thickly-shrubbed platform in front of a cliff, from which we have a view of another separate watchtower and the Iori River running in a blue ribbon along the gorge, as well as of the mountain ranges growing out of each other like giant sea waves. The view is perfect not only for the patrolling security guards, but equally so for dreamers, poets and philosophers.

Different eras have left their mark on the construction of the fortress. Several years ago, Arsen and his colleagues discovered and excavated a huge hall in the territory of the upper fortress. At first, archeologists assumed it was a place for meetings between the king and the nobility. However, after studying the architectural features of the room, the scientists concluded that it was designed to hold water.

"With this pool, we are talking about a completely unique construction not seen in the entire South Caucasus. There have been none like it found either in Azerbaijan or Armenia," Arsen explains. *"It is 22.5 meters long, 5.8 meters high and 5 meters wide. It would have held about 500 tonnes of water. The stones are laid with old Georgian masonry, the bricks are 22 centimeters long. There is blue waterproofing on the bricks so that water does not seep through the stones. There's also a place where you could collect and purify water."*

It turns out that the water was brough there through a clay aqueduct (again, Roman technology!) from a nearby mountain where there are many springs. Why did this fortress need so much water? It was used as drinking water, but also for cooking, other household needs and, last but not least, for putting out fires caused by enemy attacks. The fortress survived many such attacks. In the 10th century, Abul Qasim's army almost completely destroyed the fortress, after which it was rebuilt by King Giorgi III. The fortress was later destroyed by the Mongols and then rebuilt many times over.

Not long ago, archeologists discovered three other pools in the fortress. They are thought to have been baths from the time of Giorgi III. Arsen believes that one of the pools, which is located in the tower itself, was likely a women's bath. My wonderful guide-archeologist enthusiastically tells me how the water supply and heating system functioned, showing me a room with thick walls without doors, a treasury, as well as ways the residents could enter the upper fortress from the territory of the lower one if the latter was captured by enemies.

There are many things in this fortress that take your breath away. For example, there is one small, but absolutely unique two-story church of the 9th-12th centuries. It is built on the place where, in the 4th century, Enlightener of Georgia (Iberia) St Nino is said to have erected one of her three wooden crosses. Later, this cross was kept in a temple in Akhmeta, destined to survive until the 1920s, when, in their anti-religious frenzy, the Bolsheviks burnt it.

In this modest, quiet Ujarma church, the walls breathe peace and tranquility. It is easy to feel as if you have traveled back to the era of early Christianity, when faith in Christ was intimate, pure, and utterly honest.

Down a steep staircase leading past the massive towers, my guide and I descend to the town of Ujarma that was located in the lower fortress. This place is now covered with a forest and thickets. *"We have yet to study this place thoroughly,"* Arsen says. *"We need to work here with utmost care. We've already found deep rooms built with ashlar masonry, which apparently served as refrigerators. We assume there were many workshops and other no less important buildings within the walls of the lower fortress."*

Finally, Arsen introduces me to the artifacts found during this year's excavations. Among them are pieces of a waterpipe made of clay, a bronze bell, 9th-century tiles, 11th-century Persian and Georgian glazed tableware, Persian multi-colored glass bracelets, candlesticks, obsidian weapon tips and a bowl with a picture of a pheasant from the reign of Giorgi III and his daughter, Queen Tamar.

No artifacts of late antiquity have yet been found. But archeology is like a young beauty: it is a fledgling and capricious science, and it can be conquered only by diligence, persistence, and consistency. Only with such a purposeful approach will it reveal to the researcher the untold secrets that the Georgian land hides within.

Ujarma — Tbilisi, November 2023

The Fortress of Ujarma was the royal residence of the Goergian kings in Late Antiquity

Arsen Khatiashvili in Ujarma Fortress

The stunning Darial Gorge, carved out by the Terek River. Located right on the border between Georgia and Russia, for millennia the Darial Gorge has been one of the two most important passes through the Caucasus Mountains- a crucial route for trade, migration, and, unfortunately, invasion.

Chapter 14.
Mtianeti, Mtiuleti, and the
Georgian Military Road

The Mtianeti region occupies a prominent position among Georgia's attractions. A visit to the country is generally considered incomplete without undertaking a journey along the historic Georgian Military Road to enjoy the perpetually snow-capped summit of Mount Kazbek, and to appreciate the architectural beauty of the Gergeti Trinity Church within its evocative high-altitude setting.

Mtianeti and the Darial Gorge hold immense historical significance as a primary route between the North and South Caucasus, a geographical advantage that made it a highly contested territory. The narrow Darial Passage, or, as the Romans called it, the Caucasus Gate, through one of the world's highest mountain ranges played a pivotal role in establishing ancient Iberia as a vital strategic ally for both Rome and, later, Constantinople. The stability of the Roman Empire and surrounding regions relied heavily on securing this route against northern incursions by the Scythians, Sarmatians, and other nomadic tribes.

The function of this gorge did not change in the Middle Ages – and it remains a key location to this day, valued for the fact that it is so narrow that it can be held off from an invading army of many thousands by a relatively small force.

In antiquity, Georgian monarchs adeptly utilized this strategically significant passage as a key element in their diplomatic and military interactions with neighboring polities. This involved both the strategic closure of the passage to impede incursions, and the recruitment of mercenaries from northern regions to augment their military forces in pursuit of national objectives. Control of the Darial Gorge constituted a recurring source of conflict for Georgian royalty.

Even today, the route remains vulnerable in Russia's ongoing hybrid war against Georgia, a conflict waged not only through military pressure, but also through the manipulation of history.

The Darial Gorge

The Darial Gorge is almost an otherworldly, mystical world, made of sheer cliffs, giant stone blocks, glaciers, waterfalls and gushing waters of mountain rivers, the most important of which is the Terek (Tergi in Georgian).

Darial is stunning at any time of year, and, there, man unwillingly realizes his insignificance compared to the power of nature. The gorge is well known for its fearsome elements, and in bad weather it can panic even the most experienced traveler.

I remember when, on a walk to the Gveleti Waterfall, we were taken by surprise by the sound of an approaching thunderstorm. Eagles were soaring, carelessly disregarding the approaching elements, when the sky, which had not heralded anything bad, suddenly darkened. The booming thunder, amplified as it echoed through the mountains, brought out in us an animalistic terror. Where in the wilderness to look for salvation in the midst of nature's rampage? That day, however, we were lucky enough to escape with only a slight fright: the rain passed by without spoiling our trek.

Here is the description of the Darial Gorge I found in the 'Guide to the Caucasus,' published in 1913:

"Everything in the Darial Gorge is formidable and majestic. It is bounded on its sides by unusually high mountain hulks, plummeting downwards. It is somehow a narrow, unusually large crack; a gigantic tomb in which the traveler feels himself a weak, insignificant creature. Everything here is gloomy, severe; the southern sky appears only as a narrow blue strip; there is no sign of life around, except for the occasional mountain eagle or swift-winged swallow. Deep in the gorge, foaming fiercely, the fast-flowing Terek groans and rumbles, filling the surroundings with its loud roar. As a living protest, as a challenge to the struggle, as an embodiment of rebellion and courage, it rushes ever forward in its endeavor to expand the limits of its life, to push the boundaries of its narrow existence, and in its frenzied endeavor to do so, pushing and dragging thousand-pound stones along with it" (Guide to the Caucasus, 1913).

The Georgian Military Road

The North and South Caucasus are connected to each other by an important transport artery, which has been called the Georgian Military Road since the 19th century. It is said that shortly before the First World War, there was a plan to build a tramway between Vladikavkaz and Tbilisi along the route of that road. Can you imagine what an important political, commercial and military-strategic significance this road had if tramways were going to be laid on it, despite the great number of potential dangers — landslides, rockslides and mudflows?!

This road remains important not only for Georgia and Russia; our Armenian neighbors rightfully call the Georgian Military Road "the road of life," as it is currently Armenia's only land transport link to the outside world.

One of the main settlements in the Mtianeti region is the village of Stepantsminda (also known as Kazbegi). I first visited it shortly after we moved to Georgia in 2010. Tourism in those places was just gaining momentum back then. The Georgian Military Road was not yet overloaded with traffic, and it was possible to marvel at the mighty power of the untouched nature of these places in almost complete solitude.

Ananuri Fortress and the Zhinvali Reservoir

I will never forget my first impression of Ananuri Fortress and the Zhinvali Reservoir, with its emerald waters framed by green mountains: I was enraptured! Another legendary landscape that will stick in my memory for a long time!

In the history of Georgia, the Ananuri Fortress, with its crenelated stone walls, towers and ancient church, has long played the role of a significant strategic point on this trade route. The fortress was owned by the Aragvi eristavs, hereditary rulers of the Mtiuleti Valley, who were responsible for guarding the Georgian border from enemy raids through the Gudauri and neighboring passes.

It is noteworthy that among Persian authors, this fortress was called Kara-Kalkan-Kala, or "the fortress of the Black Shields." The Muslims called the Pshavs and Khevsurs who were part of the fighting units of the Aragvi eristavs and valiantly guarded the borders of the Georgian state, "Black Shields."

However, as is often the case in life, pretty pictures tend to have a flip side, and often it is a much less attractive one.

Let me turn to history again. Zhinvali has always been an important transport route, where roads from West to East and from North to South cross. Many ancient Iberian settlements were located here. Since the 19th century, several burial sites of antiquity, and hoards of bronze objects typical of the Colchian Bronze Culture, have been discovered in this area. Scientists have had time to study only a small part of the available archeological monuments, as much more remain underground. On the basis of these artifacts, historians have managed to learn curious details about the life of Ancient Iberia and Colchis, and about their peoples.

In the Middle Ages, Zhinvali was a lively settlement, with active trade, master builders, architects and craftsmen, temples and roads, towers and castles. Sadly, this immensely valuable historical legacy was submerged when the construction of the Zhinvali Reservoir, a water reserve for a new hydroelectric power station, was carried out in the 1970s. 18 villages, cemeteries, as well as monuments of architecture—castles, arched bridges and churches—were buried underwater. In the

The historical Georgian region of Tao, now part of modern Turkey, is home to various Georgian historical monuments. Noteworthy among them was the Chali Fortress and church, which dates back to the 10th-11th centuries. In the summer of 2023, the area was completely flooded for the new Yusufeli hydroelectric power station. Georgian historian Buba Kudava managed to take the last photos of the church, paintings and frescos before they were submerged.

vision of the Soviet authorities, the economic benefits of the power plant far outweighed the cultural losses. It is completely incomprehensible to me by which criteria one can compare the historical to the actual economic value of a place. However, such things have happened at all times in history, and they still do, and not only in Georgia.

The Georgian Military Road winds upwards along the turbulent Aragvi River. Near the village of Pasanauri, where the White and Black (Khevsur) Aragvi merge, it is impossible not to bow down before the magical power of Mother Nature. Two powerful mountain streams, meeting each other, retain their separate colors for some time, flowing in parallel as before their confluence, like two different-colored ribbons.

A Monument to a Friendship that Never Happened

On the ascent to the Jvari ("Cross") Pass (2379m), there is a monument symbolizing Russian-Georgian friendship. The monument is located above the abyss, overlooking the so-called Devil's Valley. Erected in the final years of the Soviet regime, this arch is a monument of that demonic era, and it loudly proclaims Soviet propaganda messages, boasting scenes from Russian, Georgian and common Soviet history.

Located on a high cliff in the middle of a spectacular high mountain range, it is ideal not only

The Mtiuleti Uprising of 1804 broke out west of the Darial Gorge. Local residents complained about Cossacks robbing them and, in response, two men were beaten to death with whips, several were thrown into a pit, and the rest were sent into forced labor. Women were subjected to cruel and indecent treatment. Residents of the Aragvi Valley killed several Russian soldiers. About 4000 Georgian and Ossetian rebels asked Prince Farnavaz Bagrationi to lead the revolt. Then a number of Georgian nobles joined the rebellion. On the 3rd of August 1804, rebels and Russian troops clashed in the battle of Lomisi. But the forces were unequal. The rebellion was eventually crushed, and hundreds of Georgian highlanders were bayoneted or imprisoned.

for photoshoots, but also for gaining some insight into the attitude of the empire towards its neighbors — a condescending suzerainty that this monument of Soviet architecture conveys in the best possible way. Pompous and colorful, national in spirit and Soviet in content, the monument's mosaic, whose context is difficult to accept, is nevertheless worthy of going down in history as a brilliant example of the power of propaganda through art.

For many centuries, Georgia and Russia have been neighbors with complex relations. The history of the so-called Treaty of Giorgievsk on the accession of the Georgian kingdom of Kartli-Kakheti to the Russian Empire in 1783 is extremely complicated and controversial (even back then, Europe did not pay due attention; its leaders all but ignoring the letters of King Erekle II begging for help). After the conclusion of the treaty, Russia repeatedly violated it, and the relationship between Georgian highlanders and representatives of Tsarist Russia was marked by hostility and confrontation, a fact colorfully described in the works of famous writer Alexander Kazbegi, a native of the village of Stepantsminda.

When Russia conquered the Caucasus, Russian officials of that time — with few exceptions — did not bother to study the manners and customs of the local peoples, their ancient history or culture. The Tsar's viceroys in the Caucasus considered the locals "savages," and fiercely fought with them, or pitted them against each other. The new authorities groomed the local people in their own way by all possible and impossible means, including through physical violence, cunning and deceit. Alexander Kazbegi's works — especially his novels 'Khevisberi Gocha' and 'Eliso' — are impressive to the core. The fiery patriotism of the highlanders, their adherence to ancient traditions and customs, their readiness for self-sacrifice, their legendary courage and bravery — all these are energies can still be imbibed in these lands today.

The Truso Valley

Just after the descent from the Jvari Pass, there is one striking place, hidden away from the eyes (and sins) of people: The Truso Valley, a realm of freedom, geysers and mineral springs.

A narrow gravel road leads along a turbulent river. The mountains here are "bald," without forest. But there is plenty of water in Truso, which keeps the alpine meadows blooming all summer long. Mineral waters flow so abundantly here that thick calcareous layers of travertine accumulate on the mountain slopes. As a result, there are unusual "rusty" mountains scattered here and there, through which iron mineral waters flow. It is not for nothing that Truso is called a "geological museum."

My favorite place in this valley is a small lake with sparkling mineral water gurgling in it. Depending on the time of day and the weather, it is either blue or emerald green. In spring and summer, the lake is surrounded by colorful flowers. I would happily spend whole days on the shore of this water body, tasting its healing coolness and inhaling the aromas of mountain herbs. It is said that this lake has neither shores nor bottom: under the edge of the grassy soil, there is a hollow sinking down to nowhere.

It is difficult not to get lost in time in Truso: few of the achievements of civilization have managed to make their way into this forgotten world. The Truso Valley, as well as the highest-mountain village in Georgia, called Resi (2400 meters above sea level), have been gradually emptying out since the 20th century. Its last inhabitants, Ossetians, moved to the Russian side. Before that, for centuries, the ethnic composition of the valley's population was constantly changing: Dvals, Tsanars, Alans. In addition, due to the geographical specifics of the gorge, the inhabitants of this region have always been cut off from the main transport artery, the Georgian Military Road.

The crown of the Truso Valley is the ruins of the medieval castle of Zakagori, whose towers offer inspiring views of the entire valley and the upper reaches of the Tergi River.

Truso is just one of the many gorges of Mtianeti, but I feel it is the most remarkable. Further along the Military Road are the Sno, Kobi and other gorges. Stepantsminda is just a stone's throw away from the Truso Valley.

Stepantsminda: The Way to Meet a Miracle

On our first visit to Stepantsminda (Kazbegi), we stayed in one of the few guesthouses existing at the time — with Archil and his wife Nino. Since then, I have visited this family regularly.

Archil, with his inimitable sense of humor and cheerfulness, is the standard of a true toastmaster: he drinks wine and *chacha* with his guests without getting the slightest bit drunk, and he proclaims many lavish toasts, jokes and pranks, but at the same time vigilantly monitors guests' compliance with the rules and regulations of a traditional Georgian feast. Archil is able to connect even the sullenest sociophobe to the battery of general fun. And even though this mountain Pantagruel is disappointed by my refusal to eat meat or drink *chacha*, he is magnanimously ready to forgive me my "sins," though without giving up hope that my behavior will soon be "improved."

Archil's mother and his wife Nino—both miracle workers—stay modestly behind the scenes of the festivities from morning to night. Thanks to their efforts, the family business is thriving. One day, I was lucky enough to get to help them in the kitchen. Before that, a Finnish friend of mine had also come to this family to learn the art of Georgian cookery. Archil and Nino organized a masterclass for her on how to make *mtsvadi* (Georgian barbecued meat). As a result of a fun cookery conversation with Nino, I was introduced to the tricks of making authentic Georgian *khinkali* (dumplings), and I also learned how to make a local potato pie called *khabizgini*.

Sometimes, in the morning in Tbilisi, I get out of bed feeling blue, and self-diagnose my malaise as "acute mountain insufficiency." There is only one therapy for this illness: being the next morning somewhere at high altitude, where the soul will be enobled by beautiful views and blissful silence, such as can be found at the foot of the Gergeti Trinity Church. And then I call Archil, inform him of my planned visit, throw a couple of essentials into my backpack, and drive over the Jvari Pass straight to Stepantsminda.

Recently, due to the intensification of trade traffic between Georgia and Russia, the journey to this cherished land takes much longer than it did a couple of years ago. But when my heart is bursting out of my chest, longing to experience again the indescribable feeling of freedom and even holiness, there is no other way: I head off to meet a miracle!

Once there, I spend the evening on the terrace of Nino and Archil's house, which offers a magnificent panorama of the eternally snow-capped Kazbek. There is nothing more enjoyable than contemplating sunset and dusk in this fairy-tale kingdom of mountains, glaciers and forest. The colors change almost by the minute: violet is replaced by yellow, sometimes pink, and after that- orange. Sometimes, the visibility is so crystal-clear that it seems as if you are looking at the landscape through a magnifying glass; sometimes, Kazbek is visible only through the ghostly evening haze; and sometimes, a light plume of fog lingers briefly on Kazbek's peak. How not to recall the Japanese sutra of 'Mountains and Waters,' according to which "green mountains can walk," changing during the day, throughout the year, and also depending on the mood of the contemplator?

At dawn, I hike to Gergeti Church, enjoying the crisp forest air and the silence of nature, which is interrupted only by bird-song, to experience one of the most thrilling panoramas of Georgia in the first rays of the sun.

And now I would like to confess one most intimate thing: On my first visit, when I saw that church against the backdrop of those fantastic giant peaks, I was overcome by an unbridled rush of feelings: I felt like falling onto my knees and kissing this holy land. Tears of love, awe and boundless happiness rolled down my cheeks, because, somehow, in some incredible way, I had been deemed worthy of seeing this perfect, inconceivable beauty: a symbiosis of the divine creation and the product of human hands.

Stepantsminda — Tbilisi, August 2023

Tsminda Sameba (Holy Trinity) Church in Gergeti

A grocery seller on the Georgian Military Road

Soviet Monument of "Georgian-Russian friendship" located in "Devil's Valley" close to the Jvari Pass

The town of Gori should take pride not in the controversial figure of its most fa-mous son, Joseph Stalin, but in in its great citadel, the Medieval Gori Fortress

Stalin's statue at the Stalin Museum in Gori

Chapter 15.
Shida Kartli, Home of Joseph Stalin

Any attempt to capture the essence of Georgia, to truly paint a comprehensive portrait of its tumultuous history, would be an exercise in futility without confronting the towering, if deeply controversial, figure of Joseph Stalin, for he looms over the Georgian narrative, a shadow cast across decades; a presence that refuses to be ignored or diminished.

The province of Shida Kartli holds a particularly strong connection to Stalin, one of the most influential figures of the 20th century. This connection stems from his birth in Gori, the province's capital. Stalin, whose original name was Iosif Vissarionovich Dzhugashvili, was born in Gori in 1878, a time when the region was part of the Russian Empire. His early life in this Georgian town, nestled in the heart of Shida Kartli, played a significant role in shaping his formative years. Furthermore, Gori itself maintains a tangible link to Stalin's legacy. The Stalin Museum, located in the town center, provides visitors with insights into his life, from his humble beginnings to his rise as the leader of the Soviet Union. While Stalin's legacy is deeply intertwined with Shida Kartli, it is also a source of ongoing debate and discussion, reflecting the broader complexities of 20th-century history and the impact of his rule.

A Story of the Soviet Past Bursting into the Future: The Stalin Museum

One of my first reports after moving to Georgia was from the Stalin Museum. This was in 2010, when the country was ruled by President Mikheil Saakashvili, who was known as an anti-Soviet leader, the darling of the West. One of the laws adopted under Saakashvili was a ban on the use of any Soviet symbols.

But, strangely, in this most progressive of all post-Soviet countries, in the Stalin Museum, I feel as if I am back in my Soviet childhood. There is a similar place where I grew up in Minsk- the Museum of the Great Patriotic War, which every school child was obliged to visit. However, even there the exposition was not as strongly tied to the cult of personality as you'll find in the museum in Stalin's hometown, in Gori, Georgia.

The building of the Stalin Museum is a pompous neo-Renaissance palace, a prime example of central urban planning, solemnly towering over all the surrounding buildings. Its construction began during the lifetime of the Soviet leader, and the museum was opened in 1957, four years after his death. In the courtyard there is a small house, in a room of which Iosif Dzhugashvili, the future Stalin, son of a poor shoemaker and seamstress, spent his childhood. To the side of the museum is the trailer-mounted armored railway carriage in which the head of the Soviet state used to travel.

The building itself, and its artifacts, are remarkable and even a little frightening. Most shocking was the style of the excursion offered in the museum. It was hard not to feel the strong Soviet presence, and, to me, it felt as if the collapse of the Soviet Union was someone's absurd invention or, perhaps, a dream.

Appearing to be filled with a sense of pride in the great Soviet Union and its leader, the guide spoke in detail about the milestones of the life and struggles of the "great father of the nations." In the entirety of the monumental museum, with its pompous ceremonial staircases and huge halls packed with Stalin-era artifacts, there is only one tiny room under the stairs where you can get acquainted with the fact of Stalin's repressions, the atrocities of the NKVD, with the history of the so-called Abkhaz War, and the blitzkrieg of August 2008.

After that first visit to this strange museum, my reality split in two. On the one hand, I saw I had come to live in a country whose changes for the better made even the most advanced Western powers gasp. The fight against corruption, reforms in the system of internal affairs, higher education, taxation, as well as the creation of exemplary Houses of Justice, where any document and any certificate can be issued in just half an hour—this was the business card of the new Georgia and its young president, who came to power in the course of the no less impressive and peaceful Rose Revolution. On the other hand, this exemplary Western-style country clearly had a Soviet past that was stuck in its throat like a huge undigested lump. And it still remains.

As I learned later, in those years, there were many different initiatives put forward to change the exposition of the Stalin Museum. One of them was its transformation into the Museum of Soviet Propaganda; into something akin to the Holocaust Museum. However, these attempts failed, opposed by the museum's management and the Gori locals. Instead, a separate museum was opened in Tbilisi, which you'll read about in the next pages. Perhaps those in Gori saw no need to reorganize this exposition, what with visitors already flocking to the holy of holies of the town of Gori, intent on discovering Stalin's legacy. Indeed, the Stalin Museum is today the most visited museum in Georgia!

The Museum in 2024

This year, I visited the city of Gori and the Stalin Museum once again, but found that zero changes had been made! For the sake of objectivity, I will say that our wonderful guide Olga, a museum employee with 40 years of experience, was ready to discuss several controversial issues of Soviet history and the biography of Joseph Stalin. However, as Olga told me at the very beginning of our conversation, she would not share her attitude of the Soviet leader with me. She said everyone has their own attitude towards him, and this was not our business.

Standing in front of a map of the Russian Empire, where all the locations are marked where Comrade Koba (Stalin's nickname) was arrested or exiled, it was amusing to listen to the stories about the wanderings of the future leader and his many escape attempts.

"For his revolutionary activities, Stalin was arrested seven times," Olga tells us. *"He was arrested in Batumi, then in Baku and St. Petersburg. He was exiled to Siberia several times. He managed to escape from all exiles except the last, which was near the Arctic Circle. He tried to escape twice, but both times he was caught and sent back. That last time he was so severely beaten that his left arm was permanently damaged, leaving it forever shorter than his right."*

"Were all these arrests really connected to his political activities?" I ask, pointing to the rumors that Stalin was, among other things, engaged in bank robberies- in particular, on Yerevan Square in Tbilisi.

"What are you talking about!" Olga exclaims, throwing up her hands. *"There were no crimes! And no proof of those rumors has ever been found! Stalin did no such thing! If he needed money, there were other party members. Stalin was a member of the Politburo, a great thinker, author of many important revolutionary articles!"*

"Is it true that Stalin later protected some of his fellow countrymen from the repressions?" I wonder.

"Actually, many were protected," Olga replies. *"For example, the Soviet constructor Korolev, who was exiled to the island of Sakhalin, wrote a letter to Beria, and after that he was released. But for this, it was necessary to find a way to reach the right person. Millions of people were exiled, and neither Stalin nor Beria could know who was where, or the names of all who had been exiled."*

"How surprising!" I note. "After all, Stalin was himself the 'father' of those great purges!"

"Yes, that's how they conducted politics back then," Olga answers. *"But they could not be responsible for each person specifically. The machine of purges was launched, and those who fell under it unavoidably became victims."*

The spacious halls of Stalin's Valhalla are filled with visitors. For some reason, I cannot help but notice the large groups of Indians, Thai, and Chinese. They say that schoolchildren and students in Chinese schools still study Stalin's biography in detail. So where else, if not in Gori, can one admire so many remarkable portraits of the "leader of the peoples," and learn about his countless exploits, including those during the Great Patriotic War (which in this museum they still prefer not to call World War II), which, of course, was won by none other than "the great Soviet people under the leadership of Comrade Stalin"?

This time at the museum, I learn that Comrade Stalin was "a deeply religious man" who not only prayed and attended church himself, but also personally rehabilitated the Church during the war, which "had suffered greatly after the October Revolution."

There are so many things happening in the world right now. And only this museum remains unchanged. Its last update was in 1979. Preserved in their entirety are numerous, sometimes the most incredible, gifts to Joseph Stalin from the citizens of countries all over the world.

And to this day, at the entrance to the large hall, in red and black tones, you can be seized by that feeling of immeasurable grief that was experienced by millions of Soviet citizens when they heard the news of Stalin's death. My father once told me that he retained very vivid memories of how people sobbed in the streets, listening to the news of the leader's death over loudspeakers; my father was only four years old at the time! In the museum's "mourning hall," the leader's death mask is exhibited, as is a large canvas with a painting of Stalin in his coffin, created by a Georgian artist.

I took my youngest son on this excursion. Interestingly, this was his second visit to the museum. He doesn't remember his first: then he was a three-month-old baby, and now he is almost fourteen.

In order to draw a line under my son's perception of this historical figure, I asked the guide to answer the question: "In general, was Stalin a positive or a negative political figure?"

This was clearly not to the guide's liking, and she answered evasively: "*I can't tell you for sure. Officially, Stalin is a negative personality, if we take into account the policy of our state. But for different people, Stalin is thought of differently. I never talk to anyone about Stalin. I don't even know what my friends, acquaintances, or neighbors think about him. We haven't had conversations about it.*"

Back home, I talked to my son, trying to see what he remembered from our museum tour. He admitted that it seemed to him as if he had visited not only Stalin's museum, but also the museum of Hitler. Have you ever heard of such a thing—a Hitler Museum in Germany?! Such a museum is simply unthinkable, be it in Germany or in Hitler's homeland in Austria! And who knows what might have happened if Hitler had won that terrible war...

Another thing that impressed my son was the story about how Stalin refused to release his son Yakov from German captivity. The Germans offered to exchange Yakov for their Field Marshal Paulus. "I won't exchange a soldier for a field marshal!" Stalin had replied decisively. *"That's the kind of monster he was. Cold as steel: sending his son to die without even thinking twice!"* my son remarked.

Who knows, maybe it's Stalin's relentless drive and almost superhuman qualities that still make some of his fellow countrymen, and even people around the world, look at him in awe. A little boy from Gori, who became someone the whole world feared—someone who opposed the West for so long, planted his agents there, and took down his enemies abroad!

Thus, Comrade Koba, unnoticed by many, has again found himself on a high pedestal—at least in modern Georgian (not to mention Russian) politics, as well as in the Orthodox Church.

"He received a country with a plow and left it with factories. He won the Great war, was an honest believer: a fair and modest person who wore the same uniform all his life!" These are the slogans of modern Orthodox conservative neo-Stalinists. This is how the main Soviet "werewolf," who refuses to stay stuck in the past, seems to be desperately reaching for the future.

The Museum of Soviet Occupation

There's another side to the "Georgia & Stalin" story that you should know. Younger, educated Georgians, particularly the city-dwellers, are acutely aware of the damage Stalin inflicted on their nation and the Soviet Empire as a whole. It is a tragic story well documented at the Museum of Soviet Occupation, on Rustaveli Avenue in Tbilisi. I visited the museum with film director Nika Bezhanishvili, whose documentary 'Northeast Wind' explores efforts by Stalin admirers in Gori to reinstate his statue in the town's main square after it was removed by Saakashvili's government.

At the museum, Nika and I examine photographs, documents, and archival footage detailing the 1921 Bolshevik overthrow of Georgia's legitimate social democratic government, forcing it into exile. The young republic was invaded and occupied by three Bolshevik armies, transforming the country into a virtual prison. We learn from the film director that the intellectual and artistic elite—orchestra conductors, poets, painters, and filmmakers—were particularly targeted for resisting Soviet propaganda. The resulting repressions were devastating: 80,000 Georgians were executed, 400,000 deported, and the entire nation was scarred by terror.

Nika points out that a more accurate and comprehensive museum of Soviet history in Georgia would result from combining the Stalin Museum in Gori and the Museum of Soviet Occupation in Tbilisi.

Georgia against Stalin

Not long after my visit to Gori, I met Giorgi Kandelaki, a historian from SovLab, who had recently edited Lasha Bughadze's 'Georgia Against Stalin.' The book, a product of meticulous research, and based on previously unseen documents, provides critical new perspectives that have thus far remained obscure to many Western academics.

SovLab is an NGO, also known as the Soviet Past Research Laboratory. It was established in 2010 by a group of historians, journalists, researchers, and civil society activists. Based in Tbilisi, its mission is to support a critical analysis of Georgia's past, including the Soviet system, and its implications on current social structures, beliefs, institutions and the state of democracy. The SovLab team also works to highlight the political, legal, and moral significance of this past.

I was curious why Stalin had become such a relevant figure in Georgia again. Giorgi explained that Georgia's failure to thoroughly confront Soviet-era crimes after the 1991 collapse of the USSR had opened the door to *"Russian disinformation warfare, which has been weaponizing the memories of the Soviet Union, and not only in Georgia."*

Giorgi characterizes the Russian narrative as *"focused on cultivating anti-Western, nativist, ethno-religious nationalism, presenting Western civilization as a danger to our souls, and the Russian world as salvation."*

In Georgia, the figure of Stalin is a key element of this strategy. Therefore, Giorgi argues, the Russian Stalin project functions as a symbol of this nationalism and a point of supposed Georgian national pride.

I wondered if Georgians discuss the Stalinist past, the purges, and their families' innocent victims.

Giorgi explains: *"There's a dichotomy. While the Great Terror of the 1930s-40s is generally well recognized, it is rarely linked to Stalin. It's perceived as a natural disaster- 'It just happened! But nobody is responsible!' Conversely, Stalin's specific crimes against Georgia largely go unrecognized."* In this context, Lasha Bughadze's Stalin book is crucial, as it contextualizes Stalin within Georgia—a subject surprisingly understudied, despite Stalin's global prominence.

According to Giorgi Kandelaki, *"Stalin's Georgian story is about clash and perpetual defeat."* He points out that the Bolsheviks were a minority in

Georgia, dominated by the Social Democrats. Stalin's political career was never embraced in his homeland. This unresolved conflict, Giorgi asserts, drove his determination to dismantle independent Georgia.

Giorgi adds that numerous archival documents prove the Soviet regime was imposed on Georgian society through the Red Army's invasion and war.

"Unlike the Baltic states in 1940, Georgia did not surrender!" he exclaims. *"It fought alone against Russia for a month, with French support in Abkhazia. The French navy even came, and Georgians retook Gagra after Tbilisi fell. It was a major war with heavy casualties. Not only was Georgia not a voluntary member of the Soviet Union, but it was an internationally recognized country destroyed by this invasion. And Stalin's role in this has been largely untold."*

I ask Giorgi to tell us a lesser-known Stalin story from the archives, specifically regarding his relationship with Georgia. He points to Lasha Bughadze's book, which concludes with Stalin's July 1921 visit to Tbilisi after the occupation. He arrived as a victor, and a town hall meeting was held with workers in a theater.

"We have numerous participant accounts of that first meeting, some from survivors evacuated by the Weimar Republic in 1922," Giorgi explains. *"Their memoirs provide a detailed picture of the dramatic event, where Stalin faced 80 questions. He began in Russian, was interrupted, and was forced to speak in Georgian. He was then overwhelmed by social democratic speakers and workers. One, Datiko Dvali, later executed in 1924, called him 'Satan!' and demanded, 'Why did you bring Russian soldiers here?'"* The meeting was a disaster for Stalin, a victory that felt like defeat in Tbilisi.

"It was his last public appearance in Tbilisi," Giorgi says. *"He returned to Georgia later, only briefly in 1926, and never in Tbilisi or publicly anywhere again. He was haunted by rejection."*

Careful examination of the archival documents shatters many Soviet narratives of Russo-Georgian friendship. In August 1924, the final major anti-Bolshevik uprising erupted in Georgia, spreading through various regions of the country. Kakutsa Cholokashvili, a national hero and military leader, played a prominent role in this uprising, through the Georgian Committee for Independence, a clandestine organization uniting various political factions, which included Mensheviks, nationalists, and others. The rebels engaged in armed clashes with the Red Army and the *Cheka* (Soviet secret police) forces. While initially successful in some areas, the uprising was ultimately crushed by the superior military power of the Soviets. The *Cheka* played a central role in the repression, targeting not only rebels, but also intellectuals, clergy, and other perceived opponents of the regime. The brutal suppression resulted in the execution of 51 out of 130 democratically elected members of the Georgian parliament, and the exile of 37, with five perishing abroad. The 1924 uprising and its aftermath remain a poignant reminder of Georgia's struggle for independence and the heavy price paid by its people under Soviet rule.

The writer Irakli Lomouri has a remarkable short story called 'Stalin in the Cellar' from the series 'Chronicles of a Parallel Georgia,' written in 2009 in the spirit of fantastical realism. The story takes place during World War II, when Moscow was occupied by the Germans, and the Japanese opened a second front in the Far East. Stalin was forced to leave the capital and hide in a secret shelter, which turned out to be the cellar of the house of a devoted Georgian Komsomol member, Maya Tskneteli. When the Japanese, Germans, and Spaniards occupied Georgia, Maya was suspected of partisan activity and summoned for questioning to find out where Stalin was hiding. Maya did not betray the leader, and she was allowed to go home. There, the leader of the people showered her with curses and reproaches for betraying the homeland: he did not believe that the occupiers had let her go so easily. Stalin called her a traitor and forced her to... hang herself in her own cellar! The story ends with Stalin's phrase: "...know, the Soviet people are invincible, because Stalin sits in every cellar!"

In 2017, Irakli told me that he was motivated to write this story by a desire to free himself from the heavy burden of the still uncomprehended Soviet history. "If we lose this historical memory and do not learn the lessons of the past, we will have no future, but will face the same twilight and terrible times that have already existed, in the era of totalitarianism," the writer claimed. "Stalin himself, of course, personally bears responsibility for what he did. But what is frightening is that the overwhelming majority of the population participated in this terror, either silently contributing through their conformism, or actively participating, becoming informers, secret agents, accomplices, and instruments of terror."

Irakli Lomouri had one very important idea, in my opinion—to create a subject in schools under the conditional name "anti-totalitarianism," without which "new generations will be an absolutely blank slate on which anything can be written," because unlearned lessons of the past inevitably lead to the repetition of terrible events. "All this alarms, oppresses, and torments me," Irakli shared with me, "because Stalin is still in everyone's cellar."

Tbilisi, May 2024

Inside the Stalin Museum in Gori

Giorgi Kandelaki presenting a book about the Georgians' troubled relationship with Joseph Stalin

The St. Nino Chapel at Paravani Lake

Chapter 16.
The Silk Road, Queen Tamar and Saint Nino

Samtskhe-Javakheti is a region with which the history of the Great Silk Road is closely linked. These regions in south-west Georgia have a special place in my heart.

Before my fateful visit to Aspindza, about which you will hear in the following pages, I had travelled to Javakheti many times. In the summer of 2011, for example, we spent a month in Bakuriani. The forest freshness of this resort, with its gently sloping mountains, our ride on the ancient "Cuckoo" train, the coolness of the shady Borjomi Gorge with its ancient villas, and an overnight stay in one of my first Georgian guesthouses near the entrance to the Borjomi-Kharagauli National Park — was an uplifting experience. I remember the day when, during a walk in the National Park, I sensed that the fabulous scenery of the mountain forest was being admired not only by myself, but also by my late father, walking beside me, for whom the mountains and the forest had always been favorite places.

When we are introduced to a region by people who know its innermost corners, several channels of perception open up simultaneously. This is what happened to me when my friends invited me to Aspindza, to the training base of the Georgian National Rugby Team. Our friend Irakli is one of the founders of this sports center, and his wife Eliso runs the Integration Center for members of national minorities and children with disabilities.

On our trip together, Javakheti truly won my heart. It was a sunny, but not yet hot, May, and when we passed the Borjomi Gorge, nature suddenly completely transformed, with narrow canyon and mountain slopes covered with dense forest dropping into spacious alpine meadows, on the hills of which, here and there, ruins of fortresses rose up, while, off in the distance, the mighty peaks reminded us of their great presence.

In Georgia, mountains can be contemplated from virtually anywhere. Seldom is there a place where majestic summits and ranges do not grace the view. And you know what I noticed? When there are mountains nearby, we ourselves involuntarily become stronger and more resilient.

The picturesque narrow road, framed on both sides by ancient trees, twists in an endless narrow ribbon. On its side, all the way to Akhaltsikhe, we come across small, old villages drowning in lush gardens, snuggled right up to the road.

Irakli is a master of making long journeys in record time: we covered 237 kilometers in just three hours, and he knew every kilometer of the road! It seemed that he could even drive it blind! On the way, he tells us about the local peculiarities and brings us up to date with the historical events that have happened on this land.

From Akhaltsikhe, the motorway runs along the Mtkvari River, making intricate zigzags. A little before reaching our destination, we stop for dinner at a cozy roadside restaurant. As we sit down in seats of honor usually reserved for the regulars, we gasp. The view from here is truly Tuscan: lush emerald hills and poplar and cypress trees growing in clusters; a spring-green landscape that makes me want to go back to my childhood and enjoy a little carefree tobogganing down those velvet slides and exult in the delight.

The tops of some mountain peaks are still covered with snow; others seem to have had their tops sliced off. Maybe up there is another, completely separate and inaccessible world, parallel to ours? I ask Irakli about it, and he replies that high up, there are indeed many alpine meadows, and there are actually country roads to explore up there too.

Rustaveli: Georgia's Legendary Poet

On the way, we had passed the village of Rustavi (not the town which is close to Tbilisi). It is said the great Georgian poet Shota Rustaveli came from here- one of many legends told about the famous man, who was much like his English counterpart William Shakespeare.

Little is known about Rustaveli. But it is no secret that his brilliant poems contain the highest concentration of wisdom and cosmic philosophy, as well as the ideals of love and friendship. And many other places in this region are connected with the poet's guiding star, Queen Tamar. The Golden Age of Georgian history happened during the reign of this outstanding woman, the "king in a skirt," seeing Samtskhe-Javakheti becoming one of

Shota Rustaveli was a 12th century Georgian poet, author of the poem 'The Knight in the Tiger's Skin,' one of the greatest works of Georgian and world literature. Biographical information about the poet is scarce. It is known that Rustaveli came from an influential and wealthy family, as he was educated at the Ikalto Academy in Kakheti, as well as in Greece. He served at the court of Queen Tamar as a treasurer (his signature can be seen on an act of 1190), which also testifies to his noble origin. Rustaveli devoted himself to literary activities, and then, towards the end of his life, he took monastic tonsure and began living as a monk in a Georgian monastery in Jerusalem. A fresco portraying him in old age is preserved there.

the most important regions in the country where this history was written.

Under this ruler, Georgia reached its greatest expanse, and peace and prosperity reigned throughout. In the Church of the Assumption of the Blessed Virgin Mary in the Vardzia Cave Monastery, one can admire one of the few images of the queen on a fresco painted during the lifetime of the great ruler.

Aspindza

In Persian, Aspindza means "shelter for travelers on the great road."

Today, life here flows unhurriedly, the old-fashioned way. Everything here, from the nature and the air to the marvellous climate and the ancient thermal springs, is conducive to renewal and resetting. The outlines of Aspindza are fascinating if you look at them from the meadow where the rugby base is located, on the other side of the Kura River, right in the floodplain, framed by mountains to the left. There is an unusual bridge crossing the river that looks like a railway bridge.

I have been visiting Aspindza and its rich surroundings on a regular basis for the past few years, yet I can't stop marvelling at the tranquil and gentle charm of the place. My favorite pastime is morning walks along the right bank of the river, which is choppy and full-flowing, the floodplain forming islands rich in flora. I always make a point of stopping on one of the town's vintage bridges and indulging in some quiet admiration of the flow of this magnificent river. In spring and early summer, the meadows are decorated with a blanket of purple flowers, and if you go a little further away, you can see that the grass is not green, but in fact purple with a yellow tinge.

This ancient town has its own sulphide and hydrogen sulphide healing springs, each with a touch of bromine. According to legend, the gods created them specifically to help people rid themselves of ailments such as gout, gynaecological diseases, psoriasis and arthritis. You can find the baths in an old pavilion near the sports center. After a regular visit to this spa, the body is rejuvenated, and balance is restored. No wonder some people come here for treatment even from abroad. I once conducted an experiment by taking selfies before and after my five-day treatment in the Aspindza springs. The result impressed not only me: as if by magic, five to seven years were written off!

The Battle of Aspindza and Another Russian Betrayal

A remarkable moment in Russian-Georgian relations is connected with Aspindza. Instead of a retelling, I will cite an excerpt from historian Donald

Rayfield's book 'Georgia. Crossroads of Empires. A History of Three Thousand Years':

"When Catherine II started an open war with Turkey, she declared patronage and military support to Imereti (the kingdom of, ed.). She wrote to Voltaire that she was happy to open a fourth front against the Ottomans, but that Imereti, compared to the Danube, Greece and Crimea, was a purely symbolic battlefield. King Erekle (King of Kartli-Kakheti, ed.) was also ready to fight the Turks as soon as the Russians promised to give reinforcements. On 21 May 1769, Solomon (King of Imereti, ed.) went to Tbilisi to discuss a joint campaign. Solomon wanted to crush his rebellious feudal lords with Russian arms, take the Black Sea coastal towns from the Turks, and drive the last Turk out of Western Georgia; most of all, King Erekle wanted to regain Samtskhe, suppress the Lezgins and expand southeastern Kakheti into the Caucasian foothills. Russia, however, had quite different goals: to turn the Black Sea from an Ottoman lake into a Russian lake: neither salvation, unification, nor even annexation of Georgia was yet on the agenda" (Donald Rayfield, Georgia. Crossroads of Empires. A History of Three Thousand Years).

Donald Rayfield further noted that *"of the 20,000 Russian soldiers that the Georgian tsars dreamed of, only 400 came in 1769, with cannons and officers under the command of General Totleben and Anton Mouravov (a native-born Georgian)."* Totleben, who had been sentenced to death for passing military secrets to the Prussians, was granted a stay of execution thanks to Catherine, who held the Prussians in high regard. Rayfield described Totleben as *"an arrogant, conniving, and incompetent general"* who treated the experienced Georgian kings as though they were *"savage natives."*

The Russian forces were met by Erekle's officers at the Jvari Pass, and by Solomon's soldiers on the Imeretian border. In October, a joint Russian-Imeretian-Kartelian army laid siege to the Turks at the border fortress of Shorapani. However, after four days, Totleben retreated, citing a lack of ammunition. Rayfield notes that *"in March 1770, Totleben returned, bringing another 800 soldiers and three cannons."* At this point, he informs us, Prince Dadiani of Samegrelo joined the alliance, but Totleben chose to move up the Kura (i.e. Mtkvari) River to attack Atskuri in Samtskhe, rather than head towards Imereti. He further ignored Erekle's advice to strike Akhaltsikhe and surprise the pasha. The delay allowed the pasha time to fortify Atskuri. Despite the lack of Russian support, Erekle achieved a remarkable victory near Atskuri, at Aspindza, seeing him drive the defeated Ottoman forces into the swollen Kura River, where many drowned. Totleben retreated once again, especially when the Turks sent reinforcements from Dagestan. Rayfield added that Totleben *"did not even think of attacking"* and, instead, *"having plotted the overthrow of Erekle, he forced local feudal lords to swear allegiance to the Russian Empress."*

Tmogvi Fortress

The Samtskhe-Javakheti region is rich in fortresses, and, while the majority of these unique defense structures stand in ruins, they are still easily capable of impressing the imagination.

One such citadel is the Tmogvi Fortress. Having seen it for the first time from afar while traveling along the road from Aspindza to Vardzia, I got the urge to explore Tmogvi from the inside. I have to admit that the legend about this fortress played not the least role in my obsession.

The Legend of Tmogvi

Today's village of Tmogvi was a well-known town in the old days. Its ruler lived in the impregnable Tmogvi Fortress together with his beautiful wife and the whole family. One day, the fortress was besieged by the troops of the Kyzylbash (lit. "Red-headed," Turkic nomadic tribes, later a Turkic nickname for Persians). For seven years, they did not lift their siege, and yet the fortress remained as impregnable as ever. Once, it is said, its garrison mockingly poured freshly whipped buttermilk on the heads of the enemies as a sign that the besieged did not lack a thing for being isolated.

One day, the head of the Tatar army spotted the beautiful wife of the ruler on the ramparts. The Pasha sent a secret intermediary to her with a message: *"Your doom is imminent. Think of salvation! Help me to seize the fortress and I will make you my wife."* The woman, long tired of being locked up, told the messenger to return to the Pasha with her reply: *"At (such a time), I will get the keys and open the gates of the fortress for you. Come in with your army and take me away."* At the appointed time, the Pasha threw the whole army into the attack, and the gates of the fortress were opened. Having taken the stronghold, the Pasha killed the guards and destroyed the entire garrison. The ruler of the fortress selflessly resisted the enemy until the very end: when he saw that the enemy was winning, he threw himself on horseback from the rampart into the abyss. His wife took refuge in one of the rooms and waited for the Pasha to appear. The Pasha

In the Russian empire the term "Tatars" was historically used to encompass various Turkic-speaking peoples within the empire. This could include groups in Crimea, Siberia, and other regions. The term's origins are linked to the Mongol Empire and the Golden Horde, which had a profound impact on the region. Over time, "Tatar" became associated with various Turkic populations, often those with a Muslim identity.

ordered his men to bring the widow of the ruler to him, summoned his retinue and the whole army, and said to them:

"I demand a completely honest answer. You'll lose your head if you dare to lie to me. Was this woman's husband greater than me in courage and looks?"

All were forced to unanimously affirm the truth.

"The ruler of Tmogvi surpassed thee in beauty and valor," they said. *"He was equal to five men like you. In nothing could you have surpassed him."*

"Indeed, you are correct," the Pasha replied. *"How could I ever have measured up to him? And to this most valiant of men, she proved faithless, showing utter disregard for his entire force. What should I expect from her? And what do you say to this?"* He asked, turning to the woman.

"What can I say? I have betrayed my husband, my people and my country, so kill me quickly," the woman replied.

The Pasha swung his saber and sliced off her head. Ever since, the fortress near the village of Tmogvi has been named *Damkali*, which means "Kill me" in Georgian.

The above tale was recorded by G. Gogoladze in 1936 in Baraleti village, Southern Georgia (Narrator B. Gogoladze. Published: Nar. wisdom. III, p. 270. Source: 'Georgian Folk Legends and Tales,' Moscow, Nauka, 1973 – p.367).

The majestic view of the citadel perched high above the Mtkvari River, even in its almost ruined state, makes a powerful impression. I had been warned that, during an earthquake, part of the mountain on which the citadel stood had collapsed, making it difficult and sometimes unsafe to walk through the ruins. In addition, snakes have taken a fancy to the area. But none of these warnings could relieve me of my insistence on seeing the mighty stronghold at close range.

To get to the fortress, we had to cross the river on a narrow bridge (not for the faint-hearted) and then climb up a gravel road leading to a narrow and serpentine mountain path. About halfway up, we left the car and walked the rest of the way. The wind was blowing hard that day, almost knocking us off our feet. We made it to the narrow isthmus connecting the fortress with the mountain, and then stopped- we didn't dare cross to the Tmogvi side. The stinging feeling of annoyance from the unfinished enterprise stayed with me for a long time after that, and it wasn't until a year later that we, led by Irakli, managed to climb Tmogvi at last!

As you climb up the remains of the fortress where it hangs from the mountain, you have to be extremely careful not to stumble and fall into the abyss. But when you get that cosmic view of the turbulent river winding its way through the mountains far below, it becomes clear that all the risks have paid off in full.

Tmogvi Fortress is said to have once boasted several churches and even a secret underground passage leading to the river. We never got to explore many of the ruins because they are on extremely steep ground. Even so, we had every reason to be triumphant that day! Dreams come true. The most important thing is to stay focused and not waste time on little things. Cheers to the triumph of a dream realized!

Saro Village and Fortress

Samtskhe-Javakheti is a region rich in enigmas, with hidden treasures at every step. The thrill of discovering them is intensified by the fact that these places remain largely untouched by mass tourism. It's a haven for those who truly understand its depths — and that's how I will always perceive this land. In the south-western part of Georgia, there are many structures of unknown, megalithic origin, among them the cyclopean fortresses of Saro and Abuli. When Irakli first brought me to the village of Saro, and we climbed up to one of the high plateaus, I had the feeling I had been transported to the early Christian era: squat earth houses made of huge, moss-covered boulders, a romantic church and convent, and stones scattered everywhere- building material from a once majestic fortress, about which almost nothing is known today.

Time is nonexistent here: unknown wizards have sealed this place in time forever.

Have you ever been blessed to feel the resonance of humanity's primordial energies? If not, a pilgrimage to Saro is a must! This land radiates the power and wisdom of vanished epochs.

Vanis Kvabebi

Javakheti is rich in cave monasteries. Vardzia is the most famous of them, and many people know it. It is a monastery complex which consists of a network of caves, tunnels, churches, and a defensive wall, all carved into a cliff face. But few have heard of Vanis Kvabebi, which is four centuries older than Vardzia. In 1089, an earthquake destroyed the central part of the monastery. Two centuries later, the earthquake that destroyed Vardzia and the Tmogvi Fortress once again seriously damaged the complex of Vanis Kvabebi.

There used to be a nunnery; now monks live there. The territory has yet to be turned into a paid tourist destination, and that is why the place is so quiet and peaceful.

One Easter holiday, we walked to the foot of the mountain into which the monastery is carved. The walk up required some stamina, as the slope is very steep, but the effort was worth it: there was not a soul around, and a ringing silence. At the monastery, we met two monks and some rabbits hopping peacefully on the lawn.

Unfortunately, we were unable to explore the monastery caves and tunnels of Vanis Kvabebi. Shortly before our arrival, there was a rockfall, and the caves were closed for safety reasons. Instead, we spent time in a picturesque meadow, enjoying panoramic views of the Lesser Caucasus Mountains, feeding rabbits, and finding our peace of mind.

Vardzia is not just a monastery; it's a complex of caves carved into the Erusheti Mountain, creating a multi-tiered "city." It features hundreds of cave rooms, including churches, chapels, living quarters, storage areas, and even wine cellars. It was primarily built in the 12th century, during the reigns of King Giorgi III and his daughter Queen Tamar. It was designed to provide shelter for thousands of people during times of invasion. The complex showcases impressive rock-cut architecture, with intricate tunnels, staircases, and terraces connecting the various caves. The location of Vardzia offers stunning views of the surrounding landscape.

Places as uniquely tranquil and meditatively blessed as Vanis Kvabebi are a true rarity on this Earth. We found ourselves unexpectedly overcome with a gentle envy for the monks who call this place home.

Khinkali with Goose-Meat Filling

Javakheti is not only a place of ancient monuments, but also of an unusual cuisine, with foods that are not widely eaten in other regions of Georgia. The local menu includes a wide variety of wild vegetables and fruits, such as wild asparagus and many other gifts of the forest.

In Javakheti's forests, you can find fruit trees: plum, mulberry, pear and dogwood, whose fruits are used to make exquisite and flavorful fruit vodka. As Irakli explained to me, the locals, fleeing from invaders' raids in the forests, used to take saplings with them so they could harvest apples, plums and pears if they were forced into a long stay in exile.

As Javakheti is the cradle of Georgian statehood, and Georgia is the wine cradle of mankind, it was in this area that a significant number of endemic grape varieties once grew. The riverstone terraces along the entire road from Akhaltsikhe to Aspindza testify to that fact even now. However, winemaking was forgotten here for several centuries after Muslims destroyed the vineyards during the Mongol, Persian and Turkish invasions. Following the collapse of the USSR in 1991, the vineyards began to be revived little by little, and today there are a number of enthusiasts in this region who have managed to restore many of the ancient grape varieties.

Irakli took us to Khizabavra, a small highland village, to visit his friends. There, Keti, the wife of his friend Gela, taught us the art of cooking a local speciality: stewed *khinkali* with dried goose meat. In Javakheti, goose hams are prepared in autumn, and the meat is cured in the fresh air all winter until spring.

It's not easy to mold those tiny *khinkali* parcels, which look much like Italian ravioli, around the small slice of goose ham you must pack into each one. After molding, we drop the *khinkali* into a large pot, with a little water and ghee, to stew until ready. I will leave you to discover the taste of this dish for yourself. I will simply say this: the culinary delights of different regions of Georgia can easily compete with the sophistication of world-renowned Italian cuisine!

The Way of Saint Nino

The path of Equal Apostle Saint Nino from Cappadocia to the old capital city of Mtskheta passed through Samtskhe-Javakheti and by Lake Paravani. As such, every year, on the 1st of June, the Feast of Ninoba is celebrated in Georgia, commemorating the arrival of the saint.

The Akhalkalaki—Tsalka—Tbilisi road is a pleasure for all the senses, especially if you make this journey in late spring or early summer, during the blooming season. The high-mountain plateau is like a colorful carpet, one that is woven of patterns blazing under the sun: scarlet poppies and many alpine flowers of bright yellow and violet. The villages are reminiscent of Saro, with unusual dwellings half buried in the ground and covered with turf.

Standing in the village of Poka, where St Nino's convent is located, it is hard to believe that we are still in Georgia: this harsh region is more reminiscent of Canada or northern Russia. In winter, the temperature in these places can easily drops below 20 degrees centigrade. Trees do not grow here: it is too high and cold for them, and it is not for nothing that this region is called the "Georgian Siberia."

In the middle of this fantastic lunar landscape is a vast lake fringed with emerald grass, behind which a ridge of snow-covered mountains rises, while fluffy clouds, reflected, seem to have drowned in the lake. Not so long ago, a large Bronze Age settlement and burial site was found at the bottom of this, the largest body of water in Georgia, while household utensils from the Hellenistic era had been well preserved thanks to the water. Scientists have yet to give an answer to the question of what could have caused the demise of the ancient settlement.

A solitary chapel graces the lakeshore, set against a canvas of sky, where clouds engage in a playful contest of architectural whimsy. All of this draws you deep into history, and also into the secret depths of your own soul. Here, it's easily to feel the ever-present sense of the divine.

Tbilisi, June 2020

The Megalithic-era Saro Fortress

Monks in the Vanis Kvabebi Monastery

An other-worldly landscape in Samtskhe-Javakheti, close to Paravani Lake

*Keti's khinkali mastery: Goose-meat delights from
Khizabavra*

In their distinctive national clothing,
Dukhobor women gather after a communal prayer service in the sirotskoye

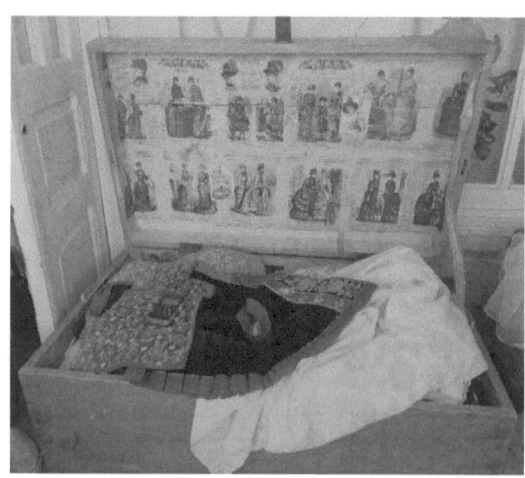

For Marina, a cher-
ished treasure is the
traditional attire of
the Dukhobors

Chapter 17.
The Dukhobors: A Handful of Russians on Georgian Soil

A friend of mine recently described Georgia in this way: *"This country is much more inside than outside."* And this is true, because Georgia is the cradle of many ethnicities and nationalities, people of different faiths, including representatives of all kinds of religious minorities.

In addition to Caucasian peoples, Germans, Estonians, Poles and Russians have long lived here. Since 1845, two Russian religious groups — Dukhobors and Molokans — have found shelter here. Like the German Protestants, about which you will learn a little later on in this book, the Russian "apostates" sought refuge in the Caucasus from persecution in their homeland.

Over time, the denomination of these "spiritual Christians" began to challenge the foundations of the Russian Orthodox Church, and started gaining more and more followers. The official church and secular authorities responded with brutal pogroms and the persecution of apostates. Count Leo Tolstoy spoke in defense of the Dukhobors and Molokans, publishing a letter in the Times newspaper protesting their persecution and comparing it to the persecution of the first Christians.

Under Tsar Alexander I, the Dukhobors and Molokans were allowed to move to the southern regions of Russia, including Crimea, where they were not persecuted. But under Tsar Nicholas I, the Dukhobors and Molokans lost favor with the authorities and were forced out into the South Caucasus. Between 1841 and 1845, five thousand Dukhobors moved to the south of Georgia, to the region of Javakheti, which neighbors Armenia and Turkey. They founded their villages in the surroundings of Lake Paravani, naming them Bogdanovka, Spasovka, Orlovka, Gorelovka, Ulyanovka, Efremovka, Kalmykovo, Troitskoe, as well as Vladimirovka, Tambovka, and Rodionovka. These villages have survived to this day, although far fewer people live there now than before.

One beautiful summer morning, my friend Elena, a photographer, and I were traveling to a land called "Dukhoboria." It was the beginning of August. The Dukhobors had invited us to stay with them in Spasovka.

The Journey to the Dukhobors

Javakheti is a high mountainous region, harsh and beautiful. The road through Tsalka is serpentine, with an altitude that rises almost impercepti-bly. After the ascent, our way lies along the spacious meadows and pas-tures of the high-mountain plateau. At the top, there is no sense of height, although we have climbed to 2000 meters above sea level. All around lie boundless expanses, a sea of colors and smells, fragrant fields; the rivers Khrami and Kstsia industriously making their way through the tall, lush grasses. The mountains are only visible from afar: in the embrace of clouds, they fringe the horizon in undulating zigzags.

In Tbilisi and its environs, the merciless sun has already burned away everything that was green. But the magic month of May still reigns at this altitude: everything that can blossom blooms at once! It's as if some magi-cian has managed to break the fields into colorful squares and rectangles: there is a sense of something cosmic everywhere. Where else did these rich scatterings of black obsidians, which we see every now and then along the road, come from?

The almost total absence of people is striking. Wilderness. A deserted land. Only occasionally on the road one meets shepherds with huge herds of cows and sheep, which they lead to one of the mountain lakes, of which there are many in this volcanic region: Madatapa, Sagamo, Paravani, Han-chali....

Before reaching the village of Ninotsminda, formerly Bogdanovka, we cross a bridge and turn left towards Spasovka. Our way leads us past villages with wide central streets and squat old houses, which often have earthen roofs. Such roofs help to keep those living there warm in harsh winters. These regions are not rich in gardens: Only the hardiest trees and people survive at this altitude.

The nature and spirit here are majestic and harsh. In winter, life here is by no means a fairytale, and it takes a tremendous effort to survive and feed oneself. Plus, the road to Akhalkalaki via Tsalka is often closed due to heavy snowfalls, leaving the villages completely cut off from the world.

On the way, Elena and I become absorbed in admiring the landscapes and forget about the time. Anna and Nikolai, the parents of an acquaint-ance of mine from Tbilisi, are waiting for us in Spasovka!

Russian Highlanders in Georgian mountains

Anna and Nikolai Kurbatov are monumental personalities. Tall, statu-
esque, with a proud posture; any artist would dream of having such mod-
els! We were especially struck by Nikolai, a big, sturdy man with bottomless, sky-blue eyes that radiate kindness.

In the yard, there are outbuildings: a barn, a chicken coop, a cow
shed. Chickens are running everywhere. Three hunting dogs are pulling at
their chains. In the middle of the yard there is a tap for drinking water.

Anna is busy with the household chores, and the first thing she does
is to feed us properly. She invites us into the kitchen, which is separate
from the house. It is modern, except for a small wood-fired iron stove in
the middle. Bread and *khachapuri* come out of this oven with an exceptional,
unforgettable flavor.

The Kurbatovs call us to the table, where new potatoes, vegetable
salad, braided cheese *chechili*, homemade sour cream, lush bread, and fish
from the local river await. After that hearty lunch, we drink tea with rasp-
berry jam and have a heart-to-heart talk. This is how the chronicle of local
life opens to us page by page.

The Dukhobors in a Time of Change

It so happens that the Kurbatovs in Spasovka are a national minority, the
only Russian family in the village. During the Soviet era, most of the villagers did not know Georgian, and it was difficult for Russian-speakers to
navigate the new realities of independent Georgia. In the early 1990s, almost all the villagers left for their historical homeland, Russia. Only the
Kurbatovs and Armenians remained in the village, having lived there since
the 19th century: after Javakheti was annexed to the Russian Empire, Christians from Turkey were settled here, while Muslims were evicted to the
Ottoman Empire.

After the Dukhobors headed back to Russia, the village was not left
empty: a group Adjarians, whose high-altitude villages had been swept
away by a land slide, were brought to Spasovka. They inherited the empty
houses of the Russian settlers. *"As if the civil war wasn't enough, and here we
have new neighbors, Muslims!"* Anna says, recalling those turbulent times
with horror.

*"At first, we were terrified of them. We'd heard they were bringing former
prisoners,"* she said. *"The men arrived first, taking over the empty houses. When
my friend and I went to the farm, the Adjarian men stared, clearly surprised to see
us working with uncovered heads, a stark contrast to their own women's attire.*

We started out avoiding them, but our fear lessened as we realized they weren't dangerous. Eventually, their families came too. The Muslim women, fully covered, were immediately put to work on the farm, as labor was scarce."

Time, with its power to both heal and reconcile, brought an unexpected friendship into Anna's life. *"My neighbor, Natela, had poor eyesight and couldn't navigate the walk home from the farm alone after dark. Her husband asked if I would accompany her,"* Anna remembers. *"And so began our daily ritual: I would fetch Natela, and together we would go to work, and at five, when darkness had already fallen, I would guide her home. For three years, we walked hand-in-hand like that."*

Before the collapse of the USSR, the Dukhobors worked on collective farms and heated their houses with coal and steam. Nikolai managed to work in various positions. He has done a lot of things in life, even artificial insemination of cows! But hunting and fursmithing are what really won his heart, he says.

During our August visit, we see the Dukhobors are in full-swing as they prepare for winter—haymaking and preparing *kizyak* (winter fuel). Every household piles huge mountains of *kizyak* in the yard. It is too expensive to use firewood, and there is almost no forest anywhere to source from. To feed themselves, each family keeps many cows, sometimes more than 10, but almost no one makes cheese for sale: they give their milk to the local farm. Anna works on the farm as a milkmaid, and in her spare time she also milks the neighbor's cows. She has strong, hardworking hands, and an even stronger character.

Gorelovka

After lunch, Anna takes us to Gorelovka to visit her relative Marina Balabanova, also a milkmaid. Anna and Marina are surprisingly similar: both are stately, russet-haired and bright-eyed Russian beauties. They could be mistaken for dancers!

Even though Marina has a house full of guests (her son and his family are visiting from Russia, having not been here for two years due to the pandemic), she is willing to carve out time for us.

We can't wait to admire her treasures, which are stored in a large traveling trunk, inside papered with old newspapers with pictures of fashionistas from the early 20th century. Marina inherited the chest from her mother-in-law. In it, she carefully stores her Dukhobor outfits: black fitted jackets (*sibirochkas*) with colorful lining, similarly fitted colored waistcoats with black velvet lining, bright woolen skirts in stripes and checks, long white cambric underdresses trimmed with braid and sewing, stockings, aprons, caps, scarves, boots and shoes.

The Dukhobors' speech is very pleasant and soft to the ear. They often use diminutive and affectionate suffixes: for example, when they talk about one of their saints, they call him *Petyushka*. The Dukhobors also have many very special words. They call a prayer service by the verb "to bow," towels as "*utirochki.*" They call a blanket a "*ryadno,*" and an apron a "curtain."

Marina clearly delights in every outfit she wears, whether for a family celebration or a religious service. "*I adore our clothes!*" she exclaims, her voice filled with warmth. "*Putting them on transforms you; you feel a sense of purity, a connection to our heritage, to something deeply cherished.*"

Despite her love for the garments, Marina is reluctant to be photographed wearing them. She was deeply upset when a visitor once shared photos of her in Dukhobor dress on social media without permission; she felt as though she had been turned into a spectacle. Marina herself avoids social media, unwilling to see the Dukhobor tradition trivialized for fleeting online attention.

The Dukhobor community maintains a firm conviction regarding the imperative to preserve the sanctity of their culturally rich traditions, challenging the growing trend toward superficial thinking we see around us in today's world.

Marina finds solace in sewing and embroidery, though she rarely has the time. Some of her most treasured garments were crafted by her grandmothers from fabrics passed down through the generations. But Marina's inheritance extends beyond material possessions; her grandmothers also bequeathed her their faith, a remarkable legacy given the prevailing atheism of her youth.

It is noteworthy that the Dukhobors' church holidays coincide with Orthodox holidays, but the Dukhobors do not go to church and do not confess to priests, because they believe that a person does not need intermediaries to communicate with the divine. In addition, the Dukhobors do not make the sign of the cross, do not worship icons, and their saints are their own wise men who once lived in their community.

Among the Dukhobors, elders and parents are always held in high esteem. They refer to their father and mother as 'little old man' and 'little old woman,' or 'dad' and 'nanny.'

I can't resist asking the question: what was Marina's dream when she was young, what did she want to become? In response, she smiles enigmatically and confesses: "*I dreamed of dancing! But, to do that, you had to enrol in a club, go there regularly. We were never asked what we wanted to be before.*

Our old people used to decide such questions for us. I was married right after grad-uating school."

Marina has two sons and a daughter. So far, only one of the sons is married and has children of his own: the other two children have not yet started their own families.

A note of bitterness enters Marina's voice as she says, *"My son, sadly, has gone to Russia. In the old days, if a family had two sons, one would remain on the family land, and the other would build his own home nearby. Families were close-knit; five sons would work together, raise their children together. It was only later that they began to disperse. There's such power in being together! As the sayings go, 'One is not a warrior in the field,' and 'Together, we are stronger.'"*

The Sirotskoye

From Marina's house, we took a walk to the sirotskoye, a former orphan-age. Founded by the Kalmykov family, who are revered as saints here, to-day the sirotskoye is used as the community hall and the Dukhobor equiv-alent of a church.

Near Gorelovka there is a special cemetery, called in Russian *mogilki*, where the graves of Dukhobor saints are located. On the saints' birthdays, people gather for general services and remember their elders. The ceme-tery, like the *sirotskoye*, is a sacred place for the Dukhobor.

At one time, the sirotskoye sat on a large plot of land, where the main buildings of the Dukhobor community were located. After the Russian Revolution, that land was taken away from them, and the buildings were converted into a kindergarten and collective farm warehouses. Some of the Dukhobor community's property was returned to the Dukhobors after the collapse of the USSR, and one building now serves as a club and an Arme-nian school.

What remains of the original community is the prayer house and the Dukhobor museum — both smart white houses with green shutters, balco-nies and doors painted in Russian patterns. It has recently been renovated, and everything is sparkling brightly.

Community houses are essentially large huts with thick walls and low ceilings. Each room has embroidered towels, or *utirochki*, on the walls, while a traditional Russian stove is obligatory.

"In the winter, it gets awfully cold here and we have to burn more fuel," Marina tells us. *"When it snows, we have snowstorms, but we still have our work to do. Even if we don't want to, we have to. Before, we used to walk to work, now they drive us there. But if there's a snowstorm, we need to go on foot, sometimes up to our waists in snow. We had such a blizzard once in winter, everything was*

covered! We cleared it, but what's the point? It just snows again! We still came on Christmas Eve to pray, though, despite the huge snowdrifts in the streets, and we were all dressed up beautifully for the holiday."

In the past, there was not enough room for everyone in the spacious prayer house for the holidays, and people had to stand in the corridor, she tells me. But times have changed: many Dukhobors have left for Russia, losing their sense of Dukhobor community. Only those who received a strong forging in the family continue to live in harmony with their Dukhobor traditions and faith. Some of the returnees have converted to Orthodoxy, and, in Javakheti, there are no more than 500 Dukhobors left.

Prayer Service in the Sirotskoye

The next morning, Elena and I were allowed to attend a Dukhobor prayer service.

At six in the morning, it's only eight degrees, though this is not surprising considering the altitude we are at. The air is fresh and crystal clear.

Before entering the large room of the community hut, we take off our shoes and then quietly go in to where the service is happening. There are no priests. On a long bench in the prayer room sit four women in Dukhobor attire, their palms on their knees. One after another, they read the psalms-instructions written in verse by the saints on how to live in harmony with the will of the Lord. After the reading, the women sing their songs, and when finished, they rise, bow to each other, and wish each other well.

The service was not long. If more people had come, it would have lasted longer, as in a Dukhobor service, the psalms should be recited by every believer present.

After the prayer service, we go out into the courtyard to warm ourselves in the sun. The silence is adorned by the chirping of birds. It is warm and blissful. A sacrament has happened. I want to tuck these subtle sensations away safe in my memory box.

The women come out onto the threshold of the hut. Three of them are elderly, one is very young. Now it is time to learn about the history of these people and the subtleties of the Dukhobor faith.

"Who wrote the marvellous texts of the Dukhobor psalms?" I ask. Tatiana, a venerable elderly woman, eagerly explains:

"They were clever people, our Dukhobors. The psalms were taken from King David's Psalter, and our saints compiled them. I know forty psalms, both long and short. In our family, we know them all."

We are told that no bell calls believers to the divine service, and the sign of the cross, and the pectoral cross itself, are also superfluous. Tatiana says:

"The cross is upon me, the cross is within me, the cross is before me, the Lord God is with me! We do not wear a physical cross, for it is the work of human hands. It is not our custom. We pray to God from the depths of our hearts. If you bear a cross, you should be, it's almost frightening to say, flawless: You should become like God! But we are all sinners on earth, for we sin when, for example, we think evil thoughts. So why wear a cross at all? There are those who kill and steal, and yet wear a cross. Therefore, God is within me, God is before me."

How do the Dukhobors themselves understand their faith?

"We are spiritual warriors!" Tatiana states plainly. *"We pray without a mediator, in solitude, with truth and reverence, humility and love."*

These days, especially in cities, there are too many distractions from communion with the divine. How can we not lose touch with the higher authorities? Wise Tatiana knows the answer: *"It is not only in the city, it happens here too, because we are often blinded by the other world. If I need to pray, I have to be alone, in solitude. In prayer, I ask God to direct my thoughts. And still, it happens that I get distracted by worldly affairs. It is difficult to rid oneself of unnecessary thoughts, but it must be done! It is possible only in solitude. They say that when we are distracted from prayer, it is Satan who disturbs us. May God help us!"*

We slowly wander out towards the big gate. On the way, the second woman, Nyura, remembers that there used to be a bust of Tsar Alexander I in the courtyard of the community. On the monument was written: "To the Pious Alexander." The Dukhobors consider this Tsar to be the Dukhobors' intercessor.

"The three regions where the Dukhobors lived, Smolensk, Ryazan and Tambov, united and asked the Tsar to exile us to good lands in the Zaporozhye region and Melitopol. But when the local people there began to join the Dukhobor community, the priests came to resent that they were losing their parish, and started to denounce us, and so we had to leave and move here. It was hard for us, of course," Nyura says.

So many sorrows and needs, so many moves! Nevertheless, the Dukhobors rarely used weapons, and only in self-defense when the Turks raided the area and they had to fight back.

"Which land do the Dukhobors consider their homeland?" I wonder.

"We have two homelands: the land of our ancestors and the land of our birth," Tatiana answers. *"We do not wish to be considered foreigners in Russia, but rather to remain nestled among these peaceful mountains. And that is how it*

has come to pass." This is not the way it worked out for everyone. The difficult life forced many to look for a new place in the sun. Some Dukhobors left for the ocean, others returned to their historical homeland.

Tatiana's granddaughter, Tatiana, or Tanya, the youngest of the women present, is only 22 years old. She also knows the psalms, thanks to her grandmother's upbringing, and recited them at this prayer service. But now Tanya is only a guest in Gorelovka: she came to visit her grandmother from Tula, in Russia, where she has been living with her parents and studying to be a lawyer for 12 years.

"In Russia, I have nowhere to go for prayer services, so I pray by myself at home. But when I am here, I breathe easier, because my real homeland is this little piece of land. My soul is purified here," Tanya tells me.

We say goodbye to the wise Russian women, a handful of Russians on Georgian soil. Along the wide country road, where storks have nested on almost every post, the Dukhobor women, side by side, slowly walk away from us towards the warm sun.

Tbilisi, November 2021

The Abastumani Observatory, once an elite Soviet scientific community

Chapter 18.
Abastumani. In Love with the Stars

We humans have an inherent attachment to all things earthly, and many of us actively seek beauty on earth. However, there are those among us for whom the source of beauty and inspiration is in the sky. Day after day, such people look up at the sky, devoting their lives to stars, planets and distant galaxies. They are called astronomers, and they live and think differently from mere mortals: their brains programed for unreachable distances.

This story is about one of the oldest observatories in the former USSR, located high above the town of Abastumani, in central south-western Georgia. It is administratively part of the Samtskhe-Javakheti region, but exists completely separate from it.

The beginnings of the observatory date to the time when Grand Duke George, brother of Russian Emperor Nicholas II, was on holiday in Abastumani being treated for tuberculosis. At the same time, the court astronomer of the royal family, Sergey Glazenap, was looking for a suitable place to build a new astronomical research station. Abastumani caught his eye, and he built there the first mountain observatory in the Russian Empire.

At first, it was a temporary observatory tower, in which he spent a year making 664 observations and taking the measurements of double stars. Glazenap realized that elsewhere on Earth it would have taken him up to five years to make such observations, and he was much aided by the fact that Abastumani has a special climate- very transparent air, which is most favorable for astronomical research. Indeed, no place like Abastumani could be found anywhere else in the entire Russian Empire. An article about Glazenap's observations was published in 1904, and attracted the attention of foreign scientists, and so it was decided to build a full-fledged observatory on the spot. The First World War and the revolution of 1917 put such plans on the backburner until the 1920s, when, under the Soviet regime, the question of building a Soviet astrophysical observatory arose again. It was then that the observations of the tsarist astronomer came to mind.

In 1932, construction of the astronomical research station began. Initially, the observatory was located in the village of Abastumani itself, but later it was moved up the Kanobili Mountain (1650 m above sea level), which is characterized by the most transparent and stable atmosphere.

During its existence, two comets, a number of minor planets, six supernovae, 17 planetary nebulae, three-star clusters and many emission-line stars have been discovered through its telescopes.

Preparing for the Trip

To be honest, before traveling to Abastumani, I was a little nervous. This often happens to me in anticipation of interesting meetings, but in this particular case, I knew my astronomical knowledge was rather poor, and one of the programs I was going there to prepare was intended for the scientific editorial office of Radio Austria-1. It is no small responsibility to tell listeners about a subject that I am not much familiar with!

I knew I needed to be particularly thorough in this endeavor. First, I decided to talk to the former director of the Abastumani Observatory, Giorgi Javakhishvili, in Tbilisi. He is a fantastic storyteller, able to explain the most complicated things simply and easily. Giorgi told me the glorious history of the "scientific town on the mountain," as astronomers lovingly call their research center.

In Soviet times, he said, scientists of many different nationalities lived and worked at the observatory. It was considered a prestigious place, and it was not easy to get a job there. The scientists and their assistants, as well as their families (totaling about 450 people) lived in the scientific campus and belonged to the very top of the Soviet elite.

The scientists were most dedicated. Giorgi tells me about one of them, Academician Rolan Kiladze: "Kiladze wore the same trainers all the time, in both summer and winter. He had no time to think about anything else but his formulas! Until his death, he lived only for his work."

Kiladze made many discoveries, Giorgi says, and was the winner of many prizes, which is probably why he was not allowed to travel abroad until 1991, lest he divulge his knowledge to enemies of the Union. Kiladze's story was very sad, as it also turned out that his parents had been killed during Stalin's time.

Once, there were 15 telescopes in Abastumani, but now only a few of them are in working order. Most of them are mechanical, which is why the scientists still live a nocturnal lifestyle: *"Imagine, be it summer or winter, as soon as a 'good sky' appears, my colleagues and I get that nervous tic: 'Why are you sitting at home? If the sky is good and you're not watching, you might miss something very important!'"* Giorgi jokes.

Not everyone can become an astronomer, just as not everyone has the nack for being a programmer or mathematician.

"Astronomers are fans of their work; they are not completely normal," Giorgi says. *"To be an astronomer, you must be a little bit crazy. Instead of sleeping at home at night in a cozy bed, you go and observe. But if you're that crazy about it, you're guaranteed a job that will give you a lifetime of joy. I can't put into words the happiness that astronomy gives me!"*

Giorgi has particular favorites he likes to observe, among them the Orion Nebula: *"It's a very beautiful nebula. Sometimes I work all night, and when I finish my observing program in the morning, I turn my telescope and just look at Orion. It's such a fascinating feeling! And I'm immensely happy when I find some new detail in my observations."*

When I learned that Giorgi not only works at the observatory but also teaches at the university, I was genuinely happy. If people like him are at the head of this science, the good old traditions will surely have a worthy continuation.

Old-Timers

After meeting Giorgi Javakhishvili, I started searching for those whose lives had been connected with this research station. It was through social media that I met Olga Sova, the daughter of an astronomer. Her childhood was spent at the Abastumani observatory. Engineer Alexander Avsajanishvili, or Shurik, as he is called by his acquaintances and friends, lived at the observatory for 10 years in the eighties, and worked in a research group studying the middle layers of the atmosphere. Shurik was an avid tourist, Olga tells me, and, together with children's and youth groups, and with his daughter in tow, he explored the full 30 kilometers of the surroundings of the observatory.

Olga and Shurik offered to accompany me on a trip to Abastumani. Olga traveled ahead with her husband and four children. Her family still had a flat in Abastumani village, which now has no more than 110 permanent residents. Shurik also has a flat on the territory of the observatory, and he drove me to Abastumani himself, via Borjomi and Akhaltsikhe, in his old Niva.

The Temple Village of Science

We arrive at the observatory late in the afternoon. *"This is our observatory! Welcome to observatory land! We are at an altitude of 1603 to 1704 meters,"* Shurik says in introduction.

After dropping our things at Shurik's flat, we headed to Olga's house, where we are met by her entire extended family. It was cold in their flat.

There has been no central heating in observatory houses since the 1990s and, today, people still heat their homes with wood stoves.

Olga also has her uncle and aunt visiting her. They live permanently at the observatory. At dinner, we talk about the old days, and it's easy for me to imagine what life used to be like "on the mountain."

After dinner, we go back to Shurik's flat. The temperature outside is close to zero. It is urgent to get the stove going so we don't freeze at night. To over-winter at the observatory, Shurik tells me, you need a reserve of two to three cubic meters of firewood. A cubic meter is approximately 800-900 kg.

"During the cold and hungry times, in the winter of 1991-92, we carried these two cubic meters of firewood home on our backs. Since you can't carry more than 20kg on your back at once, we had to make multiple trips," Shurik recalls, as he chops wood right in the middle of his bedroom, where there is a pot-belly stove. But Shurik can cope with these difficulties: it is obvious he is a hardened fighter.

While the stove is warming up, we head out to explore one of the observatory domes, as I am eager to see how the astronomers work at night.

The observatory is located right in the middle of the forest, with air that is so clean, it makes you dizzy. There's not much snow yet. The moon is out in full, and its silvery light floods the area, making the night seem like day. The sky, a clear and bottomless expanse resembling velvet scattered with diamonds, feels close enough to reach.

The pompous Stalinist buildings of the observatory look impressive in the moonlight. We approach one of the domed buildings and knock on the door, but are left waiting. Shurik makes a couple of phone calls, and we find out that the astronomers have not yet turned up for work. As we wait for them to come, Shurik smokes and I, freezing, hop from foot to foot to keep warm.

Finally, the doors are opened to us and we are invited under the dome. The telescope stands under an open retractable roof. Next to it is a computer through which observations are made. Long-time astronomer Givi Kimeridze has been working at the observatory since 1970. The scientist shows me his workstation and introduces me to the objects of his research: blazars and pulsars, using many unfamiliar-to-me scientific terms.

I'm trying my best to get into the subject, but my mind is lethargic in the cold. To dispel my fatigue, Givi, like a magician, points his telescope at the full moon and invites me to look through the eyepiece. With a sly smile, he warns that during the full moon, when the moon shines at its brightest, it becomes much harder to make out the details of its surface. The direct sunlight eliminates the shadows from the lunar mountains and craters, leaving them almost invisible. I can certainly see how the absence of shadows makes the moon appear flatter and less defined, making it difficult to distinguish its features.

"Now you see the most beautiful part of the moon," Givi tells me. *"These are the Lunar Mountains, and the sun is illuminating them. The magnification is times 250. Look at the craters. The size of the largest ones are around 400 kilometers in diameter. Craters on the moon are formed because the moon has no atmosphere."*

After contemplating the moon a while, we stand on the terrace of the dome, and Givi tells me that the observatory equipment is outdated. With science moving ever forward, in order to keep up with progress, new telescopes are much needed!

Life "on the Mountain"

When we get back to Shurik's flat, it is much warmer, but I am already cold to the bone and shivering all over. I wonder how astronomers work in such conditions. What kind of endurance must they posess?!

Shurik gives me hot tea with jam and rubs my feet with vodka, while entertaining me with memories of his observatory life in the old days. He admits that the biggest problem in such places for urban newcomers is solitude.

"The first winter I spent here alone was psychologically hard for me," he recalls. *"The canteen and shop worked, bread and groceries were brought up regularly. But the loneliness! Not everyone can bear to be alone for too long. But then I learned to play the guitar, and I had more fun.*

"Regardless of any difficulties, our observatory mountain is genuinely ideal both for scientific work and for raising children," Shurik asserts confidently. *"In this place, removed from the city's noise, nature itself is unspoiled, providing a one-of-a-kind setting for delving into scientific research. Furthermore, the ability to observe the world, yourself; to analyze and form conclusions – this is the precious gift that life in this kind of place offers."*

The next morning. Olga and I wander through the territory. She shows me the old library, primary school, shop, hotel, and the canteen where the residents used to organize all sorts of festivities. There was even a theater club-cinema in the scientific town, where entertainers would come and perform. The observatory was a very popular place during her childhood, she tells me.

But now the supply has worsened. Residents of the "mountain" have to go down to the town of Abastumani for food. Many of them use the cable car, which, thank God, still works! After lunch, Shurik and I head down to wander the small town, where tsarist dachas still stand, preserved, alongside pre-revolutionary hot spring baths and many once-popular sanatoriums.

Devoted to the Stars

The next day, scientist Eduard Dzhaniashvili, another elder resident of the research station, takes me around the museum and tells me something of the history of the place, about his own works, the working conditions of astronomers, and his dream of restoring the former scientific spirit of the town. After all, even in the difficult nineties, when scientists had to exchange their clothes for food from villagers nearby, scientific life went on as usual!

"We kept working," Eduard recalls. *"Work is in our blood. Every day, we have to do something in astronomy because the science is developing so fast. Even when we had no electricity or finances, we still did our work in anticipation of a better life in the future."*

Since the collapse of the USSR, a lot of observatory equipment has fallen into disrepair. Over the last 10 years, Eduard has often had to fix his work telescope with his own hands. He also bought an additional computer for his workplace to optimize his observations: he has only to go under the dome to adjust the telescope, and he can observe from his office. But if he had an automatic telescope, it would be possible to observe even from Tbilisi, he tells me. *"Nowadays, some Japanese amateur astronomers get better data with their pocket telescopes than we do with our observatory equipment!"* he says.

Some of Abastumani's observatory scientists, especially its astrophysicists, have gone to work abroad. But Eduard says this doesn't count as a brain drain, because the scientific exchange is ongoing.

"It is rightly said that science is for wealthy people. We, who have stayed here, hold on to our enthusiasm. Those who can't tolerate such working conditions go and look for a job that pays better, or quit science completely," Eduard tells me. *"I don't have time to look for other work, because there's still so much to be done in astronomy, and you need every minute, every second, to do it."*

When you do the work you love, time flies by. Three days at Abastumani Observatory seemed like a whole year to me! I take away with me a lot of impressions. One of them is that I got to live a little bit of the life of each of my interviewees.

As evening slowly descends upon the mountain, Shurik and I begin our journey back to Tbilisi. On the road, before my mind's eye, like legends come to life, emerge the images of astronomers—fanatics of their craft, indomitable enthusiasts, whose gaze, despite all adversities, remains perpetually drawn to the stars.

Tbilisi—Abastumani, 28th December 2015

Astronomer Eduard Dzhaniashvili,
devoted to science even in war and
hardship

The village of Dochu in the Gometsari Gorge

Joyful and cherished traditions: the Parsma village folk festival

Beautiful Tush women in the village of Dartlo

Chapter 19.
Tusheti. The Karmic Path of the Heart

There is one very special region in Georgia, special because it is so isolated from mainstream civilization, cut off by high mountains. When thinking of it, my heart overflows with almost religious awe.

What is this region where the journey there puts one's life at risk? What is this place where it is forbidden to bring pork, because the meat of an "unclean animal" could defile the sacred land? What is this strange place where men live outside most of the year and women have two identities: in the presence of men they are dutiful wives, loving mothers and caring housewives, but without their protectors, they become mythical Amazons? What kind of land is this where Christians believe in Jesus, but where St Giorgi is the highest deity? What is this tradition where people pray not only in churches, but also in pagan sanctuaries, and where sacrifices are obligatory during festivals? Who are these strange people who still live a semi-nomadic lifestyle, spending the summer in the highlands and descending to the valley for the winter?

It is not easy to write about Tusheti: hardly anyone would believe the tales. In order to verify that this paradise on Earth really exists, you have to see it with your own eyes. I will try to tell you about it based on the materials I collected during my several trips there, but you should know that these notes are unlikely to convey even a fraction of what one can see and experience in Tusheti.

The Tushs are a mountainous people. Part of them are Chagma-Tushs, a Georgian tribe which speaks a dialect of the Georgian language; the other part are Tsova-Tushs, descendants of the Ingush. Their language is Batsbi, and it belongs to the Nakh group of Caucasian languages, which also includes Chechen and Ingush. The Batsbi dialect in Georgia is called Tsova-Tush. The Batsbi came to Georgia from the Vabua region of mountainous Ingusheti. In Georgia, the Batsbi people are predominantly Christian.

Nowadays, the Tushs live in both the mountains and the valley. From the middle of the 17th century, they began to descend into neighboring Kakheti. For their valor and courage in the fight against the Persians, the Kakheti king granted them lands in the villages of Lower and Upper Alvani, Laliskuri, and part of the village of Pshaveli. These are beautiful villages, with well-built houses and neat, well-maintained garden plots.

Lessons in Tush History

Most Tushs used to live in the mountains, on their ancestral lands, as sheep farmers. In traditional Tush society, all men, as well as boys from the age of eleven, were shepherds; spending most of the year in the mountains with their flocks of sheep. It is not for nothing that the Georgian word *katsi*, "man," in the Tush dialect simultaneously means "shepherd" and "worker."

In the 1950s, the USSR leadership, suspicious of the mountain people and doubtful of their loyalty to the Soviet authorities, began a program of forced resettlement of mountain dwellers into the valleys. Both farming and cattle breeding were completely banned in the mountains, and a propaganda film called 'They Came Down from the Mountains' was played in cinemas. In the course of this violent action, most of the Tush villages were deserted, houses were abandoned, and herders were forced onto farming land and into valleys.

In the 1970s, the government came to its senses when it saw that the destruction of an ancient tradition was fraught with terrible consequences, not least that flocks of sheep were destroying the fertile lands of the Alazani Valley. So the Tushs were urged... you guessed it: to return to the mountains! Another propaganda film, 'Highlanders Return to the Mountains,' was used in this regard.

Electricity was supplied to Omalo, the central village of Tusheti, and plans for a boarding school were laid. It is said that a large military base was going to be built in Tusheti too, but they ran out of time for it, as the Soviet Union collapsed.

The Kakhetian neighbors I spoke to noted how they respect the Tushs for their diligence and friendliness, as well as for their physical and spiritual strength and endurance. Yes, these qualities of the Tush highlanders are truly admirable, as is their love for their homeland, for which a Tush would easily sacrifice his life.

The Road to the Cherished Land

It is better not to watch clips about the road over the Abano Pass (2900m). There's no need to make yourself nervous beforehand. If you have decided to see paradise with your own eyes, set to it purposefully and without looking back- you will definitely be rewarded for your determination!

From the Tush village of Alvani in Kakheti to the village of Omalo in the heart of Tusheti, there lie just 84 kilometers, but it is a road that takes no less than four hours to traverse. Before the road was built in the late

1970s, the Tushs used to climb the mountains using another path, as the road to the Abano Pass existed only on the Omalo side.

You will have to be patient and prepare well before traveling. Drivers usually take care to stock up on bread, wine, sweets, vegetables and fruit before setting out. And be sure not to forget your toothbrush, as I once did- there are no shops in Tusheti!

The road up is steep, narrow and winding, with sharp turns. There is often only enough space for one car, meaning drivers regularly have to re-verse in order for two cars to pass each other, and not every vehicle can cope with such a task- overheated brake pads are a common occurrence!

The higher we climb, the less vegetation we see, and the more often we come across memorials to people who have died on the road. Unfortu-nately, accidents are all too frequent. It is not for nothing that one of the most important toasts at the Tushino feast is raised to those who never reached their destination, and there are such people in almost every family. The road through Abano to Tusheti is called "costly." There are various reasons for the high number of casualties: unsuitable transport, inexperi-enced or inattentive drivers, as well as all kinds of force majeure circum-stances, such as rockfalls, avalanches and bad weather.

"How could you trust an inexperienced young lad driving a lorry or minibus for the first time?" you might ask in bewilderment. It's a question you'd better not ask the Tushs. But one day, we took a chance and did just that. This is the answer we got:

"For us, our home country is everything! When our hearts call us home again, and we get the chance to go, no one ever thinks to ask who the driver is, how much experience he has, or what kind of car he drives. We just really want to get home, as our hearts are always drawn to our land."

Alas, such behavior is not easy to understand for the rational and comfort-conscious inhabitants of the plains. But turn on your heart, and everything will become clear: For the Tushs, the journey home is not merely a physical displacement, but an internal karmic path that demands strength of spirit and loyalty to their roots. They follow this path, guided not by reason, but by a deep inner feeling: the call of their ancestors.

Nature, Climate and Landscape

On the road through the pass, cars stop at every turn: it's impossible to just drive past with the monumental scenery changing every few minutes. And, of course, you want to capture everything in each new picture.

The air is clean, clear, fresh and highly rarefied. But it is not the air that makes you dizzy- it is the feeling of direct contact with a higher power. Perhaps this is the drug that etches these places in your soul.

After the Pass comes the descent to Tusheti, opening access to a world of pristine, untouched nature: the whole of Tusheti is a national park, one where hunting and fishing are officially prohibited.

In alpine meadows and on mountain slopes, the grass and flowers are unusually rich in color, as if someone's invisible hand photoshopped the picture. In Tusheti, the traveler's aspirations are reduced to the elementary: to breathe, look, listen, and, filled with love, to absorb all the beauty, power and greatness of this world.

Tusheti National Park was established in 2003 to preserve the unique nature and cultural heritage of the region. Boasting 83,453 hectares, it is one of the largest protected areas in Europe. Tusheti National Park differs from other Georgian reserves in that there are unique settlements and people living on its territory. In Tusheti National Park, a 15,000-hectare pine forest turns into a birch forest as the altitude increases. The most common species are downy birch, Litvinov's birch, and Radde's birch. Rare animal species such as the Caucasian tur, chamois, mountain goat, deer, lynx, bear, and wolf inhabit here, and many unique plants grow here, 230 of which are endemic.

Tourism and Traditions

Nowadays, Tusheti survives more than anything on summer tourism. Almost every Tush is a guesthouse owner, guide or driver. It is not hard to imagine what it is like for the mothers and wives of those who drive tourists around!

Natela, from Dartlo, whose sons worked as drivers until recently, before changing careers, breathed a sigh of relief in my presence: *"Thank goodness they have other jobs now! Now I can sleep well. Before, my whole life was spent worrying about my children."*

The roads and road conditions here are unique, so you have to be prepared to pay a lot of money to travel within the region. It's understandable, though: the period of summer earnings for locals is short, and there are no petrol stations in these parts. I recommend you rely on your feet as your best means of transport, and your rucksack as your best food store. Feet help you to see and learn much more than if you drive through it all.

For the Tushs, tourism is both a source of income and a burden. The mountain dwellers themselves acknowledge that the tourism industry undermines traditional hospitality and poses a threat to the preservation of their cherished customs. Frequently, you can hear Tush residents expressing concerns about the gradual yet unavoidable shift in the traditions of their community.

"Not so long ago, no guest left our house without being fed and pampered. But now, the guest pays for every little thing!" my good friend Khatuna lamented. *"But what can you do? The world is changing, and borders between countries and traditions are disappearing. When I visited Greece, did anyone invite me to their house for coffee just once? No."*

Khatuna advised me to go to villages that are not accessible to motorized transport, as, only there can we "find truly generous and hospitable Tushs." Khatuna comes from one such abandoned village in the Gometsari Gorge, but only goes up there for short summer breaks.

Nugzar Idoidze, an Omalo anthropologist, informed me that the Tush pastoral character, in contrast to, for example, the Svan or Khevsur one, has always been known for its openness and generosity toward visitors, along with an aptitude for adjusting to evolving circumstances.

Today, the Tushs themselves complain that the flexibility of that character pushes many of them into the pursuit of material things. Those who have not found themselves in tourism go abroad to work. It is sad that there is too little work in Georgia, especially for men, while there is abroad, where the pay is much higher.

In the Gometsari Gorge, we meet a kind, glorious, 86-year-old man, Guram. He tells us, with no small amount of bitterness, about his only daughter, who had gone to work in Europe to look after the elderly and sick: *"Well, tell me, for Christ's sake, is 900 euros in Italy really a good salary?"* the old man wailed, and you could hear the pain in his voice.

Tourism — Hope or Scourge?

In Georgia, there are different categories that protect the land: national park, national reserve, cultural landscape, and protected area. In 2006, the whole Tusheti region was declared a protected area. Now, it has a unique status — it is a cultural landscape, where not only natural but also cultural values are protected.

"This is a valuable system that is connected with the development of ecotourism. We are developing ecological trails for tourists, but we still believe that our main economy is pastoralism," anthropologist Nugzar, who is also the director of the enthnographic museum in Omalo, tells me. *"In economic terms, tourism is an additional income for the Tushs. Our main activity, what we are striving to return to, is the pastoral culture, our traditions. It's just that they need to be brought as close as possible to the latest technology. There should be an understanding in the government that sheep breeding should be preserved and developed in Tusheti.*

"The fact is that shepherds are sometimes forced to leave their farms, their flocks, and go abroad to earn money. We have a popular saying: 'As soon as the last shepherd puts his staff to the wall, the history of Tusheti will be over'."

Plans, Information and Local Patriotism

Living in Georgia and making plans is a thankless task, because as soon as you make plans and tell someone about them, God will surely laugh at both you and those plans! It is simple: one proposes, God disposes. As such, in Georgia, you should learn to live spontaneously, plan a day or two ahead at most, and mentally ask for the blessing of the Universe. In the case of Tusheti, this is not advice or a rule, but the law!

Everything we had planned, including the road through the Pass itself, had to be constantly revised and adjusted. How can one not believe in the presence of a higher power when it comes to this great region under the heavens?

We were blown away by the local patriotism and pride of the inhabitants of different Tusheti gorges for their small piece of homeland. On one and the same day, yet in two different gorges, we were told to collect thyme from the village, because, according to each recommender, their thyme tea is the most delicious!

A Special Kind of Women

In these regions, girls and women, even elderly ones, are fabulously beautiful. Looking at them, one can't help imagining the heroines of the immortal Rustaveli's poem: exquisite facial features, slender, delicate, but at the same time strong and proud, with beautiful posture.

Women in Tusheti have always been not only wives, mothers and sisters, but also, if necessary, warlike protectors. It was women who set their men up for victories, for they chose only the bravest and most courageous to be their husbands. Bravery was among the most important qualities for the highlanders, for the enemy was close at hand, in Dagestan and Chechnya.

In almost every village here, there are legends about folk heroines who killed themselves and their relatives to avoid being captured by the enemy, as, in Tusheti, being captured was considered a huge disgrace, even for women.

When husbands, fathers and brothers herded sheep in the mountains, women not only raised and educated the children, but also did all the men's housework, as well as making cheese from cow's milk, weaving carpets, sewing, and knitting clothes. Pregnant women worked until they gave birth: pregnancy was no reason to shirk work. If it happened that a woman was sowing or reaping in the field and had contractions, she went away, gave birth to her child alone, wrapped it in a clean cloth, and then went to a special hut for post-partum women, where she built a fire and lived for forty days together with the newborn- all because local superstition labelled post-partum women unclean. As it turned out, however, forty days after childbirth spent away from the rest of the family gave the woman time to recover, and the child the chance to thrive. At the end of those forty days, the woman and child moved back into the common house.

Giorgi Tsotsanidze, 82, an ethnographic scholar from Tusheti, told me of his birth, right on the Abano Pass:

"I was born on the road from Tusheti to Kakheti on 4 October 1936, on the second day of the Alaverdoba holiday, when my family was descending into the valley. The weather was terrible, cold and windy. We had no midwives, but all the Tush women knew how to deliver babies. Our neighbor Sara delivered me. She wrapped me in felt that the shepherds gave her and carried me on her back, and my mum walked down with the other children."

I am constantly amazed at the slimness of the Tush women, especially considering their diet of high-calorie foods such as buttered cheese, cottage cheese in ghee, fatty meat, and potatoes. My friend Khatuna laughed when I told her my thoughts: *"It's genetics, my dear! You can't escape it! When do we ever sit down to eat? We are always on the move, and in the fresh air!"*

Khatuna, a mother of two living in Alvani, teaches physical education at the local school, and runs a grocery store and model guesthouse called Sweet Alvani. She also makes time to attend any number of training courses.

The Tush Shepherds

In traditional Tush society, sheep breeding is far from being the main source of income. However, the profession still enjoys great respect among the local population: everyone knows how difficult the labor of a shepherd is. The flock is always guarded by vicious Caucasian sheepdogs, and if the shepherd fails to see an uninvited guest in time, the dogs will tear that guest to shreds. That's why, before our trip, we were equipped with an ultrasonic dog repeller to scare the dogs away. We were also lucky in one case: one of the herders saw us in time and called off his dogs before they could attack us. Our savior was called Islam, and he spoke perfect Russian, being a 36-year-old Chechen from Grozny, who had been living in Georgia for 19 years because *"there was no place for him at home"* and because he was not ready to *"submit to the Kadyrovites."*

Islam willingly told us about how Georgia had become a second home to him, and how Georgians are "native brothers" not only for him, but also for his uncles and cousins, who all work as shepherds together with him. Since leaving Chechnya, Islam has never been back home, though he regularly meets up with family members in Minsk, who fly there especially for the reunion.

The shepherds work from dawn till dusk, and "overtime" comes as par for the course. Sheep are milked twice a day- a sheep is not a cow, I am informed, and milking them is not easy. It is not always possible to sleep at night, either, Islam tells us, as *"wolves are ever watchful!"*

Islam makes his own cheese and cares for it "like a small child" as it matures over the season. He is not afraid of hard work, especially as it pays well by Georgian standards: 1400 GEL a month. *"We will all be able to rest later, up there,"* Islam says, pointing to the sky. *"But while we're here, we have to earn a good living!"*

While Islam and I are talking, six men are shearing sheep. I worry it is hurting the defenseless animals. But, on seeing how the shepherds work with such skill, I can't help but admire their technique. Islam explains the secret: a shepherd must shear around a thousand sheep each season, and up to two thousand each year, so they are well-practised!

In parting, Islam confesses to me his only problem: *"Nothing in this life is difficult! The only thing that is difficult is picking up girls! I have yet to find a woman who will be to my heart's content, and who will agree to wait for this shepherd to come home from work."*

Pastoral Culture

The cultural values of this unique region are intrinsically linked to shepherding. Sheep, horses, Georgian sheepdogs, and even the delicious sheep's cheese made with the rarest methodology, all originate from the shepherding culture. Surprisingly, the exclusively male occupation of shepherding helped to develop women-led craftsmanship too.

Handicrafts in Tusheti are the domain of women. They weave carpets, spin yarn, sew and knit. Tusheti clothes are dark in color, or black, and there are no ornaments on their garments as there are in Khevsureti. Women wear their hair high, tied up in black shawls, and are richly decorated with silver.

Tush shepherds dress in felt clothing and impenetrable burkas made of coarse sheep's wool. This traditional attire not only protects them from the elements, it also once served as real armor. Imagine, even a sharp saber couldn't pierce the thick layer of wool with a single blow. And in severe winter frosts, such a burka is a real salvation, providing warmth and comfort.

Religion and Rituals

While Christianity began spreading through Georgia in the 1st century and became the state religion in the valleys in the 4th century, it arrived in Tusheti much later. Here, it spread on its own accord, without any formal guidance, and that's how many pagan deities in Tusheti ended up merged with Orthodox saints. It is not easy to distinguish them: for example, there is a deity called *Batoni Mtsvarieli*, and nobody knows what or who it is; they only know it as a patron of women and cows. Beliefs in such deities are still alive there today!

Mountaineers have two kinds of saints: those who became saints in their lifetimes, and those who descended from heaven to earth. The religion of the Tushs, as well as that of the Khevsurs and Pshavs, is syncretic: a fusion of the pre-Christian pantheon of deities with Christianity. According to their beliefs, the Tushs are Orthodox Christians, but the rituals they perform are certainly not Christian. They did not build churches in the mountains: more important than churches for the Tushs are *nisha* sanctuaries, from the word *nishani*, meaning sign, which are built in the open air. *"You put a stone on a stone and a white stone on top. That's the sanctuary for you,"* explains a young Tush historian.

They say that even in ancient times there were large cult buildings in Tusheti, and they were always connected only with the afterlife. The cult of ancestors is incredibly important here: at least half of all toasts are drunk to the departed during a Tush feast, as we discovered at the summer folk festival in the village of Iliurta in Gometsari Gorge.

Summer Festivals

The summer season in Tusheti, starting mid-July, is a time of holidays called *Atnigenoba*. In every village, one day of the summer is considered the day of the holy cross. In terms of scale, these festivals are comparable to our winter New Year festivities.

During these celebrations, the Tushs go to their cult crosses and pray there. The inhabitants of each village have one or more prayer cross, and consider themselves "servants" of that cross. According to Tush beliefs, the cross is a power that helps its servant, and it can appear to him in the form of a wheel of fire. There are many legends about this wheel.

A week before the Atnigenoba festival, men brew beer, and on the first day of the feast, they slaughter cattle in prayer halls, make sacrifices, and prepare a mountain of food for the many guests that are expected to come. It is always a man's job to cook the meat. On these days, the communities sing and have fun together; organizing games, contests, dances and horse races.

I bet that the majority of readers of this text, even in their most colorful fantasies, won't be able to imagine all the scope and exuberance of such a summer feast in the Tush highlands!

Devotion

Devotion to traditions, roots and origins, as well as dedication to their work — this is perhaps the main trait of the Tush character.

Bochorna is the highest-altitude village not only in Georgia, but, it is said, in the whole of Europe. It is located at an altitude of 2345 meters above sea level, and for the past seven years has been competing with Ushguli in Svaneti for the title of the highest permanently inhabited village in Europe. For many years, no one wintered in Bochorna, but for seven years now, an old country doctor, Irakli Khvedaguridze, whom I was lucky enough to meet, has been overwintering there. With his inherent sense of humor, Irakli tells me in confidence that the people of Ushguli are looking forward to his passing so that they can once again claim to have the highest inhabited village in Europe. This amazing man is already 81 years old, and he is full to the brim with energy. During his time as a doctor in those harsh winter conditions, Irakli has managed to save 34 people from death.

"How do you manage to get to other villages in winter, in deep snow and ice?" I ask.

"If there's not much snow, I ride a horse, if there's more, I go on my skis, and if there's a lot, I walk waist-deep in snow," the doctor says. "What else can I do?"

I ask Irakli why he loves his small homeland so much, and he confesses: "I was born and grew up here, and, yes, I could live anywhere, but it is in the mountains of Tusheti that I can be most use to people, saving their lives!"

Dartlo — Alvani — Tbilisi, August 2019

Irakli Khvedaguridze, a devoted country doctor

Tush shepherds and their flock at the biannual shearing

View of David Gareji Monastery

Chapter 20.
David Gareji: A Sanctuary Turned Time Bomb

The legendary Georgian monastery of David Gareji is built in the limestone caves of the driest part of Eastern Georgia, the history of it inextricably linked to the history of Christianity in Georgia and the emergence of monastic life here. My one trip to Gareji taught me something else besides history, though: How religious shrines can become time bombs.

How Religious Shrines Become Time Bombs

There are many different conflicts on the territory of the former USSR, programed unintentionally by history, or intentionally by people. Many of these conflicts—for example, the Transnistrian, Nagorno-Karabakh, Samachablo and Abkhazia conflicts —have had their hot phases, one or more. The people in these conflicts became hostages to the interests of those who claim the right to control the fate, moods and preferences of the masses.

Other conflicts, although not yet "hot," are slowly smoldering away, representing a time bomb.

One of these bombs is the territorial dispute between Georgia and Azerbaijan over the land on which an important Georgian holy site stands, the David Gareji Monastery. This is indigenous Georgian land: monastic life began here in the 6th century AD, when St David, one of the 13 Assyrian monks who came to Georgia, founded a monastery which allowed him to devote himself completely to prayers and thoughts of God. On the territory of the monastery there are many ancient chapels bearing frescos of the 11th - 14th centuries that have entered the history of fine arts as works of art of the "Gareji icon painting school."

David of Gareji was one of the 13 Assyrian Fathers and a founder of monasticism in Georgia. David lived on Mount Zadeni, near the ancient capital of Georgia - Mtskheta, then on Mount Mtatsminda in Tbilisi, where today there is a church of his name - Mamadaviti). He finally moved to the cave of Gareja in Kakheti. The name of St David of Gareji is also connected with the history of the construction of the Kashveti Church on Rustaveli Avenue in Tbilisi, as well as the Akura Church in the village of Akura, Telavi municipality. Commemoration of him in the Orthodox Church is on 7 May, according to the Julian calendar, and on Ascension Thursday (Mamadavitoba).

In the 1920s, the Bolsheviks "gifted" these lands to Soviet Azerbaijan, but at that time no one was particularly concerned with marking out the borders between the Soviet republics, as they were conditional. It meant that when the USSR collapsed, the borders between Georgia and Azerbaijan were left undemarcated. In recent decades, this frozen conflict has reared its head from time to time, either intensifying or weakening. Three years ago, the Azerbaijani government claimed that part of the Udabno (Gareji) monastery complex was Azerbaijani territory, which caused mass protests among Georgian believers. Following the rallies, the Azerbaijanis "allowed" the Georgian side access to the monastery.

Every now and then, the press flashes reports from the conflict region: this visitor was not allowed into the monastery caves, or that pilgrim was detained by Azerbaijani border guards on the new "border," one that is not recognized by anyone.

There is talk in Georgia that it is favorable for certain forces to pit Georgia against Azerbaijan, forces that seek to turn a cold territorial conflict into a hot one.

Just how serious is the territorial dispute with Azerbaijan? What is needed to prevent it from escalating into another war? These questions prompted me to go to the David Gareji monastery myself and try to get a clearer picture on the spot.

Along with me went my good friend Zurab Kikodze, a hiker with great experience who knows all the hiking trails in the country. He first visited the David Gareji complex back in the early 1970s, when Soviet troops were stationed on the territory conducting military exercises.

We had to leave Tbilisi early in order to attend the morning service. There were not many devotees there, but despite this, and even though the interior decoration of the small monastery church is rather modest (after various acts of vandalism in Soviet times, the ancient frescos have yet to be restored), the atmosphere during the service is heartfelt.

After the service, we talk to the Abbot, Mamao Iliarion (in Georgia, the priest is addressed as *Mamao*, meaning Father), who invites us into his simple, icon-decorated residence.

Mamao Iliarion tells us that the Azerbaijanis have already seized two monasteries from the complex, and plan to claim another. The two taken are the Bertubani Monastery, where a military base has already been established, and the Chichkhituri Monastery. And now they are trying to lay claim to the Udabno Monastery where we sit.

The border dispute began in the early 2000s, when Azerbaijanis occupied the first two monasteries. *"Azerbaijan's actions are unlawful, as these monasteries are Georgian holy places, part of our culture and our history,"* Mamao Iliarion asserts.

Three years ago, the Azerbaijanis set up their border posts right outside the Udabno monastery and declared that anyone who wanted to visit the temple had to first enter Azerbaijan. The monks gathered many believers and organized a mass protest, after which the Azerbaijanis relented and took down their post.

Yet, now, Georgian monks cannot visit the cave chapels seized by Azerbaijan, and they cannot take care of the valuable ancient frescos inside them.

According to the abbot, the Azerbaijanis behave as they please in this disputed area: some visitors they let in, others they don't. And sometimes they demand to see the documents of pilgrims and tourists.

Problems arise almost weekly, they say. The monks suspect that the Azerbaijanis want to accustom both visitors and monks to the idea that the territory has already been lost by Georgia. But this will never happen, Mamao Iliarion insists.

A Clash on the Georgian-Azerbaijani "Border"

After speaking to the Abbot, my old friend Zura and I, armed with water bottles, take a walk to the caves, which lie 125 meters above the level of the central monastery. The climb is quite steep and, as we are doing it on a hot July afternoon, not particularly pleasant. On the way, I wonder if we'll be lucky enough to meet border guards from at least one of the sides so I can ask them about the situation on this non-existent border.

Soon, we reach the monastery of Udabno. It is a small, old church, part of which is built into a mountain cliff. The access gate is padlocked. But next to it, in a little meager midday shade, three Georgian border guards stand guard: two soldiers and one officer. Perfect!

We say hello, and I get to questioning them: "Guys, do your Azerbaijani colleagues patrol here too?"

"They've been known to," the officer replies. *"But as long as we're standing here, they don't. This is our territory. They want to take it away from us, but they don't know how to do it. Our land used to be right up to that container over there,"* he says, pointing off to the south.

"Do you stand here every day?" I ask.

"Practically every day, yes. Sometimes we stand somewhere else, but then the Azerbaijanis, when they see we're not here, come straight over. They are Muslims," the officer replies with a smirk. *"But we Georgians are hospitable: we accept everyone peacefully."*

"Can't they let tourists through?" I wonder.

"They have no right to do so. On the other hand, they do have machine guns. What can you do against machine guns?" the officer laments. *"But if they see*

us, they immediately leave. We have Orthodox frescos here. When we were Christians, they were still savages."

I ask if we can see inside the Udabno cave-church, to which they tell us no.

"It's closed because it houses very valuable, old frescos. The day before yesterday, diplomats from Holland were here. And, as the Azerbaijanis refused to let them in, we had to call the authorities. Their soldiers know neither English nor Russian and have little education. Who knows Azerbaijani here? Nobody! So they communicate with gestures."

The soldiers tell us their job is like a diplomatic one: no conflicts should be fuelled.

Some 300 meters below us, we can see the Azerbaijani "border" outpost.

"We used to have monastery caves even further away, but then someone sold the land. Every five years, the authorities change, and everything changes. This land is strategically important. It's 125 meters above sea level. They only care about height," I'm told.

We say goodbye and walk further along the ridge to see the caves, some of which have frescos. Below us is a vast desert, and, very far away, we can see a village in Azerbaijan.

During the walk, Zura shares his memories with me: *"I used to walk here before most of these border guards were even born. This was the old Soviet border. Back then, there were no clear boundaries: 'here is a mountain, this is yours, and this is ours.' There is another huge monastery on this mountain, which can be seen in the distance, where houses stand, but we can't go there now as it's been claimed by Azerbaijan."*

David Gareji is also famous for its venomous snakes, which slide out of the shade to bask in the summer warmth from May onwards. Zura walks ahead, holding a huge stick in his hand. Once, he steps on something resembling a snake. He pokes it with the stick—it's just a shoelace! *"Snakes never come out in the high heat. They are out early in the morning and late in the evening,"* my companion reassures me.

He tells me that there used to be a huge Soviet testing ground here. *"I even have pictures of old ruined prop tanks standing there, which were used as targets. There were empty shell casings lying around, trenches, some old clothes. They were bombing, planes were flying, god knows what else happened here!"*

We move on. It's scorching hot. Cicadas are singing and birds are chirping. Zura stops me for a moment to draw my attention to the chirping of a bird: *"Do you hear that? It's a partridge. We used to hunt them here a lot. There were hares here too, and if there are hares, then there are wolves."*

On the way, we peek into the caves, seeing inscriptions on the walls in different languages, including ancient ones. Zura claims that among them we can find not only Georgian, but also Persian and even Mongolian! Zura comments on one of the inscriptions in detail, reading it first in Georgian, then translating it: "'*Monk Kalistrat Chichva. Give, O God, blessings to monk Kalistrat Chichva from Mingrelia.*' *And the year is written: 1883. You know, I was a little boy at that time and I told him: 'Chichva, what are you doing, why are you spoiling the cave?*'" Our Zura is a joker!

It's Sunday afternoon and there are a lot of tourists. They walk either in pairs or in large groups. We hear German, English, Italian and French.

Standing in one of the caves, where beautiful frescos remain well preserved, Zura points out the saints' faces, which have been deliberately damaged.

As we explore the rugged terrain, we suddenly encounter Azerbaijani border guards in wide-brimmed panamas, emerging from behind a thicket. They ask where we are from, and Zura answers, "*Georgia.*" Intrigued, I ask them which nationality isn't allowed to walk here. "*Everyone's allowed. It's a tourist zone,*" one replies in good Russian. Their questioning seemed suspicious to me, but they assure us they are just doing their job: border patrol.

Curiosity piqued, we chat with them about their work. The Georgian officer we were talking to before appears and joins in our conversation, and soon we are discussing everything from wine to military service. The two sides, despite their tense history, seem at ease, sharing stories of military life. The Georgian officer, who hails from Kakheti, jokes about the differences in their cultures: tea for Azerbaijan, wine for Georgia, and even compares their kebabs to Georgia's *mtsvadi* and *khinkali*.

"But Azerbaijan doesn't have mountains like Georgia, does it?" I throw in.

"*How not? Of course they do!*" the Georgian border guard argues. "*They have Karabakh. But it was taken away from them. Just as Abkhazia was taken from us,*" he says.

"*It's turbulent again there, in Karabakh,*" he adds. "*The day before yesterday, they showed it on TV: seven Armenians killed and one Azerbaijani soldier. It's all Russia's fault. It is Russia that bakes such 'tasty pies' – it is Russia that makes these time bombs and we who shoot at each other.*"

"*God grant you your lands back!*" one of the Azerbaijani officers, who we learn is called Samir, says abruptly.

As the sun blazes overhead, the two military men swap tales of uniforms and the heat, lightening the mood. The conversation shifts to life in their respective countries, with Samir describing the benefits of military service in Azerbaijan. Both sides agree on the need for NATO and EU membership, but express caution about dealings with Russia and America.

After an hour in the cool shade of an ancient monk's cell overlooking Azerbaijan, we reluctantly part ways, our conversation having been a surprising mix of humor, history, and diplomacy.

Down by the car park, we see a car, right out of which a young guy is selling freshly made coffee and other drinks. He even has iced coffee! What service!

"It's a great idea, you selling coffee here!" I say as I buy one, thinking 'at last, the spirit of entrepreneurship has come to Georgia!'

"But I'm not from here," the seller says. "I'm from Eastern Ukraine, from Donetsk, a refugee."

Zura and I are shocked.

"Actually, I'm a double refugee" he confesses. "I'm an Armenian from Tbilisi. We fled with our family from here to Ukraine in 1993, and now we have fled again, back to our homeland. We had to leave everything in Donetsk, and came here with nothing."

And so, sitting in the parking lot in front of the monastery, in the shade of a single tree, we spend more than half an hour talking to a handsome refugee coffee seller. We talk about the plight of his family and thousands of other similar families who have lost so much to war.

Meanwhile, up above the monastery, the border guards, nice Georgians and Azerbaijanis who made friends right before our eyes, continue their service with Kalashnikovs in their hands.

God grant their rifles remain unused toys for big boys.

Tbilisi, July 2015

Note: Sadly, since 2019, the mountain path around the monastery and the caves containing the frescos have been closed to visitors.

Georgian and Azerbajani border guards in David Gareji

A coffee vendor, who is also a double refugee, near the David Gareji Monastery

Starters at a typical Georgian supra (feast)

A cooking masterclass with Nana Nersezashvili in Leliani

A feast during a summer festival in the Tush village of Iliurta. Some toasts Georgian men must drink standing

Chapter 21.
The Culinary Landscapes of Kakheti

I prepared the following text for a photo report published in 2016 in New Spaces, a magazine printed in six languages. My goal, with photographer Mariam Sichinava, was to learn about the culinary traditions of Kakheti and their adaptation to the demands of the modern world. But in addition to the cuisine, we discovered many other treasures of Georgia's largest region, too. Now it's time to explore Kakheti!

There's a popular Georgian legend that goes like this: When the Creator was handing out lands to the people, the Georgians, as usual, arrived late. By the time they showed up, every plot of land had already been claimed. God, a little annoyed, asked why they had been so delayed. The Georgians, ever charming, replied, *"Lord, we were only late because we were toasting to Your health all the way here!"* This answer, full of warmth and good humor, pleased God immensely. With a smile, He said, *"You are a good people! There's only one piece of land left, the one I kept for myself. But I will give it to you."*

Maybe it was really so. Of all the Caucasian nations, God has truly bestowed Georgia with the most generous gifts, and this is especially true of Kakheti, the country's most popular agricultural and wine-growing region.

In Georgia, the tradition of winemaking dates back 8,000 years. In 2013, Georgian traditional winemaking was inscribed on the UNESCO list of cultural heritage.

Kakheti wine is particularly famous for its being fermented in large clay jars called *qvevri*, which are buried in the ground. The traditional Kakheti method of winemaking consists of fermenting the harvested grapes in vessels together with the pulp and seeds, giving the wine a uniquely intense taste, color and aroma. In Kakheti, almost every family makes wine using *qvevri*, and even a number of large wineries have adopted the method.

The mild climate and the fertile, mineral-rich soil of Kakheti allow for rich harvests. Fans of Georgian cuisine rightly say that, in this country, the food tastes as it did 300 years ago! Vegetables, herbs and fruits form a significant part of this cuisine: crunchy cucumbers, magically aromatic tomatoes, glossy elastic aubergines, tender spinach and beetroot, juicy pomegranates, fleshy plums, oily nuts, exotic edible plants, and the fragrance of herbs and spices.

Numerous dough and cheese dishes, as well as original meat dishes, have guests falling in love with Georgian cookery, and with Kakheti in particular.

To all of this must be added another indispensable attribute that I have mentioned before: the art of enjoying life, slowly and thoughtfully, with gusto and enthusiasm. In Kakheti, they do it exceptionally well. Indeed, in this hidden corner of the world, life flows much as it did in Southern Europe before the age of globalization.

One beautiful spring morning, our team — me, the photographer, her assistant and our driver — set off on a trip through Kakheti.

The picturesque road is lined with fortress ruins, pretty villages and cave settlements hidden in the rocks, taking us from Tbilisi through the Gombori Pass (1620 meters above sea level) to Telavi, the capital town of the Kakheti region.

Chateau Mere

We make our first stop at hotel-restaurant Chateau Mere, the home of Gia Piradashvili, who is also the owner of the Winiveria wine company. On a cozy summer terrace overlooking the Great Caucasus Ridge, we taste a light wine from his cellar, made according to European technology from mtsvane grapes. European technology means that the wine was fermented without contact with the pomace. A gourmet and hedonist, Gia Piradashvili tries to modernize traditional Georgian cuisine: reviving old recipes, or inventing his own. On his restaurant menu, we find a wide variety of vegetable and fruit purees, such as those made from bell peppers, carrots, mint and honey, which are served as a side dish to meat and fish.

Gia prepares for us an assortment of Georgian appetisers called *pkhali*. This is a traditional paste of poached vegetables, seasoned with ground walnuts, fresh herbs, and spices. In addition to traditional *pkhali*, Piradashvili's restaurant prepares a version with truffles that grow in the neighboring forest. After the appetisers, we are served fresh river trout stuffed with tarragon and orange.

"It is impossible to imagine Georgian cuisine without fresh herbs: wild thyme, red basil, dill, smooth parsley," Gia tells us. Undoubtedly, the king of herbs is young coriander, which is much more delicate in flavor than its Asian or African kin.

Alaverdi

We are planning to explore a monastery wine cellar while in the area, one of the most important holy places in Georgia: the Alaverdi Cathedral. Built in the distant 6th century, it is the jewel of the Alazani Valley. Here, in the monk-led monastery, there is an ancient, 11th-century wine cellar boasting 50 *qvevri*, each with a capacity of 60 tons. In fact, it is the oldest monastery wine cellar in Europe!

The monks make the wine from their own organic grapes. The head oenologist, Father Gerasime, tells us about the monastery's wine: "*As they did thousands of years ago, our monks place the harvested grapes in a special vessel made from a solid tree trunk. Then, as in the old days, we crush them with our bare feet so as not to damage the seeds.*"

He tells me that the monks fast strictly beforehand, then confess and receive the abbot's blessing.

Up to 10,000 bottles of wine are bottled in this monastery every year, and some wines are aged for up to three years in *qvevri* first. The wine is then collected using ladles carved from dried ornamental gourds.

During the tasting, we learn that white wines made with Kakheti methodology are called amber wines. White wine made using rkatsiteli grapes does indeed have an amber color, and its aroma includes notes of caramel, peach and dried fruits.

Red wine made from saperavi grapes is called "black" in Kakheti because of its dark red color. Its flavor is reminiscent of currants, cherries and chocolate, and it also has light tobacco notes. Traditional Kakhetian cuisine is meat-based, and red wine with a rich bouquet goes very well with it. However, according to Father Gerasime, the wine from the Alaverdi monastery goes with all dishes. It is also an integral part of the monks' diet!

Rkatsiteli (meaning "red horn/stem") is a Georgian white grape variety. It is used to produce a wide range of wines, from dry and fortified wines to brandy. It is widespread in all viticulture zones. Rkatsiteli juice is used as a base for *churchkhela*, while the berries can be consumed unprocessed. Traditionally, Rkatsiteli is used to produce amber wines in *qvevri*. Wines such as Tsinandali, Gurjaani and Vazisubani are produced from Rkatsiteli. Standard wines are neutral in flavor and it is best to drink them in their first year. Amber wines open with hints of apricots, sultanas, dried herbs and zest, and have a tannin structure, meaning they can be stored significantly longer.

In Alaverdi, the monks are not only engaged in gardening, but also in beekeeping. They collect linden, royal jelly, chestnut and meadow honey, and make wax candles and other beekeeping by-products. Hives are often taken up to alpine meadows. The head beekeeper at Alaverdi Monastery is Father Joseph, who has been involved in beekeeping since 2005. Two hundred hives are currently under his personal care.

Near the monastery is the House of Matsoni, where we make our next stop. In this restaurant, popular with tourists and pilgrims alike, we taste *matsoni*, a Georgian whole yoghurt, which is used as the main ingredient in many dishes in this restaurant. It is even used to make ice cream! We enjoy our *matsoni* in its pure form, combined with aromatic acacia honey from the monastery, and crunchy walnuts. We are also served organic dried fruits and fresh Georgian bread lavashi from a clay oven.

The Pottery Village

Along the way, we stop in the village of Vardisubani, which means "village of roses." The village is indeed well decorated with colorful rose bushes. Vardisubani has always been considered a settlement of potters. The quality of the local clay is renowned throughout Georgia, and wine producers from all over the country come here to buy the highest quality goods on the spot.

We pop in to visit father and son Tamaz and Zaza Karaulashvili, masters of pottery, who belong to an ancient pottery dynasty. Even women in the family made *qvevri*: Zaza's grandmother was a wonderful potter, he tells us. In the Karaulashvili family workshop, it is easy to get lost among the giant *qvevri*, many of which hold up to 2000 liters of liquid. It takes up to two months to work on one such giant vessel, and the breaks between successive 10cm layers of clay must not be too long, so that the clay does not dry out completely. *"The qvevri then spends up to two weeks in a kiln at temperatures of up to 200 degrees,"* Zaza tells us.

For the night, we head to Napareuli, a village in the middle of the Alazani Valley, the largest and most picturesque

Napareuli is a traditional center of Kakhetian winemaking. Wines have been made here since ancient times, mainly from the rkatsiteli and mtsvane varieties. Red wine under the Napareuli brand started to be produced in 1890 from the local saperavi grape.

valley in Georgia. An alley of old, shade-giving walnut trees leads us across the Alazani River, where we stop to enjoy a romantic sunset overlooking the vineyards and lush emerald fields.

A word of advice to those traveling through Kakheti by car: be patient, as large herds of sheep and cows will cross the highways here and there, and no one here would dream of hurrying the livestock!

It is late in the evening when we get to Napareuli. While waiting for dinner, we bake bread in a clay *tone* oven and prepare *churchkhela*, a Georgian sweet made from thickened grape juice and walnuts.

To make *churchkhela*, walnuts or hazelnuts are strung on a string in advance, then dipped in hot grape puree, then dried for up to three months to ripen. *Churchkhela* are popular at the New Year and are traditionally served on the festive table.

Our next day begins with shopping at the market in Telavi, where local farmers proudly display their wares. We admire mountains of cheese, a colorful palette of spices, fragrant wild berries, mushrooms and herbs, fresh and dried fruits and nuts. We are struck by the huge carcasses of animals on display. This market hall is an adventure in itself! You can find almost everything that Kakheti is proud of: whole chickens, geese and ducks, large jars of honey, various pickles, fresh farm eggs, clarified butter and cheese, wax candles, brooms made of natural materials, and an unimaginable mix of clothes and jewelry.

Leaving Telavi, we stop at a small cheese factory, the family business of Gocha Gogashvili, where sixty types of local cheeses are handmade. We try *sulguni* cheese, which resembles mozzarella. Sometimes it is aged in red wine or honey, or smoked and woven into thin bundles or plaits.

On a picturesque road, we pass by the royal residence and fortress of Gremi, and visit the winery of Alex Shaloshvili in the village of Shilda. The vineyards of the Shaloshvili family are located in the middle of the Alazani Valley, in the Kindzmarauli wine microzone, where the soil has a grey-blueish tint and is exceptionally rich in minerals, with a lot of pebbles and limestone. Here, saperavi grapes reach a special maturity due to the large amount of sunlight, and ferment quickly. But with the help of cooling, the fermentation is stopped, and a semi-dry Kindzmarauli wine is obtained. Kindzmarauli wine is produced according to the European method and must be drunk chilled.

Leliani

We continue our journey towards Lagodekhi, and we stop in the village of Leliani, near the national park, at the guest house of Nana Nersezashvili, where we are to take part in a Georgian cookery course.

At Nana's house, it is easy for any guest to feel that they are at Christ's side; to realize what a miracle it is to live solely on the gifts of one's own garden.

Nature has generously endowed this region with riches: cherries, apples, plums, peaches, nuts and figs, excellent vegetables, and lush meadow grass, thanks to which the cows produce unusually tasty milk. From Nana, we learn how to make Georgian cheese and soft cream cheese *nadugi*, similar in consistency to Italian ricotta. Under Nana's guidance, we prepare *charkhali*, a traditional Kakhetian dish made of beetroot, herbs, spices and plum sauce *tkemali*. *Khachapuri*, a Georgian cheese pie, which we bake right in the garden on a small stove, requires a special art. We are also taught how to put together *khinkali* filled with meat and herbs. It turns out that a *khinkali* should always have an odd number of folds: 19, 21, 23, etc.

In the evening, we celebrate with a traditional Georgian feast, called a *supra*. The head of the family, Malkhaz, is the toastmaster. Toasts are usually drunk in a strictly traditional order: to the motherland, God, ancestors, children, and then friends. We drink unpretentious white, home-made, from small shot glasses, emptied one at a time.

At this point I will allow myself a slight deviation from the story of our culinary journey through Kakheti, as here I want to touch on a related and very important issue.

The Georgian Feast: A Scientific Phenomenon

Mary Ellen Chatwin, an anthropologist from the USA, defended her thesis at the University of Basel in Switzerland on the culture of the Georgian feast. When I was preparing an edition of a radio program called 'Georgia in My Heart,' Mary Ellen and I met to talk about her curious anthropological research. It was my first 'academic' encounter with a Georgian *supra*, and I soon became friends with this remarkable scientist, who, it turned out, was as deeply in love with Georgia as I am, having lived here for over twenty years!

Our first topic of discussion is meat, which is usually prepared by men: it is men who slaughter the cattle and cut up the carcasses, it is not women's work. Such meat dishes as *khinkali* are also cooked by men. Meat and fire are dominated by men in Georgia.

According to Mary Ellen, food in Georgia is a real cultural, economic and even political occurrence. A *supra* is a strictly organized process in which nothing unforeseen happens: Sitting at a Georgian feast, one can relax, knowing ahead of time what to expect. A *supra* is the crown of any significant event in the life of a Georgian, be it a birthday, anniversary, or wedding. Even business deals are celebrated around the feast table.

During excavations of an ancient Colchian settlement in Vani, a statuette of a man with a horn in his raised hand was discovered. This image has been replicated, and similar figures on a larger scale decorate streets throughout the country. *Tamada* is the name given to this statue.

The phenomenon of the *tamada* is a real institution, one that brings structure to the process of a festive meal. A toastmaster is a form of dictator: controlling the feast, and the order and number of toasts. He is to be obeyed and not contradicted. Any bully in the presence of a toastmaster will be wary of showing his temper, and before making a toast themselves, guests must ask the *tamada* for permission to do so.

Toasts at a Georgian feast are indeed a topic for scientific research. Even the sequence of toasts has a strict order. Toasts are drunk for the actual reason of the feast: it can be the birth of a child, christening, wedding, anniversary, birthday. There are also religious moments in toasts — for example, when drinking a toast of thanksgiving to God. There are also sentimental toasts to parents, siblings, friends, children, memories, friendship and love.

Supras can go on well past midnight, and at such feasts the wine pours out in rivers. The toastmaster or his assistants are in charge of order during the feast. No guest should be seen in an embarrassing state due to intoxication; nothing should mar the mood of those present. It is also the function of the toastmaster to escort a tipsy man out, to give him a chance to get himself in order, or to help him get home safely.

Mary Ellen Chatwin observed another phenomenon: *"Toastmasters are a system of dining designed by men, for men. If you attend a supra in a small village or at someone's home, you may see men feasting in the shade, but you won't see local women at the table. For many women, a supra is a boring and very heavy event. They are the ones who prepare the food for the feast, and after a whole day or even several days of preparation, they are so tired that they have no desire to sit at the table and feast on an equal footing with the men. In the villages, while the men feast, the women sit at a distance, eating dessert or drinking a well-deserved coffee. Foreigners feel awkward when they see men sitting at the table and women running to the kitchen and back. The guests don't realize one simple thing: it would never occur to the women themselves to sit at the table with their men!"*

In a sense, such a tradition is logical. After all, if there are guests in the house, who should serve the table? That's right, the women of the family! Of course, this is not the case in a restaurant: where the feast is served by waiters, the women can sit at the table and participate in the *supra*. They don't have to cook and so they can enjoy the feast equally with their menfolk.

The famous Georgian *khinkali* is now more and more often eaten outside the home, as it is troublesome to cook *khinkali* for a horde of guests. That is why *khinkali* parlors were invented for eating them. More and more often, for large feasts, Georgians prefer to reserve a table in a restaurant. Such occasions as weddings, school banquets, anniversaries, birthdays and wakes in urban areas are celebrated in banquet halls. In villages, such occasions are prepared at home, in the family, with the help of the nearest neighbors and relatives.

It is very important to mention children in the system of organizing a feast. Teenagers usually serve as cupbearers, bringing water and soft drinks. In this way, they learn the rules of the Georgian feast, learn the stories of the family, the country, the appropriateness of quoting poems. Small children don't usually sit at the table, but even the strictest toastmaster won't keep them away: it gives them a chance to listen to the stories of their elders and learn who their ancestors were and where they come from. By school age, Georgian children tend to know their family history quite well. Who among our Western European children knows so much about their ancestors? And this knowledge is very important for the continuation of the cultural tradition of the family and society as a whole.

"There are cultures in Asia and in Africa that are also strongly tied to the theme of ancestry," Mary Ellen tells me. *"But in Georgia, it happens in a very systematic way. Not even in Georgia's neighboring countries – in Azerbaijan, Armenia, or in Russia – does this exist to such a pronounced degree. In Georgia, tamadoba and supra are elements that make this country unusually strong in terms of its own identity."*

The Supra as a Social Phenomenon

Sometimes, people with different perceptions of the world, different upbringings, different backgrounds, and different political views gather around the table. Sometimes, there are strangers sitting side by side at the same table. Thus, the table becomes a place where useful acquaintances are made, where issues are solved, and agreements are concluded. Conflict at the table is unthinkable.

The management of a feast is not only about the correct alternation of toasts: *"A toastmaster is always a diplomat,"* is another important observation Mary Ellen makes. *"Some people honor a strict toastmaster who doesn't let the rules be bent. Others like a creative toastmaster who offers lavish toasts. But I think it is rare to meet an outright bad toastmaster in Georgia. Such a person will not be invited to an important feast."*

Georgians learn the art of self-expression from their youth. At a true *supra*, you'll hear unique poems, the most beautiful Georgian songs, and numerous quotes from verses and even medieval poems. And while it is tradition, toastmasters need not be men: Mary Ellen recalls that there was once a famous female toastmaster in Kakheti.

The Tablecloth and the Feast

Supra means "tablecloth" in Georgian and Arabic. But, nowadays, the word also means "feast, banquet." When guests gather, the table is already laid with appetising dishes. Hot dishes are brought out later, when the typical European has already filled himself with salad, cheese, *khachapuri*, and other cold delights. And then he is told that the meal has, in fact, only just begun! They then proceed to bring out roasted mushrooms, meat and vegetables to tempt him further. An hour or two into the feast, they bring the *mtsvadi* — meat roasted on a spit. At the end of the feast, desserts are sometimes served, and fresh, seasonal fruit is brought to cleanse the palate.

Are there regional differences in the culture of the *supra* across Georgia? Eastern Georgia and Tbilisi were more influenced by Persian and Arab cultures, while Western Georgia was heavily influenced by Turkish culture, but there is no big difference in the tradition of feasting.

The difference in dishes or ingredients is striking, though. For example, in Western Georgia, dishes made with corn flour, such as *mchadi*, are popular, while in Eastern Georgia these dishes are rarely prepared. Or *churchkhela*: in Western Georgia, this delicacy is made with corn flour, while in Eastern Georgia it is made with wheat flour. In Samegrelo and Imereti, food is spicier, with a lot of hot pepper used. Wine in Western Georgia is lighter, and one can quickly become tipsy on it, though intoxication from such wine passes rather quickly. In the eastern Georgian regions of Kartli and Kakheti, spices are used less often and food tends to be less spicy. But, there, the dishes are meaty and fatty, and the wine served with such dishes is tannin wine: strong and fermented in *qvevri*.

Grapes do not grow in Svaneti as the conditions are too harsh for grapes and there is not enough land for vineyards. But apples grow there in abundance. In autumn, Svan apples are used to make vodka (*natkhani*) through fermentation and distilling. The quality of the drink is directly determined by the quality of the apples and the number of distillations: the more distillations, the stronger the alcohol!

The Svans boast that *natkhani* gives them almost no hangover. In general, fruit vodkas are very popular in Svaneti and other provinces of Western Georgia. A strong alcoholic vodka infused with honey is considered a luxury. Ordinary vodka is also found here, called *rakhi*. A kind of fruit vodka called *zhipitauri* is made in the mountainous regions of Pshavi, Khevsureti, Tusheti and Mtiuleti. Traditional cheese *dambalkhacho* is usually served with it.

In some mountainous regions, Georgians make home-brewed beer. You can be assured, though, that wherever there is a feast, no matter how rich or poor the table is, no matter what is poured into the glasses, Georgians are sure to make a toast and beautifully praise God!

The Drinking Culture

As a rule, at Georgian feasts, a large amount of alcohol is consumed, primarily Georgian wine, and usually light and white, as red wine is not for feasts. Men are expected to drink to the bottom of their glasses at each toast, then refill ahead of the next toast. This rule does not apply to women: no one expects a woman to drink a lot. That said, a woman's glass should be kept topped up by a man. Women should never have to pour for themselves, not even lemonade or water: all they have to do is lift their empty glass or tumbler and it will be filled immediately by the nearest attentive man.

Georgian Hospitality

"In terms of hospitality, Georgia is similar to Greece," Mary Ellen states. Some anthropologists called the Greek system of hospitality 'inglobing hospitality,' which means all-consuming hospitality. This means that once you are in someone's arms, you can't get out! Foreigners, according to Mary Ellen, often lack autonomy because they find themselves at the very center of their hosts' attention. But such hospitality should be understood and appreciated.

Seeing guests as "godsent gifts," Georgians will treat a visitor to their home with a sense of ownership. It is very important to be polite to the host and never go against what she says: this is her house, and these are her rules!

It is very common in villages for people to borrow money or borrow groceries just to be able to give a proper welcome to their guest. And if an important or high-ranking guest is expected, the entire village will come out to help prepare the feast, even if not all the villagers are invited to the table. Hospitality is a very serious phenomenon in this country!

My conclusion is this: Georgians live exclusively in the "here and now." Periods of stability in this country have never lasted long, and the people here got used to living from crisis to crisis, and that's how they learned to appreciate the present.

Tbilisi, May 2013

Bodbe Monastery

Our journey through Kakheti continues.

We head for Sighnaghi, a picturesque hilltop town surrounded by large, ancient walls. Two kilometers away is an important pilgrimage site, the Monastery (Nunnery) of Saint Nino. In this romantic place, overlooking the Alazani Valley, with a view of the Greater Caucasus Range, is the tomb of the Equal Apostle Saint who converted Georgia to Christianity in the 4th century and who spent the last years of her life here. Magical powers are attributed to this tomb, and cherished wishes are fulfilled here, especially those concerning health: childless women and men who take a dip in the icy font of the Saint Nino Spring are said to become cured of infertility, with God generously bestowing them with child. As a rule, if, thereafter, a girl is born, she is named after Saint Nino. If a boy is born, he is baptized with the name Giorgi.

At the convent, we learn about the gardening talent of the nuns and what goes into their daily diet. One of the sisters, Rachel, leads us past colorful flowerbeds into the convent garden. There are also meadows for grazing the cattle. The monastery's 10 cows produce a lot of milk!

In a dark, cool and damp room, we are shown how the nuns grow oyster mushrooms, called "wood mushrooms." Meat is never eaten in the monastery, fish is eaten only on holidays, and wine is rarely drunk. And yet the food in the monastery is varied and not at all meager, because, as Sister Rachel says, monastic life is rather monotonous, and so the food must present them some comfort. Every day, there is a delicious vegetable soup, a plethora of Kakhetian vegetable dishes, various dishes of milk and *matsoni*, beans, and bread from their own bakery.

The Sumptuous Delights of Sighnaghi and Gurjaani

The next stop is Sighnaghi itself. There are many cozy cafés and restaurants in this picturesque town. In the Pheasant's Tears winery, there is a restaurant that attracts not only tourists, but also chefs from all over the world looking for inspiration. The restaurant is run by chef Gia Rokashvili.

We sit in the beautifully manicured garden overlooking the town, while Gia spoils us with his latest creations: young green beans with mint and thyme, cucumber and tomato salad with cold-pressed Kakheti sunflower oil, juicy forest mushrooms with tarragon, rosemary and spicy green pepper, *pkhali* and *chakhokhbili*, a stew of homemade chicken with garlic and tomatoes, Georgian spices and herbs. We are also served young cabbage pickled with aniseed and beetroot, as well as mature, dry and low-salted sheep's cheese. Accompanying these delights, we enjoy Kakheti wines: white Chinuri aged in *qvevri* and red Shavkapito made from a rare endemic grape variety.

The last stop on our journey is the Chateau Zegaani winery near the town of Gurjaani. This is a recently restored winery founded back in 1820 by Georgian Prince Alexander Chavchavadze, who perfected traditional Georgian viticulture with the help of French technology.

The chateau is located in the middle of a magnificent park overlooking the Alazani Valley and the Greater Caucasus Range. The endemic grape varieties rkatsiteli and saperavi are grown here, from which wine is made using both European and traditional Kakhetian technology. European wines are aged in oak barrels, while Kakhetian wines are kept in *qvevri* for up to three years before being bottled. We visit the wine cellars during our tour of the estate.

David Tatulashvili, the new owner of the chateau, does not hide the fact that his winery's oenological products are intended for true wine connoisseurs: the price of a bottle starts at 30 euros. However, I see this as a fair price for an organic product made using ecologically clean grapes, and considering that the entire process, from harvesting to bottling from the *qvevri*, is done exclusively by hand.

Our wine tasting takes place in a luxurious royal hall with chandeliers and handmade walnut furniture. Rkatsiteli dry white wine has a golden color and an extremely intense aroma of spices and dried fruits, while the flavor of rich red Saperavi wines is spicy and laconic, with notes of rosehip, cherry and smoke.

While having our taste buds pampered with exquisite amber and "black" wines, we finally understand why Georgians call their homeland the inheritance of the Lord God!

Tbilisi — Alaverdi — Telavi — Sighnaghi — Gurjaani, June 2016

Winemaker Gerasime from the Alaverdi Monastery

Pastoral heaven in the Alazani Valley

Zaza Karaulashvili from the pottery village of Vardisubani in Kakheti

The market in Telavi

Chapter 22.
Georgia: A Paradise for Gourmets

Georgia has been actively developing its gastrotourism prospects over the past few years. My friends Kristo and Gio, owners of the legendary Tbilisi restaurant Ezo, invited me to participate in their "Ezo Tours" project, and I gladly accepted.

Kristo and Gio aim to protect their homeland from becoming a hub for mass tourism by offering a more refined, subtle, and sensual way to explore Georgia. Their approach encourages travelers to activate a deeper perception of a country they have yet to discover. This enriched experience engages not only the visual senses, but also taste and touch, incorporating aesthetic elements that enhance the journey. Kakheti, which has long been renowned as a gastronomic paradise, is the best place for such a tour.

Telavi: Exploring the Market and Tasting Khinkali

Our first stop on the Ezo Tour was the agricultural market in Telavi. I love this place, despite its apparent chaos, disorder and not at all glamorous appearance! Of course, it cannot be compared to the famous La Boqueria in Barcelona, but Telavi's market is much more authentic. You'll not find the likes of it in Tbilisi, nor the real gastronomic symphony that you can hear in the Telavi market, which has preserved the Georgian spirit of by-gone eras, a time when this country was considered an important trading center on the Silk Road.

Armed with two wicker baskets, Kristo invites us to pick out the "right" local produce, and along the way instructs us on what to choose, from which vendor, and how.

Kristo is a real find: despite her fragility, she loves quality food, and her gastronomic fervor will easily infect even the most sophisticated ascetic! Kristo opens for me another new page in my culinary experience.

In addition to numerous spices, one of the most important components of Georgian cuisine is fresh herbs. I will never cease to marvel at the care and love with which Georgian housewives choose herbs at the market! Kristo picks up, examines and smells each bundle tied with corn leaves, and then stocks up on *regani* (red basil), *tarhuna* (tarragon), green onions, coriander, mint, *kondari* (mountain thyme), and fluffy small-leaved *obamalo* (marsh mint) with its many tiny purple flowers. Marsh mint differs significantly from common mint: *"Without ombalo, you can't make green tkemali sauce or green lobio,"* Kristo explains.

A little further away, she buys juicy giant peaches, small firm aubergines, succulent onions and fragrant pink tomatoes that are as big as the peaches and just as intense in flavor.

At the long cheese counter, Kristo quickly finds her favorite vendor, from whom she usually buys sulguni. *Sulguni* is boiled and should be savored while it is still very tender, with milk oozing out between the layers. Undoubtedly, the most delicious *sulguni* is made in Samegrelo, where cows spoilt with succulent grass produce a very different quality of milk, one that is both fatty and flavorful.

"Western Georgian cheese is not easy to find in Eastern Georgia: if transported incorrectly, it overripens or spoils too quickly. But this owner's cheese is excellent," Kristo promises us. Then we buy a young sheep's cheese from Tusheti, which, according to Kristo, should be thick in texture but not oversalted. We also buy dambalkhacho—curd ripened in a clay pot buried in the ground, which tastes like a mixture of camembert and green mould cheese.

Next, our guide leads us to a stand with homemade sunflower oil, and we study its color and taste: a bright, amber-colored liquid with an intense aroma of freshly toasted seeds that tickles the tongue and awakens the appetite. Next in line is marinated *jonjoli* (Staphylea colchica). These are the pickled inflorescences of a unique endemic tree, sometimes referred to as Caucasian capers. As Kristo says, despite the pickling, a good *jonjoli* should retain the flavor of the delicate flowers. The pickles further whet our appetite. After weighing the *jonjoli*, the vendor generously treats us to pickled garlic and crunchy pickles, which are not only pickled, but even fresh: long, light green, with barely visible skins and almost entirely without seeds! These are the so-called "glass" cucumbers, which I usually take with me abroad as a souvenir.

Our baskets are already filled to the brim. Kristo teaches us how to choose walnuts by gently rubbing the walnuts with our fingers. If the walnuts are healthy and properly dried, the walnut oil will come through. Walnuts are abundant in the market. In Georgia, a salad of tomatoes, cucumbers and greens is often dressed not with vegetable oil, but with grated walnuts. Fat walnuts are also the basis for Georgia's divine dish *satsivi*—turkey or chicken in rich, savory walnut sauce.

What else do we need for our upcoming feast? Of course, honey, *chacha*, and forest and garden berries: blackberries and strawberries. We buy them on our way out of this palace of abundance.

What can I say? The Telavi market stretched our taste buds to the limit! To tame our gurgling stomachs ahead of our evening feast, Kristo and Gio take us to taste the best *khinkali* in Telavi: to a café that serves nothing but. It is a modest place, popular among the locals, where *khinkali* are cooked traditionally, with meat stuffing, as well as with *nadugi*. Kristo promises us that no better cheese *khinkali* can be found in the whole of Georgia!

Although I'm not a big fan of *khinkali*, it is hard not to admit that our guide is right: the thin dough served to us exceeded any ambitious expectations! It is served here with golden-colored melted butter, which must be poured directly into the inside of a bite of *khinkali* before you eat it all.

The Luxury Wines of Zangaura

After lunch, our way lies to Zangaura, an unusual Kakhetian village with a subtropical climate. It turns out that the inhabitants of Zangaura, like their neighbors from Leliani, come from Imereti, their ancestors having been resettled there more than a hundred years ago.

In Zangaura, we are met by the hospitable owner of the Georgian Wines winery, Merab Buzaladze, a true man of passion. In the difficult 1990s, when Georgia and its inhabitants were exhausted by civil wars, Merab, a nuclear physicist, made a bet on winemaking and, as time has shown, he did not go wrong in his choice. Merab realized not only his own plan, but also the dream of his family, having bought back 153 hectares from the state which had belonged to his family before the revolution. Now, Merab produces 15 types of wine, for which he has received top awards at both Georgian and international exhibitions. Merab makes Saperavi wine from his own grapes, and buys white grapes from farmers in Imereti and Kakheti. In addition, his land grows many fruit and melon crops, as well as nuts.

He tells us that during the construction of the winery, a lot of historical finds were made on the land: jewelry and crockery, which, according to scientists, are from 2100 to 3000 years old. Today, these finds are showcased in glass cabinets in a large, cool hall, where, after a glass of chilled water, we taste the first of his wines: a young, white, Kakhetian Mtsvane.

During a talk on the history of the winery, we are particularly impressed by a huge clay *qvevri* found during excavations. It has been placed in the same museum-hall, arranged carefully in a wooden frame.

"Why didn't you give this *qvevri* to a museum?" we ask Merab. "Isn't this exhibit of museum value?"

"Scientists, of course, came here, and they appreciated all our finds," he tells us. *"But for a museum, a qvevri of two thousand years old does not represent any special historical value."*

Indeed, if we take into account that Georgian winemaking is 8000 years old, it is easy to understand his logic!

After refreshing ourselves with that glass of young wine, we walk to the old trees, in the shade of which a luxurious table has been laid, with sun loungers and hammocks all around. Nearby, a stream gurgles, in the water of which melons and watermelons, plucked especially for us, are cooling. Here, we are to taste the rest of the wine and viands prepared for us by the tempters Gio and Kristo.

As an introduction, a brightly colored, pink, semi-dry Saperavi is perfect, with a taste that is something between forest blackberries, strawberries and fragrant peach. Here, this wine is called not "pink," but "ruby" (*lalisperi*). After a pause and another sip of cool water, we hear Merab's story about the difference between Kakhetian and Imeretian wines, and in parallel taste white wines Tsitska-Tsolikauri, Krakhuna, Khikhvi and Kisi. One succeeds the other in increasing intensity of taste, color and aroma.

The appetizers accompanying the wine are like an opera overture, each building excitement for what comes next. Kristo's milky *sulguni* with tarragon and red basil, *regani*, as well as Svan salt and homemade red *tkemali* sauce, and thin rolls of *sulguni* filled with *nadugi* and tarragon and mint, all ideally complemented by light white wines.

This extremely informative tasting in the evening sunshine is interrupted by a walk to a small lake with an island, also on Merab's land. The heat still lingers; the air is dense and humid. Every movement is a challenge, but the physical costs cannot outweigh the monumental views of the Great Caucasus Range and the seemingly endless valley. The sound of cicadas chirping and the scent of meadow flowers accompany us along the tree lines of plum and prunus.

In this small subtropical microzone, the flora and fauna are extremely rich. According to Merab, his fields are among the most important places where migratory birds flock on their way from Europe to Africa. Fifteen years ago, he succeeded in getting hunting banned in the area, prompting protests from the locals who had made a living from hunting them. The birds, however, received this change with gratitude, and their numbers are increasing by the year!

After the walk, we continue our sumptuous feast. The more intense rare wines Khihvi and Kisi are accompanied by savory Tusheti cheese, nuts, and dambalkhacho, which we dip in honey, as well as grilled aubergines with herbs, onions and fresh tomatoes.

After dusk, Merab takes us into his vineyard to show us how the saperavi grapes grow, the wine from which he is going to give us a taste of. At the beginning of each row of vines are rosebushes. It turns out that roses are not planted in vineyards for their beauty, or even for their fragrance: roses are susceptible to disease, and are the first to signal if something is wrong. They get sick much earlier than the grapes, giving farmers good warning in advance: if a farmer sees a diseased rose bush, they immediately take action to save the vine.

Merab generously shares his oenological wisdom with us. He tells us, for example, that vines should be planted in such a way that the wind, which in this area usually blows from west to east, does not damage the grapes.

Our feast is topped off with two types of Saperavi. One of them, the younger, has a bright bouquet of cherries and light spices. The other, more mature, has an aftertaste of ripe figs and plums. The wine is thick and dark red. It is not for nothing that red wines are called "black" in Georgia! The best accompaniment for red wine is meat, and our Gio has juicy mtsvadi kebabs of pork and beef just about ready.

As a rule, Georgians do not eat desserts in their classic form. After a feast like ours, it is easy to see why: a hearty meal leaves no room for sweet excesses, unless, of course, we are talking about fruit filled with juices, whose analogues cannot be found elsewhere. It's hard to deny ourselves the pleasure of tickling our taste buds with the crunch of ripe watermelon and the honeyed flavor of melon.

Our amazing day is coming to an end. It has been so full of different flavors and aromas: a real culinary ecstasy!

Telavi — Zangaura — Tbilisi, July 2018

Visiting Again

In the fall of 2024, we revisited Merab Buzaladze's Georgian Wines winery. During this second meeting, we learned about his six-year-long project to revive forgotten endemic grape varieties from different regions of Georgia and to produce wine from them. It is known that Georgian grape varieties — Chkhaveri, Rkatsiteli, Meskhuri Mtsvane — are the ancestors of many European wines. Merab obtains information for his research on the origin of grape varieties and their genetic relationships from the Max Planck Institute. He has allocated 15 hectares of land for this project, on which he has planted 50 ancient grape varieties, among them Kakhetian Kakhuri-Mtsvivani, Bodburi Chitistvala, Ikalto Tsiteli, Imeretian Tsirkvalis Tetri and Kvelouri, Meskhetian Meskhuri Mtsvane, and Kartlian Gabasha. We tasted some of these new "old" wines. And it was a very unusual experience, because the taste of many of them was quite exotic!

Despite being a small country, in Georgia there is an amazing combination of incongruity: hedonism and daily hard work. This comes from the fact that life on the plains and life in the mountains is very different. Next, we head off on our way to the land where, according to legend, the heirs of the Crusaders live.

Kristo and Gio cooking for the feast at Zangaura Wine Estate

Churchkhela and spices seller at Telavi market

Winemaker Merab Buzaladze during the wine harvest at the Zangaura Wine Estate in Kakheti

The author wearing papakha, a traditional Georgian hat, on the way to Khevsureti

Chapter 23.
Khevsureti. Heaven beneath the Clouds

Dreams of traveling to Khevsureti, located in the north-east of Georgia, have weighed on me for a long time. Not only is it one of the least accessible places in the country, its main wealth is its mountains, steep cliffs, the fortress of Shatili and Mutso, as well as endless mountain rivers, gorges, alpine meadows on steep slopes, dense forests and snow-covered peaks. There are legends about the Khevsurs, describing them as direct heirs of the crusader knights. Well, admit it: who among you would not like to communicate with the descendants of the Crusaders?

Descendants of the Crusaders

The legend that the Khevsurs originated from the Crusaders is one of the most famous and romanticized versions of the origin of this unique mountain people of Georgia. According to legend, a part of the Crusaders who participated in the Crusades became cut off from their main forces and, retreating, settled in the inaccessible mountainous regions of Khevsureti. They mixed with the local population, and their descendants became Khevsurs. Some researchers point to certain cultural features of the Khevsurs, which are believed to have Crusader origins, such as armor and weapons, flags with crosses, and certain customs, such as the veneration of flags, which have similarities to European knightly traditions. Khevsurs traditionally used chain mail, swords, and shields, reminiscent of the armaments of medieval European knights.

Nevertheless, most modern scholars consider this legend a romantic fiction. Archeological research in Khevsureti has not provided convincing evidence of the presence of Crusaders in this region.

Many Georgian and Caucasian ethnographers and historians believe that Khevsurs are an ancient Georgian people, formed in the mountainous regions of Georgia as a result of natural ethnogenesis, long before the appearance of the Crusaders. Similarities in weapons and symbols are explained by cultural contacts with neighboring peoples, including the Byzantines, who also used crosses and knightly armor.

Despite the lack of scientific confirmation, the legend of the Khevsurs' origin from the Crusaders plays an important role in their self-awareness and cultural identity. It emphasizes their militancy, independence, and connection to European culture.

***

One day, my good friend Zura delighted me with the news that he and I were finally going to that cherished Khevsureti region!

Zura is a former rugby player and theater director. He has been exploring the secrets and trails of Khevsureti since 1971, and visits the region regularly, either with his guests, or on his own. He knows the region by heart, perhaps even better than the locals themselves!

Pshav-Khevsureti is the correct name for this region. I had merely a superficial knowledge, having only once had time to visit the picturesque village of Roshka before the Datvisjvari Pass (Bear's Cross Pass). From Roshka, we went to the magnificent Abdelauri lakes. But that is a separate story.

On my first visit to Khevsureti, I did not manage to make it to Shatili, the main settlement of Khevsureti, and since then, I have been itching to go further into the region to finally see Shatili and Mutso, fortress towns with their back-to-back impregnable Medieval towers.

"Believe me, dear friend, there is a real tourist boom in Shatili! Why do we need Shatili? I'll show you places where tourists rarely set foot," Zura promised.

He lent me his huge rucksack and asked me to pack only the necessities: warm clothes, waterproof shoes, socks, hat, gloves, some food, but a minimum: a couple of tins, apples, hard-boiled eggs, tea, coffee, *khachapuri*, biscuits, and *chacha*.

"We should definitely travel light," Zura warned me. *"We'll probably leave the car about halfway to Khone, as beyond that it's off-road: the road was washed out after heavy rains last summer. And we will have to carry sleeping bags with us. We won't need tents: we'll sleep in the houses. On beds, but in sleeping bags."*

And so, one early, late-September morning, we set off. It is hot in Tbilisi and I wonder what awaits us in the mountains. We travel in my car. I drive, because Zura doesn't have a driving licence. He had convinced me that the road was "harmless" and that the pass could be dangerous only in bad weather.

The Datvisjvari (Bear's Cross) Pass

Compared to the Abano Pass, which leads from Kakheti to Tusheti, the way to Pshav-Khevsureti through the Datvisjvari Pass is really not that difficult: the ascent is not steep, and two cars can easily pass by each other on the road.

Autumn has already touched nature with gold and crimson here, but the September sun still gives the feeling of summer.

The nature of Pshavi (the region up to the pass) is characterized by soft landscapes. Of course, these are already quite high mountains, but they are not yet massive, not harsh, but are incredibly picturesque. These mountains peak out from behind each other, not obscuring the traveler's perspective. That is why it is good to go to the Georgian mountains not to get away from oneself, but to find oneself anew and discover new horizons.

Traveling Companions

On the way, we meet a young couple from Russia slowly walking up with huge rucksacks. Zura asks me to stop the car and invites them to come with us. The Muscovites are surprised at our attention, because they didn't even ask us to stop. *"We only recently got to Georgia, and haven't had time to get used to the legendary hospitality,"* our new traveling companions joke, thanking us for our help.

They have an interesting program planned: with us, they will drive to the pass to get a bird's-eye view of Khevsureti, then they will head back, walk to Roshka, and from there cross the Abdelauri lakes and the Chaukhi Pass (3338 meters above sea level) to Dzhuta, the only Khevsureti village on the other side of the Pass leading to the Mtiuleti region. From Dzhuta, they will have easy access to the village of Stepantsminda (Kazbegi), and further on—through the Darial Gorge—straight home to Russia. At the Pass (2,689 meters), after a brief photo session, we and our companions go our separate ways: passing Shatili and Mutso, Zura and I are heading to the village of Khonistsikhe, where his friends Liana and Otar live.

"Gamarjveba" Means "Victory"

On the way, Zura points towards villages completely abandoned by their people. After the Second World War, in 1952, an urbanization program was carried out, during which the Khevsurs were forcibly relocated to the valleys. An urban-type settlement called Gamarjveba was built near Tbilisi. It is a dormitory town where there is no work for the people, and where the only way to survive is through housekeeping and trading at Tbilisi's Lilo wholesale market, or by making commercial trips to and from Turkey. Only a few of the migrants regularly climb up to their native Khevsureti mountains.

Before reaching Shatili, Zura suggests we stop and explore one of the few well-preserved, free-standing watchtowers near the first village after

the Pass, Lebais Kari. We climb up the steep slope with the speed of mountain goats (though keeping up with this long-legged hiker is a challenge for
me!). The view from the top is dizzying, fantastic, my first "ooh" moment
on the other side of the Pass.

In Shatili, sixty towers huddle together. According to legend, ancient
Shatili was founded by Queen Tamar during the Golden Age of Georgian
history, but the settlement acquired its current appearance a little later, in
the 14th century, when Mongols appeared in the North Caucasus, raiding
Georgian lands. The main task of the fortress town was to defend the Georgian land from enemies, who in these parts most often came from the
North.

Almost no one lives in the towers now, and the fortress town, a can-
didate for inclusion on the UNESCO World Heritage List, has become an
open space for travelers with fantasies of historical adventure.

In Shatili, you can find
many guesthouses and cafés, and
even a good mobile signal. There
will be no such "luxury" on the
next leg of our journey.

Tamar's official title is not queen, but king.
This is how *mepe* is translated. According to
Georgian tradition, queens were wives and
mothers of kings, in Georgian *dedopali*.

Our way from Shatili lies through a beautiful forest along the river
called Arguna. On the left side are huge, sheer cliffs resembling stalactites.
It is hard to imagine that this is a creation of nature and not the work of
human hands. We pass by crypts located high above the mountain river:
people used to come here from the village of Anatori and shut themselves
away to die alone, so as to avoid infecting their families and friends. This
was the case particularly when the black pox was raging in these parts.

We continue on our way, through the abandoned fortress town of
Mutso, which suddenly grows before our eyes like a crown on the high
cliff. Mutso is believed to be an even older settlement than Shatili, thought
to have been inhabited from around the 10th to 13th centuries onwards.

Mutso is built of local, natural stones, using the principle of an eagle's
nest, on an impregnable rock. Like its counterpart in Shatili, the Mutso fortress is a single fortress house that served as a defense for all its inhabitants.
Inside the fortress are residential houses, each of which looks like a fortress
itself.

Mutso was a family castle and belonged simultaneously to three families: Daiauri, Cholokashvili and Torgva. The Cholokashvili clan later
moved to Kakheti; the Torgva clan was partially dissolved and merged
with the Chincharauli clan; and the third clan that once owned the fortress
moved to the village of the same name at the base of the fortress. At the

end of the 19th century, both the fortress of Mutso and the village of Mutso were deserted.

In 2014, the National Agency for the Preservation of Cultural Heritage of Georgia, under the Ministry of Culture and Sport of Georgia, decided to rehabilitate Mutso. With the support of charitable foundations, and with the participation of local residents, rehabilitation work and the construction of a small hydropower plant on the Andaki River began. As soon as there was running water, electricity and communication with the outside world, people started to return to the village.

Mutso was given the status of Monument of National Importance and turned into a cultural museum-reserve. The project to restore the high-mountain village of Mutso was awarded the Europa Nostra Award (European Heritage Awards / Europa Nostra Awards) in 2019, for saving this wonderful piece of history and culture from oblivion.

A Khevsur Legend about the Construction of Mutso

An invincible Khevsur warrior named Torgva built the fortress of Mutso to protect the village of Ardoti, upstream of the Andaki River.

After the erection of Mutso, Torgva summoned the Khevsurs from all the neighborhood. And they stood in a single line from Mutso all the way to Anatori. Torgva took a large stone and handed it to the Khevsur next to him. He then passed it to the man beside him. Thus, passing stones from hand to hand in a chain, the Khevsurs built a whole town in just one day.

Visiting Garcia

Zura introduced me to an old friend of his, a Khevsur by birth with the sonorous Spanish name "Garcia." Unlike the legendary Torgva, Garcia did not build his house in a day, but he did do it entirely with his own hands! Keeping to the Khevsur tradition, he made his house of woven rods and wooden blocks. The walls were then insulated with hay and covered in clay. It is a warm, nice and cozy construction, with a small kitchen, a fireplace, and a magnificent summer terrace with many flowers. I wished I could stay with Garcia for a day or two!

Before moving home to his ancestral land, Garcia lived in Gamarjveba and taught at the University of Tbilisi. However, rather than return to his native village, which is really far away in the mountains, he built a house in the gorge, right by the river, in a lushious meadow. He also built a bridge over the river all by himself.

Garcia spends most of the year in Khevsureti. *"What can I do in the city? There is dirt and hustle and bustle, but here there is silence, not even a television, and nothing to distract you from life,"* Garcia says thoughtfully.

Unspoken and unhurried, like most Khevsurs, Garcia is incredibly hospitable, treating us to vodka and delicious homemade cheese and bread that he bakes himself. Oh, it's so hard to tear yourself away from this fragrant, fluffy bread!

We spend about an hour chatting, eating mountain delicacies and making toast after toast. I don't want to leave Garcia's home, and not just because of his bread. And my gut feeling doesn't deceive me: a little later it becomes clear that this was the last haven of comfort in the Khevsureti region.

Khevsureti — Onwards and Upwards, into the Past!

We reluctantly say goodbye to the hospitable Garcia and move on. As we pass the border guards, Zura tells me that he knows many of them from his childhood. Indeed, the military men were friendly to Zura, and not only them: everywhere we went, people would rush up to and hug Zura, eager to share the latest news with him. I reminded myself that, in the mountains, there is no point trying to rush anywhere: you simply need to relax and savor every moment. That's how it is, my beloved Georgia!

The main topic of discussion was the road: had it been repaired after the bad weather? Would we be able to get to Khonischala by car, or would we have to leave it on the road? The guards tell us that someone had recently managed to drive a jeep to the village, and suggested we could try it too.

After crossing a turbulent mountain river, we try several times to drive up a steep rise on a road strewn with large, sharp stones. By the fourth attempt, we realize we can't make it: we will have to leave the car down by the river, and with our rucksacks and bags on us, walk the next kilometer to the village on foot.

Khonischala and its Inhabitants

There are only a few houses in the village of Khonistshala on the banks of the Khonistshali River, and only four of them are inhabited — the rest are empty, as most people moved to the city long ago.

Zura's friends, Liana and Otar Shetekauri, live in a small, squat house with only a few rooms: a kitchen, a dining room, and two bedrooms. Next to it are several other buildings: a barn, a stable and a building that used to be the children's room. Now, the three adult daughters live in Gamarjveba, and tourists sleep in their quarters.

Travelers come by Khonischala on their way from Tusheti to Khevsureti, or vice versa. No one can miss Khonischala.

I sleep in the former nursery. There are three old spring beds, and the walls are hung with faded posters with pictures of sportsmen and pop stars. The room is lit by a paraffin lamp. Zura sleeps in the house next to the kitchen, on the same kind of spring bed. It's cold. We both zip ourselves tight into our sleeping bags.

Highlander Life

The houses in the village are low-to-the-ground, with few or no windows. In the mountains, they save on heat, light and food. There is no electricity. In the past, rooms were lit with tinder or paraffin lamps, but now they have adapted to the times by installing solar panels. There is no gas in the mountains, so they heat the rooms and cook food with small wood stoves. There's also no running water or sewage system. I ask Zura if I can take a shower somewhere, and he laughs and replies, *"You can shower when you get back home! The Khevsurs only wash themselves in July!"*

On the road, Zura tells me at length about the difficult life of the local people. To survive, they have to work tirelessly, he says. In these places, unlike other regions of Georgia, it is incredibly difficult to support oneself completely through agriculture: you can grow only potatoes, carrots, cabbage, courgettes and herbs in a vegetable garden. The main local wealth is milk, butter and cheese. The locals stock up for the whole winter in advance, and also prepare produce to sell. There is another salvation here, too: hunting.

I ask to hear more about how they prepare for the long winters. It turns out to be a long list! They clean the stable, take the cattle to pasture, stock up on firewood, mow and dry hay in stacks, milk the cows, and make cheese and clarified butter from the resulting milk. They also dry edible and medicinal plants, pickle ramsons (bear's garlic, or Allium ursinum) and other vegetables, and make jam from forest berries. And they pray continuously that the weather does not fail them; that the summer isn't wet, and that the hay has time to dry. It is hard for us city flowers to imagine the difficult conditions in which people who can only rely on hard physical labor sometimes live.

A Khevsur Meal

Most of the day-to-day products the locals need are brought here from the city, and I see our hosts have plenty of sweets, *chacha*, sweet peppers and cucumbers. We are sorry we didn't bring much with us: we should have taken this into account in advance.

While Zura is chatting with Otar about life and living, Liana is setting the table for dinner. We have pasta soup with meat and tomato paste, pickled ramsons, cheese, and a salad of tomatoes and cucumbers (the tomatoes were brought from the city by a neighbor). We eat in semi-darkness (the light of the only bulb is very dim) and drink *chacha*, making toast after toast, as is customary in every decent Georgian family. The owners speak little Russian, but they seem to understand everything. I try to use my Georgian to the best of my ability, but when my vocabulary runs out, Zura translates my toasts.

You're Your Own Donkey

In the morning, Zura once again asks me to double-check if there is anything extra in my rucksack that I can leave behind that might otherwise weigh me down. Today, we have to climb even higher, and walk about three kilometers, to the village of Khone, to where Otar and Liana's winter residence is located. In summer, they live by the river, at an altitude of 1,700 meters above sea level. In winter, contrary to logic, they do not go down to the valley, but go up to the village of Khone, at an altitude of 2,100 meters. Why? Because their cows do not graze in Khone in summer, so they gather masses of hay there for winter, drying it and gathering it into stacks so they and their cows can survive the cold weather.

There used to be a road to Khone. Though not asphalted, it was still good enough for most vehicles to drive on. But last year it was completely washed away by heavy rains. Now, the only way to reach the village is on horseback or on foot. It's not too difficult for us with our not-too-heavy rucksacks. But how do the locals manage to do it when it's time to pack up and head up for the winter? The Shetekauri family does not have a horse: the last one died of old age and there is no money for a new one. They had a donkey, but it was eaten by wolves.

"Liana and Otar have become their own beasts of burden," Zura says with a wry smile. *"Civilization and progress haven't necessarily benefited the highlanders. Where they once only had to provide for themselves within their village, they now bear the added responsibility of supporting relatives in the city, sending them money and supplies when necessary."*

Now the most important thing is that the weather doesn't let us down. In the mountains, even in summer, the weather is impossible to predict, and even more so in autumn. After breakfast, we look at the sky: will it rain or not? As soon as the clouds are dispersed by the wind, Zura gives a command: *"Onwards and upwards!"* We say goodbye to our hosts until an indefinite "later," as we don't yet know how long we will stay up there.

Crossing Bridges

Liana explained to us that we first had to walk along the river and cross three bridges before the upward climb would begin.

I find the first bridge dubiously unreliable: the wooden beams between the large flat stones wobble and creak so terribly, I just can't find my balance, and my huge rucksack makes it even worse! Zura, however, crosses the bridge playfully and commands me: *"Come on! Take off your rucksack and cross the bridge without it! Then you'll feel more confident and can go back for your rucksack."*

What a strategy! And then I come up with a strategy of my own: I decide to crawl across. It's easier to feel stable on all fours, surely? A deceptive feeling... But I did make it to the other side. We cross the river two more times on the same wobbly bridges, and then we start climbing.

You can't see the paths, and Zura leads me along by instinct. The views are getting more and more dizzying, and the river already seems like a thin, winding ribbon far below us. We don't head toward the top of the mountain, but turn sideways onto a narrow path, the mountain on the left and the abyss on the right. The path is overgrown with grass, so the drop-off is barely visible. *"Careful!"* Zura warns me. *"If you stumble, you'll slide straight down, and then no-one will be able to help you!"*

I remember what I was once taught by a St. Petersburg parkourist: *"When you are high up and get scared, never look down, but try to focus on things at eye level. That way, the fear will pass."* So that's what I do. Now the main thing is not to stumble. Of course, I want to admire the view, but I'm not up to it yet. On the way, I keep thinking how nice it would be to learn to combine pleasure and caution.

Zura points out the main chapel of the area, named in honor of Saint Athenogenes, who, in the 4th century, preached Christianity in Khevsureti, a gift for which he was burned. The chapel is about thirty meters up the hill from us, but I can't go there: women are not allowed to approach, let alone enter, the shrines. Zura comforts me by promising to show me a photograph of the place once we get back home.

We're walking on a windswept section, the wind pounding us. It's not easy to stay on the path, and when we turn into the birch forest, I breathe a sigh of relief. The trees here are not tall; they all lean to the ground, the way the wind has shaped them. Just as us humans are shaped by our destiny, I think to myself.

It is almost windless in the forest now, and it smells pleasantly of spicy autumn leaves.

After passing through the forest, we cross the river once more and emerge into a sun-drenched alpine meadow. What a wonderful reward for the journey!

Khone

The village we come to is tiny: there are more haystacks than houses. In the meadow, men have huge piles of hay on their backs. Zura explains that this is how they carry the hay from the meadows to the village. They used to grow wheat and potatoes there, but there are too few people now, so they have abandoned the practice. I look down at them, working like ants, and I don't understand how on such steep slopes it is possible not only to do something productive, but to remain on one's feet while doing so! The locals don't even have horses, and I'm told each sheaf weighs at least 40 kilos. Can you imagine how much weight the Khevsurs carry every day? But the mountaineers are a hard-working, resilient and unbending people.

Zura tells me a sad story. In May last year, a local from the Shetekauri clan was herding sheep to another gorge: 400 sheep and 40 young bulls and heifers. At night, a landslide came down and covered all the livestock, together with the shepherd. Only a few cows survived. The brothers found the place where the shepherd's hut was and managed to recover his body. The family lost both a loved one and their sole source of income, and yet received no help from the state. And that same year, in August, another landslide swept away the road from Khone to Khonishchala, washing away the iron bridge, which has yet to be restored.

Our Khevsur Life

We got into the village before the rain started. Zura even had time to chop some wood for the evening.

We enter Otar and Liana's winter home and start to settle in: Zura gives me the room with the wood stove, and he lies down on the bed in the hallway. Zura's room smells mercilessly of garlic, as it is where they store the pickled ramsons. The Khevsurs also keep a constant supply of ghee, cheese and potatoes in their houses.

The house is even more squat than Otar and Liana's summer dwelling in Khonischala: it is a real dugout, with an earthen floor. In addition to beds, there is an old wardrobe, a couple of tables and chairs, and two benches by the stove. The conditions in Khone are truly spartan. I go outside. There is another bench in front of the house, and I sit down on it and gaze, mesmerized, at the panorama of mountains and clouds. It's already dark, and it looks like the stars are just a stone's throw away.

A Fugitive

On the way to the village, we met a swarthy, wind-dried man of about 55, called Valiko, carrying bundles of hay. I learn something curious about this Valiko, that he is not a local but a "refugee." Not from Abkhazia, though: from the world!

Genatsvale is a Georgian expression that's very difficult to translate directly, as it carries a lot of emotional weight and cultural nuance. It's a term of endearment and affection, and it can be used in a variety of situations. While not a perfect translation, it roughly translates to "I'll take your place" or "I'll take your pain." This implies a deep sense of care and willingness to sacrifice for the other person. It's used as a term of affection, similar to "darling," "sweetheart," or "my dear," but with a stronger sense of warmth and respect. *Genatsvale* is a very versatile and expressive word that reflects the warmth and hospitality of Georgian culture. It's a way of showing that you care deeply about someone.

"Valiko fled here from the world about sixteen years ago. The locals took him in, and now he's almost like one of their own: he works and lives with everyone else."

I ask why he fled the world. It turns out he lost at a game of cards.

"So he decided to run to the mountains to cure himself of an incurable card addiction?" I ask Zura.

"It's much simpler than that, genatsvale!" he replies. *"If Valiko hadn't run away, he would have been killed for his debts!"*

A Birthday Party

Our stove hadn't really heated up properly by the time it started to get dark. I was just starting to get uncomfortable, when our "refugee" Valiko popped his head round the door and invited us to a birthday party. The evening was saved! Well, of course, how can you be in Georgia without going to visit people?! It turned out a local guy was celebrating his 23rd birthday, and we had been invited to join the fun. We grabbed the Estonian chocolate bars I had brought and the Krakow sausage Zura had saved, and with these gifts we set off.

The neighboring dugout, similar to ours, is half-dark, but it is heated and smells deliciously of freshly cooked food.

At the stove sits an elderly man, joined by Valiko, and three young boys, including the birthday boy. A slumped old woman, dried out by the weather and life's hardships, silently serves food into metal bowls for us.

We are treated to chowder made of young *lobio* (green beans), with potatoes, cheese and homemade bread, as well as delicious fruit vodka. Toast after toast, time flies by. For dessert: candies. Looking like Santa Claus handing out presents, Valiko takes candies out of a bag and passes them round.

They have a radio, and it catches a Chechen channel which occasionally broadcasts Georgian music. We are warm, cozy, and having fun. When I get tired of following the conversation, I lean back on the bed and start taking notes. *"What are you writing there?"* Zurab asks me. "Poems," I reply. *"Poems are good! But don't read them to us now!"* he says. The reason for his request is simple: none of the people present except for Zura understand my native tongue!

And Up Again, Under the Clouds!

The next day, the weather favors us, and we set off on the hike that Zura and I had long planned. My friend will take me far, far away, to the foot of Tebulo (4492 meters), the highest mountain in north-eastern Georgia, with Chechnya just behind its snowy peak. It will take about five hours to walk there.

"What if it rains?" I ask.

"Then we'll get wet," Zura replies calmly.

The thought that we might not reach our destination because of the weather makes me uncomfortable. How frustrating it is not to reach your goals! Wouldn't it be better not to try at all? I realize I'm being silly, or at least asking inappropriate questions. But it is in the mountains that all our fears manifest themselves. Or maybe in ordinary life we just don't realize the fears we're carrying around.

We're walking upwards. There is no path again: we walk wherever our eyes and feet lead us. There is tall grass and very loose ground everywhere. We are surrounded by open space and phenomenal views! However, in Khevsureti, where the mountains are crowded, the feeling of space and openness is less than it is in Tusheti or Svaneti, pushing you to go higher to try to see farther.

The climb is steep. Zura teaches me not to walk in spurts, but to move slowly, without stopping.

The higher we climb, the lower the grass and the colder and windier it gets. Vladimir Vysotsky's songs about mountains buzz around in my head. I have already put on all the warm clothes I packed: a hooded sweatshirt and a windbreaker. Heavy black clouds begin to thicken in the sky. Now the thought of going higher makes me feel quite uncomfortable.

> **Vladimir Vysotsky** (1938 -1980) was a highly influential Soviet singer-song-writer, poet, and actor. He was renowned for his distinctive, raspy voice and his deeply emotional and socially conscious lyrics. He was a prolific songwriter, penning over 600 songs that often explored themes of everyday life, social injustice, and human struggle. Vysotsky was a passionate mountaineer. This personal experience heavily influenced his creative output. Essentially, the mountains were a strong metaphor within his work, representing a space for true human experience and a place to test the limits of the human character.

I timidly articulate these concerns to Zura, but he ignores them completely. Two hours later, in a meadow, Zura finally suggests we take a break and have a snack. We hide from the wind behind huge boulders. Lying on the sun-heated rocks feels so good! I thaw out a little and start to come back to life. Zura shares with me a *khabizgina* pie filled with potatoes and cheese.

We are already at an altitude of 2,100 meters, but Zura is aiming higher. He tells me he has often spent nights alone in the caves up there, and in the mornings he has watched mountain goats and aurochs or roe deer playing.

"You'll never see such things down here!" he says. *"The chance of encountering people here is much less than encountering a bear or auroch."*

Then he exclaims: *"Look, it looks like a bear was lying right in this spot, and recently too!"* Indeed, in many places the grass appears squashed.

I ask how dangerous it would be to actually meet a bear out here.

"If the bear isn't hungry, and if you don't attack it yourself, and if it's not a female bear with a cub, then no, it's not dangerous," Zura says calmly.

I wonder if he gets scared of bears when he's out here alone.

"If I go into the mountains for a long time and alone, I usually take some kind of weapon with me, like a knife," he tells me.

Looking at the thickening clouds, I convince Zura we should start heading back down to humanity. I'm afraid the rain will catch us on the road, and end up with us stuck in a cave somewhere. Zura grudgingly agrees with my reasoning. If I had taken my chances and pushed on, we'd have got to Mount Tebula in an hour and a half to two hours, we'd have seen the Khuro Gorge, where there were landslides last year, and, if we'd kept climbing, we'd eventually have come to the Chechen border.

But these are all places we are stocking up for our next foray under less ominous clouds.

On the way back, we stop every now and then to bask in the sun. The clouds are gradually parting, and the sun is beginning to shine. It will rain only in the evening and will be pouring all night. But for now — bliss!

On the way down, I realize how important the practice of mountain marching is in hiking. It's not just cardio exercise, but a specialized technique, good for heading both up and down.

"You can easily spot inexperienced hikers on their way down," Zura says, as if reading my mind. *"You shouldn't walk, but run down in zigzags, as if you are skiing."* He demonstrates the technique, and I realize I need many more hours of training!

We get home in the evening. We stoke the stove and, while our dinner is boiling, drink tea on our luxurious "terrace" with its panoramic view. We have a royal dinner — boiled potatoes with melted butter, cheese and eggs. We don't have much else to do, and the hot food in our stomachs makes us sleepy. Time for an early night!

Back to "Civilization"!

When I wake up at seven the next day, I hear a troubling sound. Peeking out the door, I see is rain, and a lot of it! It is dripping through the roof in the room where my friend is spending the night, into a bucket placed purposefully under the hole. Zura, wrapped up like a baby in his sleeping bag, is still snoozing sweetly in his bed. I go back to my own bed, but can't find sleep again. I want to go down already. What could we do in this mountain dugout in the pouring rain? We had no more city food left, the tea and coffee had all been drunk, the fruit and vegetables had been eaten. We had only an inviolable reserve of ramsons, ghee and potatoes.

"It's raining," my friend states when he finally wakes up. *"So we'll sleep on! What else can we do?"*

Oh, my God! What sleep?! All we've done for the last three days is sleep: early to bed, late to rise! I want to go swimming! And to find out what happened in the world during these three days. We have no connection with civilization and I'm on edge. What if the rain washes out the road and our one path back? We've got to get down now. Right now!

But Zura is unfazed. He burrows back into his sleeping bag. *"Take your time,"* he tells me. *"If the rain doesn't stop today, it will tomorrow. Don't worry, we will definitely reach Tbilisi by the eighth of March."*

It is clear to me that Zura is in no rush to leave. For him, the Khevsureti mountains are always a paradise, no matter the weather. That's what I call true love!

I persuade him up when the rain turns to a drizzle two hours later. We are accompanied on our walk down by a small dog, who runs ahead of us, wagging her tail merrily. Although it is damp and quite cold, we are again walking, with birds singing in our hearts!

We get to the bridge I crawled across. And on the other side, Liana meets us. I cheer, and find myself shouting out my desire for hot coffee. She leads us back to her home and indulges us. The Indian instant coffee over hot, fresh milk, that she made for us that day in Khonischala was the most delicious coffee I have ever had in my life! And when we reached the car, I had the feeling that we were almost home in Tbilisi.

On the road, near Shatili, the mobile signal reconnected, and "civilization," with all the power of its sms messages and missed calls, came pouring down on our poor heads.

Reflecting on Khevsureti

Khevsureti greeted me not only with harsh weather; the trip there coincided with a personal storm in my life, and so anxieties and doubts tormented me, and the fear of bad weather wouldn't let go. But it is in moments like those, I later realized, that it is especially important to challenge yourself, even if the challenge is small. Only by overcoming obstacles do we realize how much we sometimes exaggerate our everyday problems. And the mountains help you to see your life from a different perspective. The harsh life of the Khevsurs, their resilience in the face of difficulties, became a healing lesson for me, helping me to overcome my own adversities.

Advanced information on Khevsureti

The unapproachable and harsh, yet mesmerizing region of Khevsureti, with its legends and unique traditions, definitely deserves a closer attention of travelers and researchers. This story presented my personal experience of discoveries and adventures. For those who wish to delve deeper into everything Khevsureti, I recommend looking into the works of people who have made significant contributions to the study of the region, among them Georgian historian Ivane Javakhishvili; Russian-German researcher Gustav Radde; director of the Caucasus Museum, who traveled through Khevsureti and left behind the monograph 'Khevsureti and the Khevsurs'

(1878); Yan Marr, a Georgian-born orientalist, linguist, and ethnographer of Georgian-Scottish origin; and Georgian poet and writer Vazha-Pshavela (Luka Razikashvili), who was considered a great expert on Khevsureti. Vazha-Pshavela's works, such as the poem 'Aluda Ketelauri,' are based on a deep understanding of Khevsur customs and traditions. Vazha-Pshavela's works can be considered invaluable ethnographic material.

Khonischala—Khone—Tbilisi, September – October 2016

Zura crossing a stormy Khevsur river

Zura (on the left) in the house of Liana and Otar Shetekauri

Pastoral perfection in the Khevsur village of Roshka

Visiting Garcia (on the left)

German timber-framed houses in the village of Bolnisi, former Katharinenfeld

German wine-cellar in the village of Asureti, former Elisabethtal

Chapter 24.
Kvemo Kartli: The Story of the German Settlements

The South Caucasus has for centuries been a melting pot of various nationalities. The Kvemo Kartli region in southeastern Georgia is a perfect example of this. Here, on the border with Armenia, numerous Azerbaijanis, Armenians and Greeks live alongside Georgians. And remarkable traces of German history can be found in this region too!

Indeed, the German cultural heritage here is over 200 years old. It was primarily the Protestant Württemberg Swabians who settled in the South Caucasus and built churches and German villages of half-timbered houses which bore German names.

The first German colonists were invited to the South Caucasus at the beginning of the 19th century by Russian Tsar Alexander I, who wanted to secure the newly acquired territories on the periphery of the empire in the South Caucasus with loyal Christians who were also considered extremely diligent and hardworking. The Swabians from Württemberg, who suffered hardship and persecution at home, were granted privileges in the Russian Empire, including freedom of religion and exemption from taxes and military service. There was also another group of immigrants—deeply religious people, the Pietists—who believed that the end of the world was imminent and that all who wanted to be saved had to be near Jerusalem.

Thus, at the beginning of the 19th century, five German settlements were established east of Tbilisi: Elisabethtal, Mariendorf, Katharinenfeld, Annenfeld, Helenendorf, and Traubenfeld. By the beginning of the 20th century, the number of German villages in the South Caucasus had grown to 25.

A Modern-Day German "Colonist" in the Village of Elisabethtal

Studying the history of Germans in Georgia led me to the village of Asureti, formerly Elisabethtal. It is a neat, architecturally well-structured village, truly German in spirit.

Although in the early 1990s, most of the descendants of Georgian Germans returned to their historical homeland, one colorful personality, the "colonist" of our time, pensioner Manfred Tikhonov, settled in this village. In 2004, Manfred bought an old, solid, half-timbered house from a German family leaving for Germany, completely renovated it, took up winemaking, and began hosting guests.

Since then, everyone interested in the history of the German settlers in the Caucasus has chosen to make their way to the hospitable Manfred Tikhonov. Over all these years, Manfred has managed to become a local attraction himself, being a kind of encyclopedia of German history in the Caucasus. He is especially revered among German tourists.

I have also been a guest of his many times, and each time it seemed to me that during the fifty-minute trip from Tbilisi to Asureti, I managed to make a forced march straight into Germany.

Manfred Tikhonov is originally from the German federal state of Mecklenburg-Vorpommern. His veins carry German, Polish, and even Russian blood. As it turned out, Manfred's father, whom he never saw in his life, was a Soviet officer during World War II.

Manfred ended up in Georgia shortly after the reunification of Germany. At first, he had his own advertising company in Tbilisi, where he appeared regularly on visits. But subsequently, he decided to settle in Georgia altogether. *"Nature, landscapes, and a little bit the people too, conquered me. Here, I have much less stress and life is calmer. I have my own vineyards, and I make wine and chacha myself,"* Manfred tells me.

Manfred's house previously belonged to a German family, descendants of colonists. It wasn't the elderly members of the family who wanted to move to Germany, but the younger generation, and the elderly had to comply, after selling their old family home.

In Northern Germany, Manfred's fellow countrymen are not familiar with the art of winemaking, because their region is a land of beer. Before moving to Georgia, Manfred only knew about the intricacies of making Bacchus' drink by hearsay. His Georgian neighbors quickly brought him up to speed, however, soon helping him to master winemaking. Now, each season, the modern-day colonist produces up to 1,000 liters of wine, both in oak barrels and in traditional *qvevri*.

In Manfred's old house, there is a substantial wine cellar, where you can find everything necessary for making wine in the European and Georgian traditions.

The newly minted winemaker considers himself a worthy successor of German traditions on Georgian soil.

"Do you know who supplied the army casinos with wine in tsarist times?" he asks. *"It was the Georgian Germans! They grafted local grapes onto wild grapevines, and an excellent new variety came out, which was called 'Black Shala.' At*

first, there were private wineries here, and after collectivization in 1931, a winery was built. The winery building itself was unique: it had three long underground tunnels, fifty meters long, six meters high, and twelve meters wide. Until the 1980s, it operated at full capacity."

The Georgian Germans were famous for their legendary love of order and hard work. It is no coincidence that most of the colonists were Swabians, from southwestern Germany, where the people are considered honed for work and success in business.

Manfred proudly tells me about the renovation of his house, built in 1870. It took a lot of effort to bring it to a presentable condition, but the house itself "helped" him in this: the substance is solid, the walls are almost a meter thick, and the quality of construction is excellent. According to the new owner, all the beams for new houses, without exception, were numbered according to a special system by the Swabian colonists and brought to Georgia from Germany. His house is a clear example of this: the numbering of the beams is still preserved on the timbers.

German Cultural Heritage in the South Caucasus

Professor Oliver Reisner of Ilia State University in Tbilisi has been committed for years to the research, documentation, and preservation of German cultural heritage in the South Caucasus. This heritage includes, among other things, the typical architecture of the former German settlements, those half-timbered houses, and also of agricultural methods and cultural traditions. He emphasizes with enthusiasm that the history of the German settlers is still alive today, preserved within numerous buildings, church records, and other testimonies.

In the summer semester of 2024, I took a seminar with Professor Reisner on the history and culture of the German settlers in the South Caucasus. As part of this seminar, we took a field trip to the former German villages in the Kvemo Kartli region. As chairman of the Association for the Preservation of German Cultural Heritage in the South Caucasus, the professor played a key role in ensuring that the Protestant church in the village of Asureti, formerly Elisabethtal, received a new dome, an important step toward restoring the historical appearance of the church, which had been badly damaged during the Soviet era.

Asureti is characterized by solid building fabric: the streets are straight, and the half-timbered houses, with pretty gardens, were built along a wide street. A perfect German village in the middle of the South Caucasus! The streets of Asureti bear German names- the central street of the village is called Schwabenstraße (Swabian Street). And in the historic

German cemetery, the inscriptions and symbols on the gravestones reveal many exciting secrets. For example, you can see that many children of the settlers died at a young age due to the difficult living conditions and diseases. The gravestones also reflect the growing prosperity of the colonists: while early gravestones are often simple, later ones feature more elaborate decorations and higher-quality materials.

The life and suffering of the Germans in the South Caucasus is concisely summarized by Professor Reisner:

"The first generation: death, the second generation: hardship, and the third generation: prosperity. A generation is 20 to 25 years. They came in 1818. When they finally gave up the idea of going to Jerusalem, they began to 'schaffe, schaffe, Häusle baue' (Swabian for 'work, work, build a house'). And all these houses you see today are from that time- no longer the earthen huts in which they lived at first, but two-story houses. These show that there was prosperity."

The German settlements in the South Caucasus, with their sense of community and their work ethic, were considered model villages. With their German wine, produced in Georgia, the German farmers supplied the entire Russian army. In addition, the German milk and cheese products of the Caucasus Germans were popular throughout the Empire.

It took several more decades before Georgia became attractive to German scientists, writers, architects, artists, and businesspeople. As high officials in the tsarist administration, Germans from the Baltic region also began moving to the South Caucasus.

German-Georgian Wine: A Blend of Traditions

In his memoirs 'Elisabethtal. Our Healthy Homeland. The Life of the Germans in the South Caucasus,' Ernst Schlecht, one of the descendants of the German settlers, described German viniculture in the South Caucasus. By writing his memoirs, Schlecht preserved valuable first-hand accounts of the German communities in the South Caucasus:

"In the village of Elisabethtal, the following grape varieties were cultivated: Muscatel, Rkatsiteli, Black Shalla (Shalla Schwarz), as well as Blauhölzer, Roter Elber, and Runder Weißer. By 1886, viticulture had become the pride of the villagers. The entire economic and social standing of the farmers depended on it. In the early 1930s, the farmers built a public wine cellar that could store 1.8 million liters of wine. There was also a room just for producing cognac. Every farmer had a wine cellar in his house. Until 1929, the farmers measured the amount of wine they produced in buckets- one bucket held 10 liters. Each winegrower had between 500 and 1500 buckets in his cellar. A liter of 'black' wine cost up to 6 rubles, a liter of

white wine up to 5 rubles" (Ernst Schlecht, Elisabethtal. Our Healthy Homeland. The Life of the Germans in the South Caucasus).

During our excursion, we paid a visit to the house-museum and winery of Immanuel Walker, a German winemaker from Katharinenfeld, today Bolnisi. The original furnishings and the many historical photos show how German farmers lived and worked in Georgia. During the wine tasting, we tried Riesling-Rkatsiteli, a Georgian wine with a German accent. Winemaker Guram Avkopashvili tells us the story of an incredible cultural symbiosis:

"The German settlers liked the beautiful color of Georgian wine, but not its taste, which they found too strong. That is why they did not make their wine in clay vessels, qvevri, but in oak barrels. However, as with Georgian winemaking, they fermented the grape skins in the oak barrels and in this way obtained an amber-colored wine with a milder taste, made according to Swabian technology, yet with a Georgian accent."

Painful Years for the German Settlers

With the establishment of Soviet power in Georgia in 1921, the active cultural and economic life of the German community ended abruptly. Within the framework of Soviet religious policy, which aimed at the suppression of religion, the German colonies lost their economic and religious autonomy, and in 1931, the services and gatherings of the Lutheran Church in Tbilisi were banned. Then the elder pastor of the community, Richard Meyer, like many other Lutheran clergymen, fell victim to the regime's repressions. The consequences of collectivization and expropriation, seeing the German colonists dispossessed of their land and forcibly incorporated into collective farms (*kolkhozes*), led to a severe famine in the years 1932-33, the first in the history of the German colonies.

And these events were only the prelude to further persecution: With Hitler's declaration of war on the Soviet Union in 1941, the peaceful life of the German settlers came to a complete close. Overnight, they were declared Hitler's allies and, in October 1941, were deported to Kazakhstan and Siberia. Families from the northern Georgian highlands were then moved into the empty German villages by a Soviet government eager to bring all mountain dwellers under strict state control, something that was easier to achieve in the lowlands.

As part of his research on the history of German settlers in the South Caucasus, Oliver Reisner has recorded many impressive stories. One of them tells what the new settlers found in the abandoned German houses in Asureti in the winter of 1941/42: filled cellars, in which everything was prepared for the long winter — wine, preserved vegetables, and fruit. The Germans had had to leave all of this behind during their deportation in 1941.

"A granddaughter of the new settlers reported that her ancestors felt like they were in paradise, and this in the middle of World War II, a time of great hardship," the professor told me.

In Asureti, I met Guram Schall, one of the last descendants of those Georgian Germans. The fate of his family is deeply tragic.

"During the war, my grandfather was arrested and imprisoned 'for having connections with Germany,'" Guram told me. *"When he was released, he had neither a home nor a family. The whole family had been deported. It was very difficult for him to come back here, particularly psychologically, as the locals continued to call him 'fascist.' And when he was released, his documents were changed so he could no longer claim anything. He built himself a small house near the forest, then bought this plot and built this house in which there isn't even a foundation. I still live here with my son."*

It is sad that Guram Schall grew up at a time when knowing German was considered unsafe. In his family, which was Georgian-Khevsurian, they didn't speak German. Guram considers himself completely detached from his roots.

Only those German women who were married to Georgians were allowed to stay. These women played a special role in Tbilisi in the 1950s and 1960s: they offered informal childcare in their private homes, which soon became known as "German kindergartens." These were mostly informal gatherings in private homes, where Georgian children learned about German culture through Christmas traditions, and German books and songs. Among the Tbilisi elite of that time, it was fashionable to send one's children to these informal childcare facilities, where, in addition to the German language and culture, they were also taught values and knowledge that were considered part of a "proper European education." Many representatives of today's intellectual elite of Georgia were pupils of these "German aunts," as these women were affectionately called in Tbilisi.

The German documentary filmmaker Stefan Tolz, who has lived in Georgia for over 30 years, created a memorial to the German aunts and the vanished German village life in his 1992 film 'The Georgian Feast.' Stefan portrays one of them, Lena, as the last Swabian from the village of Rosenfeld, today Sartichala. With great pride, Lena recounts in the film the bells of her village church. Whenever these bells rang, all the villagers would return from their fields to the village and cultivate their community.

"The Germans were deported in 1941, and when some of them returned in the 1970s, there was no church left, and there was no longer that German village

life that had existed until the 1930s," Stefan says. *"In my film, I showed how Lena sang Swabian folk songs. This means that until the late 1920s, there were still beautiful Swabian folk songs and poems in Georgia that followed the old Swabian song tradition."*

Since their houses were already inhabited by others, not all Germans returned to their villages from exile. After the collapse of the Soviet Union, they relocated to Germany, so that today there are hardly any direct descendants of the German settlers left in Georgia.

German Influences in Georgia's Cultural Heritage

Not only rural areas were shaped by the German settlers: the capital Tbilisi also bears traces of German history. Some districts of Tbilisi, among them Kukia (formerly Neu-Tiflis) and Didube (formerly Alexanderdorf), were once German villages, having been founded at the beginning of the 19th century on the left bank of the Mtkvari River as part of the German immigration.

Architect and art historian Nestan Tatarashvili is passionate about the German history of Georgia and, in her free time, guides tourists on the trail of the German settlers in the Caucasus. She finds the Neu-Tiflis district particularly interesting, as it was there that the European character of the city was especially evident. I learned from Nestan that today's Kote Marjanishvili Square was formerly called Kirchenplatz (Church Square) and was located in the center of Neu-Tiflis. The Evangelical Lutheran St. Peter and Paul's Church once stood here, a project by the German architect Otto Jakobson, executed by his German colleague Leopold Bielfeld in 1897. As a result of Soviet religious policy, which aimed at the removal of religious buildings, the church was demolished in 1946, after World War II. Interestingly, the demolition was carried out by German prisoners of war. *"Unfortunately, not much of old Neu-Tiflis is left today, as this district was later incorporated and fell victim to the urban development processes of the time,"* Nestan tells me.

It was precisely in Neu-Tiflis that almost all skilled tradespeople and businesspeople from throughout Germany, as well as Germans from Russia and the Baltic region, settled. There were German master tailors, watchmakers, bookbinders, shoemakers…and they would employ young Georgians as apprentices, so these professions spread quickly in Georgia. Thanks to the Germans, there was a significant change in various trades: Asian influences noticeably decreased, while European influences increased. The first urban brewery, for example, was opened by the Germans. Until then, Georgians had only brewed beer in the mountains. There were also German bakeries, pharmacies, piano shops, and hotels in Neu-Tiflis. A branch of the Siemens family, which was responsible for the electrification of the country and the construction of the telegraph lines, also lived there.

There was a German school in Neu-Tiflis, which was also accessible to Georgian children. This had a formative influence on many young Georgians, and some of its students went to Germany to study. Many famous Georgian scientists and politicians studied at German universities.

German scholars, artists and writers made a significant contribution to popularizing the South Caucasus in Europe. In the 19th century, a time of growing interest in foreign cultures and languages, some German intellectuals devoted themselves intensively to exploring this region. A prominent example is the German publicist and writer Arthur Leist (1852-1927), who dedicated his life to Georgia and died in Tbilisi. In close collaboration with Ilia Chavchavadze, a central figure of the Georgian national movement, he created the first German-language anthology of Georgian poetry. Leist also translated Shota Rustaveli's masterpiece 'The Knight in the Tiger's Skin,' the Georgian national epic, into German, and wrote numerous works about the land and people of Georgia. In his 1893 book 'The Georgian People,' he created a comprehensive compendium of Georgian history, geography, ethnography, and literary tradition. These works made a significant contribution to disseminating knowledge about the South Caucasus in the German-speaking world, and to arousing interest in the region. Here is an excerpt from his texts:

"Georgia is one of the most beautiful countries on earth, and possesses everything that can satisfy and delight even the most demanding of nature lovers. Its mountain landscapes are as magnificent as those of Switzerland, its lowlands almost as lush as those of Northern Italy; it has water-rich rivers, a diverse flora, and beautiful seashores. Only one adornment is missing for perfect beauty, namely the lakes, of which it possesses only a few of very insignificant size. The traveler who, coming across the Black Sea, enters the country in Batumi, believes himself transported to paradise (...).

"In the brief description of Georgia's nature, the reader may have recognized some similarities with Italy, and I found many occasions for comparison during my stay in the dolce terra latina. The Gurian-Mingrelian lowland on the Black Sea vividly recalls the swampy region between Taranto and Brindisi, or that near Mestre; the rocky, treeless valley of the Kura near Tbilisi resembles the barren landscapes of Campania. The lush and fertile valleys of Kartli and especially Kakheti also exhibit characteristics of Italian nature. The same can be said of the flora" (Arthur Leist, The Georgian People).

Arthur Leist published the only German-language newspaper, 'Kaukasische Post' in Tbilisi, for sixteen years. Unfortunately, the life and work of this Georgia enthusiast, who is buried in the Didube cemetery, remains largely unexplored.

Many other German intellectual giants from science and art promoted Georgia's cultural and scientific rapprochement with Europe in the 19th century. The tireless work of polymath Gustav Radde (1831-1903), a naturalist, zoologist, and founding director of the Caucasian Museum, is responsible for the country receiving its first museum of this kind in 1867. The Caucasian Museum quickly developed into an important center for research on the Caucasus. On the occasion of the Fifth Archeological Congress in Tbilisi in 1881, the Viennese history painter August von Siegen (1850-1910) decorated the walls of the Caucasian Museum with impressive paintings from ancient mythology, the Old Testament, and Georgian history: Prometheus chained to the rock, the arrival of the Argonauts in Colchis, Jason and Medea in the sanctuary of Hecate, Noah with the vine, Amazons on their horses, as well as the Georgian kings David the Builder and King Tamar. Although von Siegen's paintings have not been preserved, this museum still exists today under the name Georgian National Museum, and it continues to be an important research and exhibition center.

Germans in Georgia Now

In Georgia, Germany is often regarded as an important role model due to its economic strength and its role in EU integration. Like from the 1900s to 1920s, today, Georgia's youth are once again showing a strong preference for studying at German universities. Living in a modern democratic society and experiencing European values and freedoms in Germany has a formative influence on new generations of Georgians, and promotes an understanding of European standards, thus contributing to the strengthening of the country's European orientation.

The interest is mutual, as a growing number of Germans have settled in Georgia over the past decades and are active in various professions, including in business, skilled labor in the economy, art and politics, teaching, and IT expertise. This development may be attributed to Georgia's economic opportunities, cultural interests, and relaxed lifestyle. Whether this new German presence in Georgia will be permanent entirely depends on the country's political and economic development.

Tbilisi, May 2024

View of Tbilisi old town and Narikala Fortress

Chapter 25.
Reflections on the Soul of Tbilisi

It so happened that for many years I loved Georgia and Tbilisi in absentia. All my ideas about this country were purely speculative: I only knew about it from books, films and friends' stories. In addition, somewhere in Europe, from time to time, I managed to come into contact with Georgia during spontaneous meetings with its inhabitants. Over time, my desire to live in Georgia grew stronger and more compelling. Although I had no solid or convincing reasons to move, there was one driving force: I felt a deep need to experience Georgia and write about it. I suppose my heart and intuition were guiding me.

After a long "battle for Tbilisi," and thanks to a happy coincidence, we finally came to live here. And, once again, I was incredibly lucky: this country has in no way failed my expectations. You must agree that such love is rare: when you first love someone in absentia, and after meeting them in person, you love them at first sight and forever.

In Tbilisi, I was captivated by the calm, unhurried life near nature, the hospitable people who idolize small children. I enjoyed immersing myself in its warmth, sunshine and friendliness: true zen! That's how it was then, and that's how it is now. In Tbilisi, I became convinced that the south is filled with positivity, joy and love. In addition, for me, the south is the freedom that comes from close contact with nature, as well as freedom from often superfluous frameworks, rules, regulations and reproaches.

After so many years, I have managed to see, learn and rethink many things. Let me share my reflections on my understanding of the spirit and essence of the capital of the Caucasus, our "warm city," which I think I already have the right to call my own. I confess, though, that my perception of Tbilisi is now strongly influenced by the people with whom I interact both in my daily life and in the course of my work.

One of the first phenomena that surprised and captivated me in Tbilisi was the widespread, airborne tolerance towards other religions, languages and nationalities, expressed both in everyday interactions and in the history and architecture of the city: Georgian orthodox churches stand alongside Armenian and Catholic churches and synagogues. There is even a mosque, a Yezidi temple and a defunct fire worshippers' temple, called Ateshga. For centuries, in the quarters of Old Tbilisi and its Italian courtyards, a strikingly friendly neighborhood of different nations and ethnicities has existed, all blending together.

Many travelers have written about this special spirit of the capital of the Caucasus. One of them was the English diplomat Sir John Oliver Wardrop (1864-1948), who left us the following reminiscence about Tbilisi: *"The population of 105,000 consists not only of Georgians, but of Russians (civil servants and soldiers), Armenians (traders and money-lenders), Persians, Tatars, and a few Europeans, viz. Germans (colonists from Suabia), Frenchmen (milliners, hotel-keepers), &c... The effect which Tiflis produces on the mind of the stranger is perfectly unique; its position, its surroundings, the varied nature of its street-life, the gaiety and simplicity of its social life, all combine to form a most powerful and most pleasurable impression... Tiflis is a city where one can live for a long time without suffering from ennui..."* (Sir John Oliver Wardrop, The Kingdom of Georgia).

At this point, I will allow myself to make a lyrical digression again to tell you a remarkable story I experienced in Tbilisi.

There Is Only One Nationality in the City of Tbilisi — Tbilisian!

Two years ago, despite the pandemic, the conflict in Nagorno-Karabakh (in Armenian: Artsakh) flared up with renewed vigor. I decided I should write about how Armenians and Azerbaijanis have lived side by side in Tbilisi for centuries, without conflict or territorial dispute, and, to this end, I went in search of Armenian-Azerbaijani couples.

Acquaintances and social networks helped me find one such couple living in a certain street in a certain house in the old town. Since I didn't have their phone number, I had to turn up as an unexpected guest knocking at their door. I brought some cakes to offer them.

In the many Italian courtyards of the Sololaki district, many families live together. This was no exception, with 12 of the residents being "old-timers." And, of course, all the neighbors know each other by name and surname. Family histories are no secret either. In such yards, neighbors share with each other joy and grief, worries and fears. And if one of the neighbors has guests, it means that there will be a party for everyone!

In a gazebo in the middle of the courtyard, two middle-aged men are leisurely discussing something. I approach and ask if, by any chance, there is an old Armenian-Azerbaijani couple among their neighbors. I am a journalist, I tell them, and I want to record a radio story about them.

One of them introduces himself as Gocha and exclaims happily: *"Of course there is! Jews, Azerbaijanis, Armenians, Yezidis, Kurds, Ukrainians, Belarusians — whoever lives here, we are all like one family. Our grandfathers and fathers were friends in these Old Tbilisi courtyards, and we are friends, and we have children and grandchildren who are friends. We are like relatives. We've known each other for fifty years!"*

How fortunate I was to find the people I was looking for so quickly! It seems that my new acquaintance, Gocha, was also happy that his help was needed, and he called out to his neighbors: *"Karimovich! Kary-Mogly! Roziko! Come out! We have a guest!"*

After a minute or two, a thin, elderly man of medium height, wearing jeans and a black jacket over a checked shirt, comes out of a basement flat. I can tell from his open, good-natured smile that he is surprised by my unexpected visit, but nevertheless open to conversation. After a quick study of me, the man introduces himself: *"I am Gaji Agra Yusuf Kory Moghly. I have a long surname, but everyone just calls me Yusuf Karimovich. My father was from Iran. He moved to Georgia in 1913, when the southern part of Azerbaijan was given to Persia. He was a very young boy then, my father, when he moved to Georgia."*

What an interesting beginning to this story, I think, handing him the box of cakes.

He asks if I am from Baku. To my negation, he guesses *"Armenia then?"* Again, I answer no. *"Then you're Georgian, aren't you?!"* he says. Wrong again! Since, in Tbilisi, representatives of all nations are treated equally warmly and cordially, I, a stranger with cakes, am welcomed as one of their own, and the doors of their souls open for me.

It is a warm, sunny winter, and the weather is glorious. The two neighbors apologise for not inviting me into their houses, because of the pandemic, but they readily suggest we have coffee in the courtyard.

"Roziko, come out!" Yusuf shouts to his wife. *"We have a guest!"* A few moments later, a small, elderly woman with a short haircut comes out of the house, squinting. *"I am Roza Sarkhoshan, it's my maiden name, and by marriage I am Gadjieva,"* she says in introduction.

Gently throwing a warm blanket over his wife's shoulders, Yusuf hugs her and says with pride: *"This is my Roziko! She is Armenian and I am Azerbaijani. She is 76 years old and I am 77. We have lived together for 53 years and almost never quarrelled. I cherish her like the apple of my eye. Last January, she had a stroke, she was in hospital for a month, and she has problems with her eyes. That's why I hide her away, so that she doesn't get sick, God forbid."*

How touching it is to see married couples who, at such an advanced age, have lost neither their warmth nor their desire to care for each other! But the story of their life and love is not so unusual, especially when you consider that in Soviet times there were many such stories, when religion or nationality rarely stood in the way of two loving hearts.

Yusuf met Roza when, after serving in the army, he stayed to work as a chauffeur in a military unit. Roza was working there as a pharmacist. Love bloomed.

At first, Yusuf admits, neither family was happy with the match. When he went with 10 relatives to ask Roza's father for her hand in marriage, he was very nervous, he recalls. However, his knowledge of languages, including Armenian, was to work to his advantage.

In the Sololaki district of Old Tbilisi, people used to speak many languages: Georgian, Russian, Armenian, Azeri, Yiddish and even Kurdish!

"All my childhood friends were Armenian," Yusuf tells me, then lists them: *"Roma, Kitai, Zhorik, Robert, another Zhorik, Ferduz, who is no longer alive. There were seven of us. All of them studied at the 40th Armenian school on Lermontov Street. I studied Russian at the 45th school. But I was friends with them. For some reason it happened, I don't know. And I'm still friends with them!"*

Before they were married, Roza and Yusuf met in secret. Only Roza's older sister knew about these secret rendezvous. We, sitting in the courtyard with our coffee and cakes, all listen with bated breath, even though the neighbors likely already know this beautiful story and its details by heart.

By chance, neither finances, religion nor nationality prevented their marriage. *"When my relatives from Baku call us, their first question is: 'How is our Rozochka?'"* says Yusuf.

"I have never regretted marrying him," Roza tells me. *"We have both Christian and Muslim traditions in our family. I have many icons hanging above my bed, and my husband has never been against it. He is a very, very good man! And God has given us two sons and six grandchildren!"*

I ask Roza what her happiest time was. *"The first time I laid with him!"* she replies merrily, and winks. Everyone laughs.

But for Yusuf, the happiest time of his life was the birth of their sons in 1967 and 1970. Then, before they knew it, grandchildren came along too.

I wonder by what tradition they celebrate religious holidays.

"According to all traditions!" Yusuf exclaims. *"In March, my Bayram, and in April, we celebrate Easter at home and Roza paints eggs. Here, our local Armenians do everything according to Georgian customs, with a week's difference. For our Bayram, we cook pilaf, and for theirs we cook their dishes."*

"When you have such a multicultural family, and right next door, in Nagorno-Karabakh, people of both nations are fighting each other, who does your heart ache for more?" I ask.

"This is a very painful topic in our family," Yusuf says, and sighs. *"I was very worried for both sides. I didn't even want to tell Rozochka about the conflict because she was ill. Her neighbors later told her about it without my knowledge. I*

feel sorry for these young guys who die for nothing because of those damned politicians- it's all their fault. 30 years and they still can't agree! They need to assert their power. I don't think anyone really needs that land, and only Russia needs the war. They have put so many troops there that I don't think they will ever get them out, just like they couldn't get them out of Georgia."

During this conflict, Yusuf says he realized something else: he is not a true Azerbaijani patriot. *"I consider Georgia my homeland. I was born here. And Roza's grandmother, an Armenian, was born here. Oh, how my soul aches for our peoples! If I have to fight tomorrow, I will fight for this land, not for Azerbaijan. I wouldn't even let my son go there to fight."*

Here, Gocha's neighbor makes one important remark: *"This family is incredibly happy. These wise people have given their children a free choice of religion. One of their sons is a Christian, the other Muslim. Can you imagine? They were allowed to choose their own religion! We have one God, and this land belongs to God. If we all thought like that, we would have no war, no bad things. We come to this world for just a little while. That's why we should love, go out, drink and have fun. That's the most important thing. We live once, and how quickly our life flies by!"*

The story I heard in that Sololaki courtyard strikes me as vividly characteristic of the Tbilisi soul, its essence, even. For centuries, the residents of this city have not labeled or judged anyone based on language, nationality, or religion. In the worldview of Tbilisians, love for one's neighbor, for the essence rather than the packaging, has always been and remains paramount. Who knows, perhaps this is why the Tbilisi land is so generous with the talents of various nationalities and faiths.

Tbilisi, January 2021 – April 2023

In Continuation of the Topic of Tbilisi — Tbilisi as a Synergy of Tradition and Modernity

How has Tbilisi managed to maintain its ability to nurture and attract so many talented personalities over the centuries? Could the answer lie in its "holy mountain," Mtatsminda, whose grandeur and history give the city a special, unique energy?

Driving through the old town along the Mtkvari embankment, enchanted by the view of the high cliff with the Metekhi Church perched on top beside the skillful cluster of houses with carved balconies clinging to the mountainside, I always think about how harmoniously East and West, tradition and modernity, coexist in this city.

What fascinates me about this unique city is the opportunity to travel to different eras and styles one after the other: the unpredictably whimsical streets of the Avlabari and Kala districts lead to the more orderly and sometimes even solemn Sololaki, Mtatsminda and Vere. These neighborhoods are built in styles that were fashionable at the turn of the 20th century: pseudo-Moorish, neoclassicism, neo-Gothic, and Art Nouveau, with lodging houses, pompous front rooms, wall frescos, wrought iron patterned staircases, colored stained glass windows and the obligatory greeting at the entrance: "Salve."

> Mtatsminda translates from Georgian as "holy mountain." On the slope of the mountain is the church of St David of Gareji, a holy man who lived here in the 6th century. The church is surrounded by the Mtatsminda Pantheon, where numerous renowned Georgian artists are buried. At the top of the mountain is a TV tower, theme park, restaurants and cafes that offer a panorama of Tbilisi. It is connected to the city by a funicular railway line. Mtatsminda is referenced in poems and songs. It has and continues to be the favorite recreation place of Tbilisians of many generations.

During the Soviet period, these houses, as well as their front rooms, became dilapidated. The architecture of the early 20th century was perceived by the communist ideology as "decadent," and therefore no funds were allocated for the restoration of such housing stock. The houses and their entrances were repaired only as a last resort, and paintings in the once chic front rooms were painted over with cheap Soviet paint, which ruined the marvelous frescos.

More than once, I was lucky enough to observe the painstaking work of restorers bringing back the former beauty and luxury of Tbilisi's mansions and state rooms. At the Tbilisi Academy of Arts, the students entrusted with the restoration of the interior of their alma mater worked day after day under the high ceilings, bringing the wall paintings and mirror mosaics of the mansion back to life. The building of the Academy of Arts is one of the most beautiful in "bourgeois Tiflis," built in the 1850s by architect Grigory Ivanov for the Armenian merchant Vardan Arshakuni. In the 1860s-80s, the Tiflis Artistic Circle was located here, and from the beginning of the 20th century — the Higher Women's Courses.

One of the restorers of the mansion, Khatia Lazurashvili, told me that during a survey of the halls of the palace, four layers of paint were discovered, which had to be removed before the original silver and even gold paintings

> Vardan Arshakuni was a rich Tbilisi merchant, Armenian by birth. In 1856-1860, he served as the Mayor of Tbilisi. Dreaming to build a palace for himself in the Persian style, he spared no expense for the construction, inviting masters from Persia and Europe to work on it. The facade and interior of the palace incorporated elements of classicism, baroque and Islamic architecture. The construction and finishing of the house took so long that Arshakuni did not live to see his palace in its finished form. The facade of the palace was changed during restoration works in Soviet times.

could be cleaned. The restorers then had to preserve the original paints and use watercolor and tempera to retouch the works.

The example of the front room at 18 G. Tabidze Street shows how rich and modern the city of Tbilisi was at the turn of the century. There, an unknown artist depicted an allegory of four continents on the walls of the entrance to the building: Europe, America, Africa and Australia.

The restoration project manager, Lia Bokuchava, from the organization ICOMOS, told me that the entire stairwell of this house was once decorated with paintings, mosaics and stucco. The top floor of the house was crowned by a glass dome, through which daylight illuminated the entire entrance. The railings and floors in this mansion were made of

Michele De Lucchi is an Italian architect. He owns his own design studio, Produzione Privata, in Milan and is a professor at the Milan University of Technology. His designs in Georgia include the Peace Bridge and the Presidential Palace in Tbilisi, the Palace of Justice in Batumi and the Medea Hotel.

expensive materials, while the staircase was made of marble. And at the entrance, there were lamps made of cast iron.

At any time of the year, I am inspired to walk around the upper part of the old town, through Sololaki and the Bethlemi neighborhood. From there, not only is the panorama of Old Tbilisi best viewed from above, but the inclusions of newer times in the body of the city also become noticeable: these include buildings from Stalin's monumentalist era, modern skyscrapers, the glass Peace Bridge over the Mtkvari River by Italian Michele De Lucchi, and the unruly "Gulliver's Trumpets" of the empty Rike concert hall.

I know that, for many Tbilisians, such innovative experiments on the image of the city seem almost akin to a crime. Yet I tend to share the opinion of Tbilisi artist Vato Tsereteli: Once, during an author's tour of the city called 'Vertical Tbilisi,' we stood at the top station of the cable car at the Narikala fortress and looked down on the crazy Tbilisi-mix of styles and eras (which, unlike the Babylonian mix of languages, did not lead to any disagreements). Against the picture of the old city, the skyscraper of the seven-star Biltmore Hotel, built by Arab sheikhs, seemed to us an impudent slap in the face to the great creations of our ancestors. But then Vato casually remarked: *"In principle, all these buildings, old and new, are logical for Tbilisi, and the appearance of skyscrapers in Tbilisi is a phenomenon to expect, because our city has been a hub for centuries, the most important hub of the region."*

His words made me think. Indeed, in a city at the crossroads of trade, transport, art and intellectual flows, new trends of fashion and style are bound to linger and take root.

In 2017, Vato shared a striking idea with me, which, considering the current events in the country and the world — Russia's war against Ukraine and the mass influx of freethinkers from Russia and Belarus into Georgia — has taken on an unexpectedly prophetic power: *"Tbilisi is slowly resuming its historical significance as a free city, a Caucasian platform for communication and the exchange of information. We used to be home to Muslims, Jews, Armenians, Georgians, Kurds, Azerbaijanis, Poles and Russians. Representatives of different nationalities continue to come here to live. Tbilisi today welcomes Muslims, Jews, Christians, and all those who are looking for a new home here, with equal warmth. Many of them become Tbilisians. After all, Tbilisi is not only the capital of Georgia, but also a place where freedom reigns and where different religions and cultures can easily communicate and interact with each other."*

The artist shared with me his dream of a new function for his hometown as a platform for negotiations in various world and regional conflicts. I would very much like to see this beautiful idea helped to be realized.

Tbilisi is a city of bright colors; colors that give birth to no less bright, extraordinary personalities. Perhaps it is because of the warm hydrogen sulphide springs on which Tbilisi stands? Maybe it is they that contribute to the exuberant growth of plants and talent!

I never tire of marveling at the grapevines winding along the facades of houses, the many fig trees, and the abundance of scented blossom in spring. They pamper the senses, make you forget vanity, mediocrity and stupidity, and direct your focus to the main thing: the enjoyment of being; the ability to appreciate beauty and celebrate life. In spring and autumn in Tbilisi, you want to spend time in contact with nature, in the forest, on the lake, and in the mountains. Thank God that the latter can be miraculously found right within the city limits!

I could talk about the Tbilisi talent endlessly. In my next book, I will introduce each of the talented individuals I met while preparing my series of radio programs about Tbilisi. They were people with specialized education, as well as naturals and visionaries engaged in both traditional fields and innovative areas of art and science.

One example is Malkhaz, the choir director at the Mama Daviti Church on Mtatsminda mountain, who has been involved in reviving ancient church hymns since his youth. He explained to me how true-believing Georgians engage in "practical theology": *"Georgians from century to century, have been engaged in practical theology, which is a love of God and love of one's neighbor; hospitality, mercy, generosity. That is why God has rewarded us with a form of polyphony that is a symbolic analogy of the Holy Trinity itself."*

At the same time, for many modern music lovers, Tbilisi, with its legendary Bassiani club and innovative composers, is a world center for electronic music. Composer Nika Machaidze, who has been composing such tunes since the mid-1990s, is renowned far beyond the borders of his country, and is even titled "the father of electronic music."

Nika told me an anecdote: *"When I won the Grand Prix at the 1999 Electronic Music Festival in Paris, my friend David Sikvarulidze jokingly pointed out that I, a man from a country where there is no electricity, was winning a prize at an electronic music festival!"* This, perhaps, says it all about the talent of Georgians. When speaking with me, Nika compares the Georgian culture and mentality to a trout that manoeuvres between different currents: between East and West. I see Tbilisi as an exemplary representative of just such a trout!

Even though Georgians are great traditionalists, there are often nuggets of innovation among them who challenge the established traditions. I include all those who have the courage to transform and improve the heritage of their great ancestors. Restaurateur and owner of a number of innovative restaurants, Tekuna Gachechiladze is a vivid example of this.

Tekuna is a Doctor of Psychology, having graduated from the University of Heidelberg. She wrote her thesis in New York in parallel to studying at the Culinary Academy there. After returning to her homeland, she devoted herself to transforming traditional cuisine, that holy of holies of all Georgians. In her café *Littera*, located in Writer's House on Machabeli Street, Tbilisi, in the former mansion of businessman-philanthropist David Sarajishvili, the fusion-style cuisine she offers is a real sensation. Tekuna easily conjures up completely unfamiliar variations on Georgian cuisine from familiar products: *chakapuli* with mussels, beetroot with goat's cheese, caramelized onions and pomegranates, *ghomi* chips, *kharcho* with shrimps…and the mouth-watering list goes on.

Tekuna's audacity is that she challenges not only the notions of what Georgian cuisine should be, but the entire Soviet legacy in Georgian gastronomy.

"For seventy years, there was stagnation in Soviet cookery," she says. *"Everything was mixed in one pot, and all dishes had a similar flavor. However, if you look in old cookbooks, you will find many interesting recipes, from bechamel sauce to plombier. Before the Communists came here, for example, French cuisine was very popular. And a French cook also worked here in the house of Sarajishvili."*

With her culinary creations, Tekuna reminds us that Georgian cuisine has always been a hub of different flavors and influences. The country's location on the Silk Road has played a big role in this.

"If you look at Georgian classical cuisine, it is a mixture of Persian, Indian, Chinese, European and Russian," Tekuna says. *"We have skilfully adopted all the achievements of others and made our own unique cuisine out of them. Today, I am deliberately doing what we Georgians have been doing for centuries."*

Tbilisi, immersing me in an atmosphere of tradition and innovation, a leisurely pace of life, eclecticism, meditative tranquility, and sincere kindness, allowed me to feel that a life away from art and creativity is emptiness, a missed opportunity to touch the eternal, a neglect of a greater gift. Art in this context isn't necessarily about creating masterpieces. Of course, transforming the world with your ideas or actions is a great fortune, but often it's enough to simply be aware of the incredible beauty and perfection of the world every day, finding personal harmony with the universe in that feeling.

Tbilisi gave me the ability to see deeper, to understand the hidden meanings of events, phenomena, and people. It is a priceless gift, and I continue to learn from this amazing city with love and gratitude.

Tbilisi, April 2024

View of Mtatsminda, Tbilisi´s "holy mountain"

The lovely Armenian-Azerbaijani couple in Tbilisi, Roza and Yusuf

Tekuna Gachechiladze, owner of Café Littera, is a master of blending culinary traditions

Artist Vato Tsereteli. Background: Tbilisi Old Town

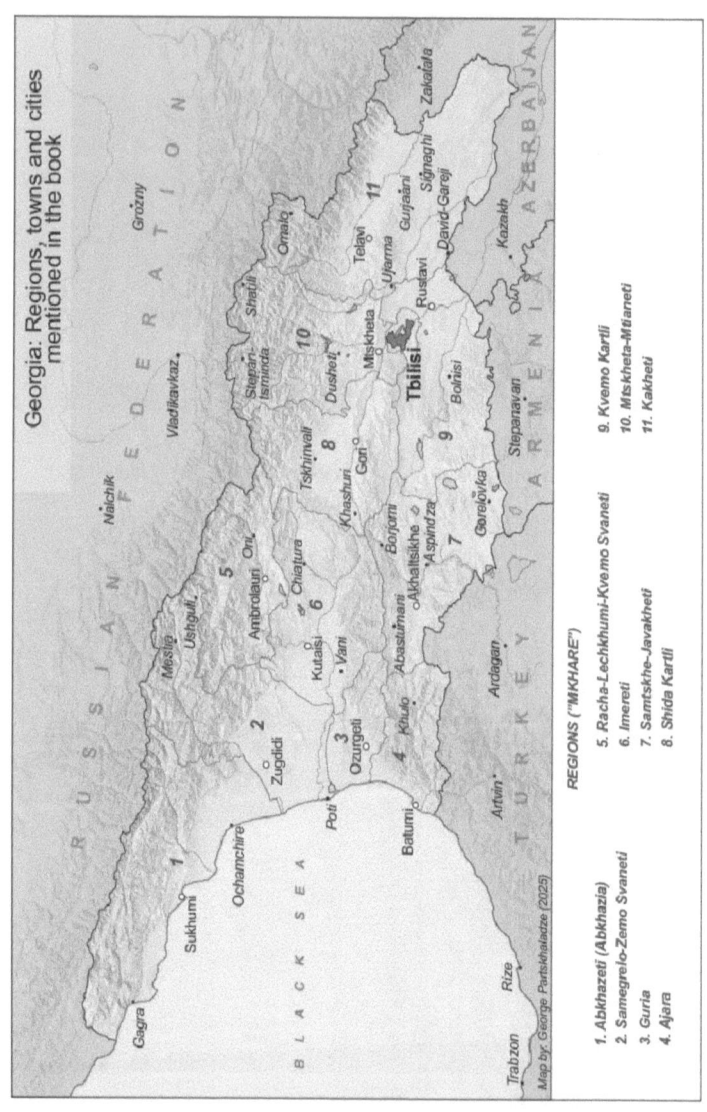

Georgia: Regions, towns and cities mentioned in the book

REGIONS ("MKHARE")

1. Abkhazeti (Abkhazia)
2. Samegrelo-Zemo Svaneti
3. Guria
4. Ajara
5. Racha-Lechkhumi-Kvemo Svaneti
6. Imereti
7. Samtskhe-Javakheti
8. Shida Kartli
9. Kvemo Kartli
10. Mtskheta-Mtianeti
11. Kakheti

Map by: George Partskhaladze (2025)

Georgia: regions, towns and cities mentioned in the book. Map by George Partskhaladze

Epilogue

Dear Reader,

These stories I have shared with you were born from my sincere desire to introduce Georgia to the world, to tell you about its bountiful land, ancient history, and living traditions. I hope my stories have helped you understand why this country is worth appreciating and loving.

Colleagues from Germany and Austria often asked me on the radio: "Why is it absolutely necessary to visit Georgia?" My answers seemed to take the listeners' breath away. They couldn't believe that on such a small piece of land–after all, Georgia is only the size of Ireland–there could be so many wonders. After the broadcasts, I received many enthusiastic responses: listeners were either rushing to pack their bags or were already returning from Georgia, full of admiration.

At the time of writing this book, Georgia finds itself at a crossroads, in a critically important phase of its history, where fateful decisions are being made that will determine the country's trajectory for decades to come. This period is marked not only by internal challenges, but also by global trends that are having a significant impact on Georgia's future.

Georgia is not alone in its trials. The world is experiencing a period of profound transformations related to shifts in the geopolitical landscape, the technological revolution, and environmental issues. Global trends such as the rise of populism, the weakening of international institutions, and cyber threats are also affecting Georgia. As a country located at the crossroads of Europe and Asia, Georgia is particularly susceptible to the influence of such processes.

However, in these challenging times, when the world is gripped by uncertainty and rapid change, it is more important than ever for people to feel support, to have something tangible, familiar, and reliable that gives them the strength to live, hope, and move forward, regardless of the difficulties. I am deeply convinced that Georgia, with its benevolent, hospitable people, its centuries-old traditions, and its rich historical and cultural heritage, represents a kind of anchor in the turbulent ocean of change.

In the mountains of Georgia, deep within its free and untamed nature, it is easier to find not only physical, but also spiritual healing, inner harmony and peace of mind. Not only the mountains and nature, but also the ancient temples, monasteries, fortresses, vineyards, unique cuisine, distinctive culture, folk crafts, music, and dances — all of these create a unique atmosphere that attracts and inspires.

I want to steadfastly believe in the victory of the forces of truth, goodness, and progress in this momentous confrontation.

Georgia and its people are something that my heart aches for with particular intensity. The English diplomat and Caucasus enthusiast's observations about this country still resonate today: *"Georgia's chief attraction lies in its people; the Georgians are not only fair to look upon, but they are essentially a lovable people; to live among such gay, open-hearted, open-handed, honest, innocent folk is the best cure for melancholy and misanthropy that could well be imagined"* (Oliver Wardrop, The Kingdom of Georgia).

I wholeheartedly wish that more people, from all over the world, might discover this ancient land, with its majestic mountains, fertile valleys, ancient temples, and fortresses. May they, like me almost fifteen years ago, be enchanted by the fantastic diversity of landscapes, the unique aromas of spices, bread and wine, and the melodiousness of Georgian songs. Above all, may they experience the profound warmth and lovability of the Georgians, allowing their hearts to thaw in the glow of such a genuine embrace — the truly lovable spirit of this country!

Tbilisi, March 2025

References

1. Чиладзе, Отар «Шел по дороге человек». Тбилиси «Мерани», 1985 [Otar Chiladze «Shel po doroge chelovek». Tbilisi «Merani», 1985] (Chiladze, O.: *A Man Walked on the Road*. Tbilisi, Merani, 1985)

2. «Батумское побережье «Русские тропики»». Сборник статей под редакцией С. А. Анисимова. Батум, Типография Г.С. Таварткиладзе, 1911 [«Batumskoe poberezh'e «Russkie tropiki»». Sbornik statej pod redakciej S. A. Anisimova. Batum, Tipografija G.S. Tavartkiladze, 1911] (Anisimov, S.A.: *Batumi Coast 'Russian Tropics'*. A Collection of Edited Articles. Batumi, G.S. Tavartkiladze Printing House, 1911)

3. «Батум и окрестности. Издание батумского городского общественного управления. К 25-летию присоединения г. Батума к Российской Империи». Батум, типография Киладзе и Таварткиладзе, 1906 [«Batum i okrestnosti. Izdanie batumskogo gorodskogo obshhestvennogo upravlenija. K 25-letiju prisoedinenija g. Batuma k Rossijskoj Imperii». Batum, tipografija Kiladze i Tavartkiladze, 1906] (*Batumi and its Vicinity*. Publication of Batumi City Public Administration on the 25th Anniversary of Batum's Joining the Russian Empire. Batumi, Kiladze and Tavartkiladze Printing House, 1906)

4. Каневский И. «Любопытные уголки Кавказа. Батумский округ. Сванетия. Очерки жизни и природы И. Каневского». Тифлис, типография Канцелярии [«Ljubopytnye ugolki Kavkaza. Batumskij okrug. Svanetija. Ocherki zhizni i prirody I. Kanevskogo». Tiflis, tipografija Kanceljarii] (Kanevsky, I.: *Noteworthy Corners of the Caucasus. Batum district. Svaneti. Sketches of life and nature*. Tiflis, Printing house of the Chancellery of the Civil Chief in the Caucasus, 1886)

5. Р. Д. кн. Эристов «Заметки о Сванетии». Тифлис, типография М. Шаридзе и К, 1898 [R. D. kn. Jeristov «Zametki o Svanetii». Tiflis, tipografija M. Sharidze i K, 1898] (Eristov, P. D. pr.: *Notes on Svaneti*. Tiflis, M. Sharidze and K Printing House, 1898)

6. Ковалевский, Борис «Страна снегов и башен. Очерки сванской культуры». Предисловие Акад. Н.Я. Марра с картой Сванетии и 43 фото автора и др. Издательство «Прибой», 1930 [Boris Kovalevskij «Strana snegov i bashen. Ocherki svanskoj kul'tury». Predislovie Akad. N.Ja. Marra s kartoj Svanetii i 43 foto avtora i dr. Izdatel'stvo «Priboj», 1930] (Kovalevsky, B.: *The Land of Snow and Towers. Sketches of Svan Culture*. Preface by Acad. N.Y. Marr, with a map of Svanetia and 43 photos by the author. Priboy Publishing House, 1930)

7. «Поездка в Пшавию, Хевсуретию и Сванетию графини П. С. Уваровой». Материалы по археологии Кавказа. Выпуск X. Москва—1904. Типография общества распространения полезных книг. [«Poezdka v Pshaviju, Hevsuretiju i Svanetiju grafini P. S. Uvarovoj». Materialy po arheologii Kavkaza. Vypusk H. Moskva—1904. Tipografija obshhestva rasprostranenija poleznyh knig] (Countess Uvarova, P. S.: *A trip to Pshavia, Khevsuretia and Svanetia. Materials on the Archeology of the Caucasus*. Issue X. Typography of the Society for the Distribution of Useful Books. Moscow, 1904)

8. Г. Лежава и М. Джандиери «Архитектура Сванетии». Издательство Всесоюзной Академии Архитектуры, 1938 [G. Lezhava i M. Dzhandieri «Arhitektura Svanetii». Izdatel'stvo Vsesojuznoj Akademii Arhitektury, 1938] (Lezhava, G. and Jandieri, M.: *Architecture of Svaneti*. Publishing House of the All-Union Academy of Architecture, 1938)

9. «Кавказ. Рача, Горийский уезд, горы Осетии, Пшавия, Хевсуретия и Сванетия. Путевые заметки графини Уваровой». Часть III. Москва, 1904. Типография общества распространения полезных книг. [«Kavkaz. Racha, Gorijskij uezd, gory Osetii, Pshavija, Hevsuretija i Svanetija. Putevye zametki grafini Uvarovoj». Chast' III. Moskva, 1904. Tipografija obshhestva rasprostranenija poleznyh knig] (*Caucasus. Racha, Gori district, Ossetian Mountains, Pshavia, Khevsuretia and Svanetia. Traveling Notes of Countess Uvarova*. Part III. Typography of the Society for the Distribution of Useful Books. Moscow, 1904)

10. «Археологическое путешествие по Гурии и Ачаре Дм. Бакрадзе». Санкт-Петербург, типография императорской академии наук, 1878 [«Arheologicheskoe puteshestvie po Gurii i Achare Dm. Bakradze». Sankt-Peterburg, tipografija imperatorskoj akademii nauk, 1878] (Bakradze, Dm.: *Archeological Journey through Guria and Achara*. St. Petersburg, Printing House of the Imperial Academy of Sciences, 1878)

11. В. Бочкарев. «Древняя и Новая Колхида (ныне Кутаисская губерния). Историко-географический очерк». Выпуск I. Кутаис, типография Зедгинидзе и Перадзе, 1889 [V. Bochkarev. «Drevnjaja i Novaja Kolhida (nyne Kutaisskaja gubernija). Istoriko-geograficheskij ocherk». Vypusk I. Kutais, tipografija Zedginidze i Peradze, 1889] (Bochkarev, B.: *Ancient and New Colchis (now Kutaisi Province). Historical and Geographical Sketches*. Issue I. Kutaisi, Zedginidze and Peradze Printing House, 1889)

12. «Города, существовавшие и существующие в Грузии. Сочинение Платона Иоселиани». Тифлис, в типографии канцелярии Наместника Кавказского, 1850 [«Goroda, sushhestvovavshie i sushhestvujushhie v Gruzii. Sochinenie Platona Ioseliani». Tiflis, v tipografii kanceljarii Namestnika Kavkazskogo, 1850] (Ioseliani, P.: *Cities that existed and exist in Georgia*. Composition. Tiflis, Printing house of the Chancellery of the Caucasian Governor, 1850)

13. П. Бирюков «Духоборцы. Сборник статей, воспоминаний, писем и других документов». Москва: Изд. "Посредник", 1908 [P. Birjukov «Duhoborcy. Sbornik statej, vospominanij, pisem i drugih dokumentov». Moskva: Izd. "Posrednik", 1908] (Biryukov, P.: *Dukhobors. Collection of articles, memoirs, letters and other documents*. Moscow, Izd. Posrednik, 1908)

14. «Путеводитель по Кавказу». Е. Вейденбаум. Тифлис, 1888 [«Putevoditel' po Kavkazu». E. Vejdenbaum. Tiflis, 1888] (Veidenbaum, E. A.: *Guide to the Caucasus*. Tiflis, 1888)

15. Rayfield, Donald. Georgia. Crossroads of Empires. A History of Three Thousand Years. Donald Rayfield Edge of Empires: *A History of Georgia*. 2012 Russian language edition. Azbuka Atticus Publishing Group LLC, CoLibri. 2017.

16. Отар Лордкипанидзе «Наследие Древней Грузии». Тбилиси «Мецниереба», 1989 [Otar Lordkipanidze «Nasledie Drevnej Gruzii». Tbilisi «Mecniereba», 1989] (Lordkipanidze, O.: *The Heritage of Ancient Georgia*. Tbilisi, Metsniereba, 1989)

17. "Иллюстрированный практический путеводитель по Черноморскому побережью" СПб, Редакция путеводителей, 1914 Автор: Москвич Григорий Георгиевич ["Illjustrirovannyj prakticheskij putevoditel' po Chernomorskomu poberezh'ju" SPb, Redakcija putevoditelej, 1914 Avtor: Moskvich Grigorij Georgievich] (Moskvich, G. G. : *Illustrated Practical Guide to the Black Sea Coast.* Editorial Office of Guides, St. Petersburg, 1914)

18. Braund, D.: Georgia in Antiquity: A History of Colchis. Transcaucasian Iberia, 550 BC-562 AD. Oxford, Clarendon Press, 1994.

19. Лордкипанидзе О. Д. «Город-храм Колхиды». (История археологических раскопок в Вани) / О. Д. Лордкипанидзе; Отв. редактор: И. В. Можейко. Москва «Наука», 1984 [Lordkipanidze O. D. «Gorod-hram Kolhidy». (Istorija arheologicheskih raskopok v Vani) / O. D. Lordkipanidze; Otv. redaktor: I. V. Mozhejko. Moskva «Nauka», 1984] (Lordkipanidze, O.: *The Temple City of Colchis. History of Archaeological Excavations in Vani.* Editor-in-Chief: I. V. Mozheiko. Nauka. Moscow, 1984)

20. Материалы по истории Грузии и Кавказа, выпуск II. М.Л. Меликсет-Беков «Армазни. Историко-археологический очерк». Издательство грузинского филиала Академии Наук СССР. Тбилиси, 1938 [Materialy po istorii Gruzii i Kavkaza, vypusk II. M.L. Melikset-Bekov «Armazni. Istoriko-arheologicheskij ocherk». Izdatel'stvo gruzinskogo filiala Akademii Nauk SSSR. Tbilisi, 1938] (Melikset-Bekov Armazni, M. L.: *Materials on the History of Georgia and the Caucasus, Issue II. Historical and archeological sketches.* Tbilisi, Publishing house of the Georgian branch of the Academy of Sciences of the USSR, 1938)

21. Отар Лордкипанидзе «Древняя Колхида. Миф и археология». «Сабчота Сакартвело», Тбилиси, 1979 [Otar Lordkipanidze «Drevnjaja Kolhida. Mif i arheologija». «Sabchota Sakartvelo», Tbilisi, 1979] (Lordkipanidze, O.: *Ancient Colchis. Myth and Archeology.* Tbilisi, Sabchota Sakartvelo, 1979)

22. Wardrop, Oliver John. The Kingdom of Georgia. Notes Notes of travel in a land of women, wine, and song. London, 1880; The Project Gutenberg EBook

23. Leist, Arthur „Das georgische Volk", Dresden, 1903 (Leist A.: *The Georgian People.* Dresden, 1903)

24. Бакрадзе, Димитри «Сванети» Тифлис, 1877: Типография Главный управ. Наместника Кавказа [Bakradze, Dimitri «Svaneti» Tiflis, 1877: Tipografija Glavnyj uprav. Namestnika Kavkaza] (Bakradze, Dimitri: *Svaneti,* Tiflis, 1877)